Advance Praise for *Raising Hell for Jesus*

Raising Hell for Jesus will challenge your preconceived notions of what it means to follow Jesus of Nazareth. Rev. Fred Morris, a United Methodist pastor, missionary, entrepreneur, and teacher, relates more than a memoir as he shares his story with daring honesty and vulnerability about what it means to stay committed to God's love and liberation for all. I knew of Fred as a pastor of a local church in the heart of Chicago, addressing racism, homophobia, unjust working conditions, and an option for the poor. I never forgot his courage as a missionary in Brazil under an oppressive government ministering to the people, only to face imprisonment and torture. For all who yearn for a Church that lives justice and truth, heals the suffering, and speaks for the voiceless—you will find Rev. Morris' life story a real example of living the Gospel.

—*Rev. Betty Jo "B.J." Birkhahn-Rommelfanger, United Methodist Ordained Elder in Northern IL Conference*

When it comes to the dream of faith-rooted social justice and fundamental human rights for all, there is no one whose life is a greater example than Rev. Fred Morris. As a preacher's kid with a big heart, as a pastor in both rural and urban settings, as a missionary and human rights activist in Latin America, and as a follower of the healing Christ of all compassion and no B.S., Rev. Morris learned early to dream big and to join with others in a persistent struggle to make that dream come true.

Without a wasted word, Fred continues to grab the reader's heart as we follow his journey of following the Christ who comforts the afflicted and afflicts the comfortable. Fred's impact on developing an effective ministry of welcome and empowerment with immigrants through the churches in Southern California was central. His dream lives on among us and gives us guidance and strength in these difficult days.

I encourage you to open your mind and your heart to the story and the dream that Rev. Morris shares in *Raising Hell for Jesus*. You will be both challenged and blessed.

—Rev. David K. Farley, Pastor Emeritus, Echo Park United Methodist, Los Angeles, CA, former Director of Justice & Compassion Ministries, California-Pacific Conference, United Methodist Church

Rev. Fred Morris tells a fascinating story, ranging from the heavenly interventions of the Holy Spirit to the crushing abandonment of colleagues on earth. He worked with famous leaders but often lived near poverty. He faced the torture of body and spirit, but he would not quit because love and justice matter. This book reminds us that the greatest leaders of the church are people with giant flaws but with an out-sized passion for truth and love. Like Rev. Morris, they were offensive to those trying to avoid responsibility but were beloved by those who knew them well.

—Rev. Dr. Joel C. Hunter, Pastor of Community Benefit, Action Church

This book recounts a lifetime punctuated by trauma, tragedy, and betrayal yet marked by exceptional resilience and deeply rooted Christian commitment. Fred testifies to the pain routinely inflicted on the poor in Latin America by an imperial power whose own citizens are unaware of the damage done in their name. He recounts how institutional Christianity has all too often lost sight of the life and teaching of Jesus Christ. Yet he also vividly testifies to the reality of the living Christ that is alive and well in those who still practice Jesus' preferential option for the poor and marginalized. This is the story of Fred Morris, a man like Jesus Christ who truly bears the very marks of the Gospel on his own body.

—Bishop Chuck Leigh

I am convinced that the ensuing pages, which carry a riveting account of history entwined with Fred Morris' own integrity, will serve to engross and challenge you as they did for me. His story pursues justice and crosses numerous boundaries. I believe you, too, will be left in awe of the number of encounters Fred faced on his faith journey. His experiences range from good to bad, often complicated and terrifying, but are also bolstered with the quintessential story of resilience that is worth sharing. Fred's long journey of faith and witness will leave an indelible mark on you as it did me to be better and require better.

—Myron F. McCoy, Senior Pastor First United Methodist Church at the Chicago Temple, Chicago, IL

In *Raising Hell for Jesus,* Rev. Morris explores what it means to follow Jesus. Spirituality and justice are the two poles guiding and shaping his understanding of ministry. He seeks to remain faithful to both.

Rev. Morris's passion for spirituality and justice led him to Brazil, where he befriended Archbishop Dom Hélder Câmara, one of the chief proponents of Liberation theology. This association with Archbishop Câmara got him in trouble with the United Methodist Church and made him a target of the Brazilian government.

To stand in solidarity with the poor means that one cannot be complicit in the oppression of the poor. The compelling challenge of Jesus is to stand in solidarity with the poor, to become good news for the poor. And that challenge is non-negotiable.

Rev. Morris didn't just hear the challenge. He lived it. His journey is a testament to his unwavering commitment to his beliefs. This book is both a worthy read and a timely call to action, especially amid the ongoing debate about what it means to be Christian in the context of Christian nationalism.

—Rev. Kenneth W. Wheeler, author of "US: The Resurrection of American Terror"

Following Jesus as faithfully as one can is an adventure. This statement is made true through the stories that Rev. Fred Morris shares in *Raising Hell for Jesus.* His commitment to Jesus has led him to encounter people from all walks and stages of life on multiple continents. He offers unflinching yet insightful stories about people, politics, institutions, religion, and more. Let Rev. Fred take you on an adventure and inspire you to live out your own adventure.

—Joseph Yoo, priest & planter of Mosaic Episcopal Church, Pearland, TX, author of "When the Saints Go Flying In"

Raising Hell for Jesus intersects the essence of social justice, the power of the Holy Spirit, and global missions that are deeply rooted in Methodism. The theological training throughout this career and call had a profound impact on his insights and actions. This moral courage prevailed but was often challenged. Fred's story illuminates the historical and theological underpinnings of missionary endeavors, highlighting a commitment to social transformation and demonstrating prevenient grace. This compelling narrative demonstrates how the Holy Spirit has empowered a witness and advocacy worldwide to champion justice, equality, and compassion in one's community and around the world. This book is a call to action, inspiring readers to replicate a legacy of social activism, spiritual passion, and unconditional love for all. It is a must-read for anyone passionate about social justice, spiritual empowerment, and global mission.

—Rev. Dr. Adrienne Zackery, Lead Pastor Crossroads UMC, Compton, CA

Raising Hell for Jesus

RAISING HELL FOR JESUS

Seven Decades of Faith, Courage, and Chasing the Impossible Dream

REV. FRED MORRIS

Foreword by Bishop Cedrick Bridgeforth

PRECOCITY PRESS

Published by Precocity Press, Los Angeles, CA
Developmental Editor: Sara Volle
Copyeditor: Victoria Brock
Creative Director: Susan Shankin
Cover Concept: Sara Volle
Cover Designer: Tim Kummerow
Interior Designer and Typesetter: Susan Shankin

ISBN: 979-8-9898304-8-0 (Trade Paperback)
ISBN: 979-8-9898304-9-7 (eBook)
Library of Congress Control Number: 2024909833
First edition. Printed and bound in the United States of America

Dedication

I want to dedicate this work to my wonderful wife and companion of the past 40 years. She has been a true gift from God, proving that, as St. Paul said in Romans, "all things work together for good for those that love the Lord." After a series of totally calamitous events occurred in my life, she appeared in an unpredictable and unexpected fashion and has been providing me with love and support in unexpected and unimagined ways.

Contents

Foreword by Bishop Cedrick Bridgeforth xii
Introduction xvii
Prologue xxi

CHAPTER 1: Growing Up—Forever 1
CHAPTER 2: Awakening the Healing Light 15
CHAPTER 3: Our Move to Teresópolis 36
CHAPTER 4: Our Return to Brazil 53
CHAPTER 5: The Beginning of the Beginning 74
CHAPTER 6: Now What? 106
CHAPTER 7: How We Got to Costa Rica 134
CHAPTER 8: Rosa Argentina Molina Marín 158
CHAPTER 9: Brasil Bloque 162
CHAPTER 10: Praise the Lord! 186
CHAPTER 11: Florida Council of Churches 197

CHAPTER 12: How We Got to Panama 223

CHAPTER 13: How We Got to Nicaragua 230

CHAPTER 14: How Rancho Don Quijote Came to Be 238

CHAPTER 15: Homesickness Leads Us to California 244

CHAPTER 16: Final Roundup 257

CHAPTER 17: Religion Is mostly BS, but . . . 272

Epilogue 289

Appendix 295

Endnotes 301

Acknowledgments 307

About the Author 309

Foreword by Bishop Cedrick Bridgeforth

"If you need someone to lead a ministry with Spanish-speaking communities, I may know someone," Bishop Minerva Carcaño told me over a phone call in 2013.

"Who?" I asked.

"Reverend Fred Morris," she said. "I met him over 40 years ago. He has a fascinating story from his time in Brazil and beyond. You should call him and see if Shandon is right for him."

I read Fred's letter of interest to Bishop Carcaño and wondered why this 80-year-old retired pastor who had been living in Nicaragua would be interested in returning to the United States to pastor a church. I emailed him to inquire if he would be open to a phone conversation. Within minutes, he replied, and we scheduled a phone conversation for the next day.

I prepared to speak with a retired United Methodist pastor who happened to be fluent in Spanish, had experience as a missionary, and might be interested in pastoring a church in Southern California. I was under the impression that the impetus and driving force for his openness to serve in Southern California was to be near some of his children. What I learned quickly was that Fred Morris was not a regular retiree. As varied as his career had been, his life journey was even more arduous and circuitous.

Within minutes of exchanging pleasantries on that first phone call, Fred began recounting his life story. More than an hour later, we agreed he would be an excellent fit for the congregation in Shandon, California. It had the potential to be a place where a Spanish-speaking pastor could build on the church's long history and help the Shandon congregation become open to serving Spanish-speaking families in the town.

As frank as Fred was over the phone, he was even more frank and resolute in person and throughout his year of service to the Shandon congregation. When we secured funding and solidified our partnership with North Valley Caring Services, we knew we needed someone with experience serving in tough communities who would also honor the people's culture and needs. Although Fred and his wife, Argentina, were only in their first year in Shandon, it was obvious to me that Fred was the perfect person to bridge the gap between what was happening on the site of the former Sepulveda United Methodist Church and what could be a transformative ministry.

Fred's stories about the Honduran and/or Guatemalan and Salvadoran gangs that President Ronald Reagan's deportation policies created in the 1980s, his direct engagement with base communities, and asset-based community development filled in the picture for me. I could see how the amalgamation of his experiences would transform an underutilized church property and bring new life to the community.

Although the congregation in Shandon did not receive the news of Fred's departure from Shandon well, the team responsible for getting a new ministry launched at North Hills was ecstatic. They could not believe that a man with so many accomplishments would humble himself enough to step into this community to start something new. Fred quickly found a way to befriend and advocate for the local merchants, advocate for undocumented community members, and act as a bridge between the facility users and community groups.

Fred Morris' lived experiences as a missionary for the United Methodist Church, a political prisoner in Brazil, a renowned advocate for justice and peace internationally, and a pastor of several churches in various parts of the country qualify him to speak up and to speak out. He shares himself in profound and vulnerable ways. His young marriage and parenthood with someone he would eventually divorce qualify him to talk about perseverance and courage. His fierce approach to ministry qualifies him to inform others of what he learned as an 80-year-old new ministry pastor.

As a follower of Jesus of Nazareth, Fred distinguishes himself among those who identify their faith practice ahead of their faith tradition. The unfolding of his story, from his childhood in Illinois to his homestead in Nicaragua, demonstrates the many layers that make Fred Morris as he reveals the mishaps, missed opportunities, and triumphs that inform his identities.

When I asked Fred to consider moving from Shandon to North Hills, I did so because I believed he was the right person to be there. He was not given a ministry plan or a list of metrics to hit. Instead, he was challenged to be one with the people and let the people give shape to the ministry. That's exactly what he did by ministering to the vendors in the parking lot, providing spiritual support for families in distress, offering communion to those who could not access it anywhere else, and opening a place of refuge for children on the move to find safety from violence and poverty.

As you read these pages, you'll move closer in proximity to Jesus of Nazareth via the life, ministry, and witness of Reverend Fred Morris.

Introduction

WHATEVER ELSE ONE CAN SAY about my life, it has not been boring. I can't help but think that my life experiences, my adventure through life seeking to follow in the footsteps of Jesus of Nazareth, may be helpful to others seeking to do the same. This adventure has been guided by two major themes, or cords: spirituality and social justice.

From my earliest memories, I have deeply yearned for things that today we call "spiritual." My father was a Methodist preacher from the age of 19. He was also Dean of the summer Methodist Church camp in New Lenox, IL. It was a week-long camp for high schoolers, but I got to go at age nine because my parents didn't have anything else they could do with me that week. One night, the speaker was Paul Schmucker, a Methodist missionary to an island in Malaysia. He showed hundreds of 35mm Kodachrome slides and gave an altar call at the end of his talk, inviting anyone present to go forward and commit to being a missionary for Jesus. Before long, I found myself kneeling at the altar. I recall feeling somewhat disappointed that "nothing happened." I don't know what I expected, but it seemed like such an important decision would result in *something*. It didn't. That was my first memory of some kind of "spiritual" yearning.

I was raised in a primarily non-political environment. Being from Texas, my parents had grown up in a racially segregated

Jim Crow society. At the time, a racially divided society was the norm. The Korean War began just as I graduated from high school. College became a good way for me to avoid the war. In 1952, my friends and I all "liked Ike" and hoped President Eisenhower ended the war before we graduated. The "rightness" of the US military action was never discussed or even questioned. After all, we were clearly fighting Communism. This was amid Senator Joe McCarthy's witch-hunts for Communists in the US government. It didn't matter that we had no idea what Communism was; we just knew we were against it.

At Drew University, I experienced what I call my "political epiphany." Dr. Howard Clark Kee[1] was my New Testament professor who opened my eyes to a world of political reality I'd never seen before. I recall very clearly that day in October of 1955 when Dr. Kee was talking about the First Century context of the New Testament. He then began a discussion of Palestine in those days. This was just seven years after the formation of Israel as a state in Palestine. Virtually all of the students were supporters of Israel. We'd never really thought about the subject and knew very little of the history of the new state of Israel and absolutely nothing about Zionism.

One of the students made a comment about the problems the Israelis were having with the Palestinians. In his quiet and unassuming way, Dr. Kee said, "Well, there is more to this than meets your eyes." He shared that he'd been in Palestine in 1948 for an archaeological dig at Shechem, a significant place in Old Testament history. That was the same year the U.N. declared Israel a State and, in effect, gave a large part of Palestine to the new country. Dr. Kee said the first thing the Israeli army did was round up nearly a million Palestinians and put them into concentration camps, bulldozing their homes in hundreds of villages around the country. "Then," he said, "as soon as they had most of them behind barbed wire, they cut off the electricity and water."

This account felt like a bomb going off in my mind. The US media hadn't reported on it. But here was our New Testament professor telling us what he'd seen with his own eyes. We bombarded him with questions, and he shared a bit more before moving along with his lecture. But that was enough for me. For the first time, it made me aware that any accepted ideology should never be accepted without question.

From that day forward, my life has been an intertwining of my spiritual quest for God and God's purpose and an equally deep hunger for justice for all people.

Prologue

We achieve greatness by caring more than others think is wise, risking more than others think is safe, dreaming more than others think is practical, and expecting more than others think is possible.

—ARISTOTLE

IT WAS BY THE MEREST CHANCE that I ran into my good friend Luis Soares de Lima that fateful Monday morning in September 1974. As usual, I went to the Camaragibe, Brazil factory at seven o'clock. I had been General Manager there for slightly more than a year. The telephone was out of order, so two hours later, I got into my car and started toward Recife, about twenty minutes away, where I planned to make some calls from my apartment. That's when I saw Luis walking along the side of the road. I stopped and honked, and he got in the car.

Nearly a year prior, Luis had moved over 100 miles away to Joäo Pessoa. I saw him only occasionally when he returned to visit his girlfriend. We talked about her as we drove to my house, and he inquired about Tereza, my fiancée. At the apartment, I made four calls, then, at ten a.m., I looked at my watch. I had to be at the Bank of Brazil in ten minutes. Luis said he would get off on the way, do some errands, then return for lunch.

As we left, I noticed a well-dressed man with a beard coming up the stairs. I nodded to him and proceeded to my car. Just as I opened the door, the bearded man rushed up behind Luis, pointed a revolver at his back, and yelled something I couldn't understand. Soon, we were surrounded by three men armed with machine guns. I looked at Luis. *It was now our turn.*

Late at night over a beer, Luis and I had often talked about the people we knew who'd been imprisoned and tortured by the Brazilian Army and its secret police apparatus. Luis knew a man who chose to die under torture rather than betray his friends.

The Army had been interested in me for several months, ever since the June 24, 1974 issue of *Time* published a story about Dom Hélder Câmara, the Archbishop of Olinda and Recife. I was the *Associated Press (AP)* and *Time*'s stringer in Recife, so the Army erroneously assumed the story was mine. Colonel Meziat, head of Fourth Army Intelligence in Recife, called me in three times for questioning. Though cold at first, Colonel Meziat became quite *simpático*. He finally said that if I avoided communicating with the Archbishop and ceased to meddle in journalism, I'd have no problems.

I sent word to Dom Hélder and simply stopped filing material with *Time* and *AP*. I was not happy with this kind of censorship and control, but I wanted to stay in Brazil and would pay the price to do so. I'd been there for over a decade, primarily as a missionary of the United Methodist Church. In 1970, I was assigned to Recife to organize a Community Center and improve ecumenical relations with the Roman Catholic community, which is how I became a close friend of Dom Hélder, an outspoken critic of the military regime in Brazil.

Nine months before my arrest, I took a leave of absence from the Methodist Board of Global Ministries and went to work in a small industrial firm. Apparently, however, neither my new "civilian" status nor my promise to sever contact with Dom Hélder satisfied the authorities. So, it was that on September 30, 1974, they came to get me.

CHAPTER 1

Growing Up—Forever

My earliest memories are of Hunter, Oklahoma, the center of the dust bowl. Massive and frightening storms would blow up so much dust that red clouds would blot out the sun. When I was an infant, my mother had to put a damp dish towel over my crib during those storms to keep me from suffocating.

More than one trip in our Model A Ford had to be canceled halfway to Enid due to a dust storm approaching. My dad would race that car for all it was worth down the dirt roads to get home before the storm caught us. We were poor. My dad was paid $30 monthly plus the parsonage, which had no electricity or indoor plumbing.

I still remember the stress of using the outhouse. We learned to take some newspaper, set it on fire, put it inside the hole, and move it around to kill off any black widow spiders. A significant celebration was in order when the house finally got indoor plumbing and electricity.

We survived because the farmers in the church would often bring in vegetables and a chicken or two. My mother also had a garden in the backyard and canned all sorts of vegetables in the fall. She would keep them in the storm cellar.

When I was two, I came down with Scarlet Fever. The family doctor was afraid I wouldn't survive. My mom prayed long and fervently for me. Years later, after I became an ordained minister of the Methodist Church, she said she'd promised to dedicate me to God's service if I survived.

My parents married in 1929 when they were both 19 years old. The following year, my mother became pregnant with my brother Hughes Bentley Morris, Jr. He was born on November 8, 1931. I followed nearly two years later, on October 30, 1933. My father had felt a call to the ministry, following in the footsteps of his father, the Rev. Dr. Otho Birten Morris. He took appointments to churches in rural Oklahoma to maintain his family while slowly doing his college work, first at Enid, Oklahoma, and then at Oklahoma City University. It took him ten years to get his college degree to go to seminary.

In the meantime, he did a correspondence course the Methodist Church had established to prepare men (no women clergy in those days) for ministry. It was for people who couldn't make it to a regular seminary. He finished in 1939, the same year he graduated from college, and was ordained an Elder of the Methodist Church. In the Fall of 1940, he was able to study at Garrett Biblical Institute on the campus of Northwestern University in Evanston, Illinois. So he and my mother packed everything they owned, and we journeyed to Steward, a small town about 100 miles west of Chicago.

My father was in the city every week, Monday through Friday. He would come home each weekend to fulfill his church ministerial duties and spend time with his family. My mother, a bookkeeper, got a job in the local grain elevator. Essentially a single mom during those three years, she cared for me and my brother, worked full-time, and maintained our home. The parsonage had a coal-fired furnace, which had to be fed thrice daily in winter. The house had no insulation. If the fire went out, we risked freezing.

In 1942, my father was assigned to pastor the First Methodist Church in Plainfield. The church in Plainfield was made of Indiana limestone blocks with a beautiful spire reaching into the sky. Halfway up the spire, a set of carillon bells was played by hand by pushing down on a different lever for each note in the scale. Every Sunday morning at nine a.m., my father climbed the stairs inside the steeple to the bell room and for 20 minutes would play a series of hymns on the carillon, following the "Push-by-Number" instructions of the carillon hymn book.

On the first day of school in Plainfield, I was beaten up by a couple of the local bullies. Over the next few years, it became a pattern. My awareness grew of a reality faced by many preachers' kids: we were always the new kids. Perpetual outsiders. I did have a good experience with Boy Scouts. We got to go to camp where we'd swim, learn to shoot on the rifle range, and hear many dirty stories from our Scoutmaster, a WWII vet.

My dad graduated from Garrett in June 1943. Most graduates were in their early to mid-20s, while my dad was 32. He was the only one already an Elder in the Methodist Church. Two years after his graduation, he was appointed pastor of the First Methodist Church in Rochelle about six miles from Steward. I started eighth grade in Rochelle, again the new kid in town. I avoided the bullies, made a few friends, got crushes on girls, went to school dances, and lettered in football and tennis.

I ended my high school career in the number two spot among the boys, just behind Jerry Marxman who later went to Jet Propulsion Labs to invent some critical things for the NASA space program. After that, he became a co-founder of the petition-promoting website, Care2.com. I played trumpet and tuba in the band, the string bass in the orchestra, and sang in the chorus and in a male quartet under the gifted leadership of Leonard Gieske, our high school music teacher.

Like every other high schooler in town, I worked 15–18 hour days canning sweet peas and sweet corn during the summer for Del Monte, which had its Midwest headquarters and two large canning plants in Rochelle. We were paid 85¢ an hour, but there was a union, so we got overtime, which amounted to a pretty good wage. When the canning season was over, I went to the Rochelle Airport and plunked down my money for flying lessons. I made friends with my instructor, Clarence Staten, the owner-operator of the airport and a former P-47 pilot in World War II. He agreed to let me work at the airport for three hours after school every afternoon and take my wages in flying time.

I managed to rack up enough hours flying, so at age 17, a week after my high school graduation, I flew to Dixon, Illinois, took my flight exam, and got my private license. With my pilot's license and high school diploma, it was time to begin college and a new chapter of my life.

From the dusty plains of Hunter, Oklahoma, to the farmlands of Rochelle, Illinois, it's safe to say I experienced the full spectrum of ups and downs that come with growing up as a preacher's kid. I learned to understand the power of resilience and the importance of belonging. Finding solace in the Boy Scouts, school, music, and the pursuit of aviation, I owe a debt of gratitude to the many teachers and mentors I had along the way. They helped lay the foundation for my life of service and thirst for adventure.

Cornell College

During our last year in high school, my friend Dick Sherwood and I made a plan to take a year off before going to college. We were accepted to Cornell College, a small midwestern Methodist liberal arts school. We decided we'd go to Australia. We'd hitchhike to San Francisco and take a cargo ship, working as deckhands to pay our fare. But then along came the Korean War. We faced a decision: either go to college or be drafted into the army. It wasn't a tough decision. We went to Cornell.

Dick and I both moved into Merner Hall, one of the men's dorms. I had a job waiting tables at Pfeiffer Hall, a girls' dorm with a co-ed dining hall. Dick didn't need a job. His roommate was Virgil Vochaska, who became a prominent lawyer in Alaska. My roommate was a young Iowan named John Lively, destined to become a P.R. guy at 3M in Minnesota.

For the first time, I was on equal footing with everyone else. We were all freshmen—no one had been there forever. I started going out with girls—only a few of the 300 or so females on the campus of 600 students came with a boyfriend. I was amazed that I was not unattractive to some of them. I wanted to be an aeronautical engineer to join the space age. I declared a math major and started out toward engineering. In my sophomore year, I hit the wall with calculus. The teacher had a most unorthodox teaching manner, so I managed to get an A in the course, but I didn't know what I was doing. When I faced Calculus II with another professor, I realized I'd never make it.

I took a course in Milton that same year with Mr. Howard Lane, head of the English department, which gave me a glimpse into a whole new world of human experience. I had my "intellectual epiphany" during that course. Mr. Lane was the most brilliant professor I've ever had in my academic career, including at Cornell, Drew University, and the University of Chicago. He never got his doctorate because after working for nearly three years on his dissertation, he tore it up and never submitted it because he decided it was "no good."

I recall with a great deal of pride my one-page answer to Mr. Lane's essay exam on Milton's trilogy. *Paradise Lost:* Shouldn't, but did; *Paradise Regained:* Shouldn't and didn't; *Samson Agonistes:* Should and did. Mr. Lane's only comment: "Looks like Fred wins the trip to England." This is the finest accolade I ever received for my intellectual efforts.

I changed my major from Math to English Literature, with a minor in History. Mr. Lane insisted I write my undergraduate thesis on the writings of a then-pretty obscure writer, Franz Kafka. With a prophetic glance toward my own future, the title of my thesis was "Suffering as the Way into Life as Seen in the Writings of Franz Kafka."

An Encounter with God's Spirit

During my sophomore year, two young Presbyterian pastors, recent graduates of Princeton—Renwick Jackson and Bill Cohea—came to Cornell for a three-day "mission." After one of their presentations, I asked Ren Jackson for a private conference. He helped me see that I'd been "missing the mark" (the biblical definition of sin) in my life. Though my life was boringly "clean" and straightforward (I didn't smoke or drink or have sex), it was also nearly totally self-centered. I was not seeking or finding God's purpose for my life. Ren Jackson deftly pointed out that the solution was to commit myself to something or Someone greater than myself. He helped me decide to seek to follow Jesus Christ in my life from that moment on.

It was as though I'd just gotten a new pair of glasses. Everything was clearer, brighter, and more beautiful than before. Following Christ meant turning away from a self-centered life toward a *life for others,* to use the phrase made famous by Dietrich Bonhoeffer. This gave me a focus for everything I did from that point on in my life. I began looking at the meaning of human existence. A group of fellow students, including Tom Wharton, Bob Engel, Tom Stewart, Wayne Wasta, Ross Ludeman, John Tisdale, and Leo Riefer, began meeting regularly for Bible study, seeking to help each other figure out what this all meant.

My brother decided to follow my father into the church ministry a year earlier. I decided that was to be my path as well. The decision to follow Christ was profound and total and has shaped my life since the age of 19. The one persistent and consistent factor in my life has been my desire to find and follow God's purpose and to be a faithful follower of Jesus of Nazareth.

Carol

I met Carol Hills in Rochelle just before I entered eighth grade. She was one of three daughters of the school principal, C.A. Hills. The Hills family were members of the First Methodist Church. C.A. was extremely proud of his three beautiful daughters and sat with them in church every Sunday. Carol was popular in high school, always had a boyfriend, and seemed a bit stuck up.

I dated Mary, Carol's younger sister, a few times. She was about as shy as I was, so we never got far in our relationship. Sandra Newlin was my date for the junior prom. That was pretty much a disaster. She lived in Davis Junction, about 12 miles north of Rochelle. After saving my money for months, I bought us tickets for the after-prom dinner at the Rochelle Country Club. Hoping for warmth and affection after the dance and dinner, I was dismayed when she told me about 30 minutes before the Prom dance ended that she had to go right home, as her mother wouldn't let her be out after midnight.

I was relatively chubby throughout grade school. By 14, I'd grown taller and slimmed down but still had a self-image of being fat. I thought I was unattractive to girls. I didn't ask Carol Hills to go to a movie with me until college. Surprisingly, she said yes, and we had our first date. Next, I asked her to go to a football game and another movie with me. By that time, we were holding hands. I began to think maybe something would come of it. When I started kissing Carol, I thought the sky was falling. After three passionate years of dating, loving, and dreaming, we were finally married in the Rochelle Methodist Church on August 22, 1954. It was the summer before our senior year of college.

We arranged to live in the "Married Barracks" at Cornell during our Senior year. These were small one-bedroom units in converted army barracks left over from WWII. Our wedding was a big affair, complete with all the trimmings. My mother-in-law, Grace, drove everyone nuts getting ready for the event. Her husband, Carol's father, died in 1950 at the age of 49, and this was the first wedding among her daughters. It was a lovely wedding, presided over by my father, Hughes Bentley Morris, Sr. My brother was my best man, and Ross Ludeman and Tom Wharton, college roommates, were my attendants. Carol was attended by some Cornell classmates and her sisters.

Stanwood Methodist Church

In September 1953, at age 19, I began my career as a Methodist preacher. I was appointed student pastor at the Stanwood Methodist Church, a farming community about 15 miles from Mount Vernon on Old Highway 30. Most members were wonderful and open-hearted folk, typical of rural Iowa. Still, like many such congregations, it was controlled by a handful of people who'd long ago gotten their hands on the levers of power in that community and were determined to hold onto them at all costs.

In my youthful enthusiasm, I was determined to tithe my $1,500/year income, giving $150/year to the church I was serving. Much to my dismay, I discovered this made me the most significant contributor to the church. As I watched the good folks of Stanwood arrive in their Cadillacs with their wives draped in furs, I felt a great deal of resentment at their stinginess. However, they seemed to like my preaching. They liked Carol, and the Women's Society gave us a check for $7.50 as a wedding present, splitting the difference between those who wanted to give us $10 and those who thought $5 would be enough.

The decision to go into the Methodist ministry meant going to seminary. Dr. Arthur Whitney, a recruiter from Drew University, came to Cornell, and I decided to go to New Jersey for theological studies. The fact that Drew was in the New York City metropolitan area was an attraction to a country boy from the Midwest. Carol had gotten a job from the Board of Education of Chatham, New

Jersey, to teach a fourth-grade class. I got a job for the summer as a replacement guard at the Iowa State Reformatory in Anamosa. It was a medium-security prison, and I worked from two p.m. until ten p.m. each day, substituting for the regular guards who took their summer vacations. With no training and very little orientation, I was told to stand in the prison yard during the afternoon, watching the inmates lift weights and play baseball.

Most of the inmates were young men, many about my age, who'd "gone wrong" by swiping some farmer's car for a joy ride, abandoning the vehicle, usually unharmed, a few hours later. Of course, several career criminal inmates in the prison served as role models and provided a school for crime to the joyriders. Too many of that group learned how to pursue a career of crime while in the Reformatory.

I established a friendship with Jim Renfro, one of the few lifers in the prison. He was in his late thirties, having been imprisoned at the age of 19 for murder. While on leave from the Navy, he and his best buddy got drunk. When they ran out of money, they decided to rob a gas station to continue their binge. Jim's buddy got a gun from somewhere, and they staggered into the gas station. Unfortunately for them, the attendant grabbed his own gun, which led Jim's buddy to shoot him.

After nearly 20 years in prison, Jim had read almost all the books in the library. He seemed remarkably free of bitterness but was aware that he'd wasted his life. He was intrigued by my decision to go into the ministry. We had long conversations, which got me a reprimand from the Warden's office for fraternizing with the inmates. The whole system seemed to me to be counterproductive. Nothing in the system remotely resembled rehabilitation for these men who had "gone wrong."

Drew Theological School

Carol and I moved into married campus housing—a small, furnished one-bedroom apartment—at Drew. We were soon joined by newlyweds Gil and Miriam Dawes, and Bob and Beth Engel. Miriam was teaching to support her husband. Carol and Miriam soon met Jody McMullen, a fellow teacher whose husband, Bud, was also a student at Drew. Bud, Gil, Bob, and I became close friends. After working two or three jobs throughout my time at Cornell, I was delighted to be able to dedicate all of my time and energy to my studies at Drew. We could get by with the scholarship I'd received and Carol's income.

At the time, Drew had the best faculty among all 12 Methodist seminaries. Dr. Carl Michalson was one of the most creative young theologians in the US and a marvelous teacher. Dr. Howard Clark Kee was a brilliant light among New Testament scholars, while Dr. Lawrence Tombs was an inspiring Old Testament teacher, and Dr. John Patterson was a longtime star of Old Testament studies. Dr. Bernard Anderson, a highly renowned Biblical scholar and a creative teacher, was also the dean of the seminary. Dr. William Farmer taught New Testament, and though not as scholarly as others, he could connect the world of Jesus' time and what was happening in our world in a way that some of his colleagues could not. I studied Biblical languages—Greek and Hebrew—taking an intensive course in Hebrew over the summer that packed a year's worth of study into six weeks.

In January of 1956, at the beginning of my second semester, Dr. Whitney, who had inspired me to go to Drew, called me into his office and asked if I'd be interested in a part-time position as Chaplain at a home for the aged in Morristown, about 15 miles away. It would involve one afternoon and one Sunday a week at the home and another afternoon with Dr. Keith Keidel, the Chaplain of the Greystone State Mental Hospital. This could be a valuable learning opportunity, and the stipend would be helpful for our expenses. So, after talking it over with Carol, I accepted the job.

The Morris County Home provided care for 125 patients. To be admitted, one had to be over 65 and need medical assistance with no family that could provide care. The director, Miss Byram, was a caring registered nurse specializing in geriatric nursing. But I found the whole place intimidating. Many of the patients were stroke victims or had Alzheimer's (though that disease had not been named in those days), so they couldn't communicate well, if at all. At 22, I was full of vim, vigor, and vinegar, and didn't know how to relate to what I was witnessing at the home. On Sundays, I arrived with a brief worship service and a mini-sermon. Miss Byram would play piano for the hymns, and I often sang a solo as folks could not follow along in the hymnal.

Miss Byram insisted this was a wonderful gift, and the folks greatly appreciated my pastoral visits. Most of them had outlived their families or the interest of their families in them. One afternoon, one of the patients shared her scrapbook with me. She'd been a silent movie star in Hollywood in her 20s. I was nearly overwhelmed looking at her past and seeing her alone in the world. On Thursday afternoons, I would meet with Dr. Keith Keidel at Greystone to evaluate my work at the home. He assisted me in processing what was going on with me and the good folks at the home. This experience, along with my formative years at Drew, helped lay the foundation for my theological journey ahead.

Franklin Memorial Methodist Church

Toward the end of my second year at Drew, Carol and I thought about starting our family. I decided to take a parish for my senior year so Carol could stop working. I made contacts through Dr. Arthur Whitney at Drew's field placement office with Methodist District Superintendents (D.S.) in the area. In relatively short order, a D.S. from Queens contacted me. We drove into the city for a meeting with the congregation. They had a potluck supper and we met with the Pastoral Relations Committee. We were somewhat put off when we discovered most of the good folks in the church had never been to Manhattan Island. Even though it was in New York City, it seemed like the parochial and limited-vision group of folks in Stanwood, Iowa, where I'd served my very first church.

I remember saying specifically in my prayers, "If we don't get an obvious signal before ten a.m. tomorrow, I'm going to call the D.S. and accept." I had learned from Glenn Clark's remarkable book, *I Will Lift Up Mine Eyes,* how to make that kind of prayer for guidance. At exactly nine a.m. the following day, I got a phone call from the D.S. of the Newark District, asking if I'd be willing to accept an appointment at Franklin Memorial Methodist Church. He told me about the history of the church—the oldest Methodist Church in New Jersey, founded in 1831. We agreed to meet with the Pastoral Relations Committee the following evening. It turned out to be one man, Roy Harrison, one of the longtime pillars of the church.

I then had to call the D.S. in Queens to tell him we'd need a couple of days before we could give him an answer. He said he couldn't wait and we had to decide immediately. So, I said "no," albeit with some fear and trepidation as we turned down a sure thing for something we didn't know. The next evening, we drove to the Franklin Memorial Methodist Church site. The building was beautiful, a traditional New England church with white columns in the front holding up the steeple. The basement had a large fellowship hall and a kitchen ready to handle potluck and roast beef dinners. The church property extended to the end of the block with a large open area and a lovely, though neglected, rose garden.

Franklin Church had about 165 members, down from its glory days of more than 300. Most of the members were over 50 and no longer lived in the neighborhood that was now predominantly Jewish. After we toured the church, Roy took us to see the parsonage, a typical 1920s neighborhood house with a wide porch across the front. Without further ado, we announced to Roy we would be happy to serve Franklin Memorial Methodist Church. It was agreed that I would preach my first sermon at Franklin on the second Sunday of June 1957. Thus began three wonderfully satisfying years in my ministry. The people of Franklin responded enthusiastically to my preaching efforts and surrounded us with their love and care.

Feeling very strongly about my call to preach the Good News of God's love for us all, I wanted to do evangelistic work in the area. We organized a "religious census" of the neighborhood to determine potential new participants. In the eight-block area between the church and the parsonage, there were just five persons who were not Jewish: A Methodist couple who lived across the street from us, Carol and I, and a Catholic man who was married to a Jewish woman. I did not feel compelled to try to convert Jews to Christianity. I was already rejecting the feelings expressed by some of my classmates that if you weren't a Christian, you were doomed to Hell. That thought didn't fit what I'd been studying in the Gospels.

I had to accept that there wasn't room for growth in the membership, but I did learn a lot about pastoral care. During my three years at Franklin, I had a total of 18 funerals. I also got a lot of practice making calls to 26 different hospitals in the Newark/New York area. There were few children in the congregation. Except for an Adult Bible Class, the Sunday School was practically nonexistent.

During that first summer, Dick Critz, a classmate of mine at Drew, asked if there would be any possibility of working with me at Franklin. Dick was the most unusual student on campus. He was ten years older than the rest of us and married to a woman 15 years older than him. Dick had flown B-24s in World War II and received a Silver Star at the age of 19 for bringing his plane home after his pilot had been killed flying over the Ploesti oil fields in Romania. He had a degree in architecture from Yale, *magna cum laude*. He also had little tolerance for fools and was one of the most abrasive and outspoken people around, which resulted in being almost impossible to place in any congregation for fieldwork.

It happened that Franklin had an item in its budget to pay a teacher for the adult Bible class, so I suggested to Dick that he could fill that post. Dick was highly appreciative of my willingness to help him and became fascinated with the messages I was bringing to the congregation. Sometime in October, he gave me *The Lost Shepherd,* a book by Agnes Sanford, an author I'd never heard of. It was a novel about a pastor who couldn't quite find his way in his ministry until a young woman helped him discover God's healing power through prayer.

In my religious pilgrimage, I'd been seeking a way to experience the spiritual power described on nearly every page of the New Testament. Apparently, Dick had seen my concern and thought that Agnes Sanford might be of help. After reading the book, I told him I found it immensely exciting but frustrating. I didn't know how to get "there" from "here." He knew Agnes Sanford personally and had gone to a couple of her schools for Pastoral Care. He contacted her and got a scholarship for me to attend one of the schools in December 1957 at her home parish in Whitinsville, Massachusetts. That week was to forever change my life and ministry.

CHAPTER 2

Awakening the Healing Light

WHITINSVILLE IS A SMALL TOWN in western Massachusetts, taken from a New England calendar. I arrived at the Western Diocese Retreat Center of the Episcopal Church—a converted three-story home that once belonged to one of the movers and shakers of Whitinsville. A broad porch went around two sides of the house.

The group gathered in the library, and Agnes strolled in. She must have been about 55, with short black hair beginning to show some gray. Most of the men had beards and long hair and smoked pipes. Several mentioned they had been in ministry for more than 20 years and felt frustrated they weren't more effective in meeting the needs of their flocks. A couple said they'd attended the school before and were back for a "second dose." When it was my turn, I simply said I was preparing for ministry and was puzzled that the churches I knew didn't show any of the spiritual power we see in the New Testament. I said I wanted to learn more about how to get in touch with that power for my ministry.

Agnes took the floor at the head of the circle of chairs where we were seated. She talked quietly but with authority. She started by reminding us that for the first three hundred years of the Church's existence, healings, and other miracles were pretty much the order of the day. After Constantine declared Christianity to be the Roman Empire's official religion, it became politically convenient for people to become Christians. What had been a persecuted movement soon became a road to political power and success. The spiritual power all but faded away. At this same time, "doctrines" became important. Agnes then pointed out the times of revival, such as St. Francis of Assisi's attempts to reform the Church, the Lutheran revolt, and the Wesleyan Revival. In the mid-1800s, the churches agreed on adopting what she called the 19th Century Heresy—that if people weren't healed, it was because it was *not* God's will.

Much of Agnes' personal life is reflected in her book *The Lost Shepherd,* as the heroine struggles with depression and suicidal tendencies, then tells the story of how she regained her sanity and found a purpose for her life by taking seriously the messages of the New Testament. Agnes asserted that the most crucial first step was to break with the tradition of the 19th Century heresy that illness might somehow be God's will. She embraced wholeheartedly the idea that Jesus presented that God is our "Father" (Abba) who loves us beyond imagining.

"Can you imagine," she asked, "a human father giving his child leukemia to 'teach him something?'" But that's what the churches often tell people when tragedy strikes. "Because we don't know how to channel God's power for healing," she continued, "we invent excuses for why healing doesn't occur. The most convenient excuse is that it's not God's will." She added that God's will is *always* for good things to happen in our lives. If they don't happen, it is not because God doesn't want them to but because something or someone—including ourselves—has gotten in the way of God's will for us.

"Do any of you think God doesn't want to save everyone?" she asked. "Let me remind all of you clergy who have studied Greek and Hebrew that the word for salvation in the Bible is the same root word as healing, wholeness, peace, or abundant life. If that is what God clearly wants for all humanity, then we must seek to become instruments of God's power here and now for God's will of salvation, healing, and wholeness to become a reality in the lives of our people.

"When a table lamp doesn't work in our home," she continued, "we don't automatically assume that the power company has gone out of business. No, we check to see if the lamp is plugged in and the bulb is good. Then, we might check the fuse box or the circuit breaker. Finally, we'd check to see if we forgot to pay the bill. But we would never assume the electricity company has stopped supplying power. So why do we assume that God has gone out of business because we don't see God's power at work?" asked Agnes.

"Doesn't it make more sense," she said, "to continue to assume that God is still in the healing and saving business and start to check out our connections to the source of power?"

The rest of the week was dedicated to showing us how to make contact with God's power and let it flow through us for the healing of the people we seek to minister. This was precisely what I had been hoping to find in seminary. People needed healing, love, and support to deal with situations of abuse and exploitation or moments of financial crisis. Why was the church so willing to be concerned about the "next life" and not about people's suffering in this life? It seemed to me that the church—and the churches—were more concerned about their own institutional life and growth than in their ability to channel God's power to enable people to embrace and enjoy the abundant life that Jesus proclaimed and lived, even while living in poverty and under an oppressive regime in the First Century. And now, here was Agnes Sanford offering guidance for how to become agents of God's power here and now.

The Healing Light

Agnes found that the image of light, with which the author(s) of the *Book of Genesis* begin the Creation stories, helps us understand how God's power can be channeled through us to perform God's will for Abundant Life. She discovered that as she came into God's Presence, she brought the person needing God's healing into that presence. Agnes saw the person surrounded by the light of God's infinite love. Walking us through such a prayer, she showed us how to see that healing light flowing into us, through us, and into every part of the body of the suffering person. She had us visualize that light was flowing with the bloodstream of the person, reaching into every cell of the body, revitalizing, nourishing, and healing whatever was not perfect.

She demonstrated by leading a healing prayer for a minister with an arthritic knee. Rejecting prayers with doubt, Agnes emphasized trusting in God's will for wholeness. After the prayer, the minister reported significant relief, exemplifying the effectiveness of persistent faith.

Agnes was particularly critical of the typical church prayer that ended with "If it be Thy will." She would not allow us to add that escape clause. "If you have any doubt that God wants to heal the person in question, then don't pray for them," she said. Simply offer them to God. But if we understand that God *always* wills health, wholeness, and healing, then we pray with trust in God and end our prayer with heartfelt thanks that God is moving in and through us to carry out God's will of wholeness.

A Second Blessing

Agnes took a shine to me and my enthusiasm. During our afternoon coffee break one day, she invited me to an upper room experience the following day. She shared how she asked a few good friends to join her for a prayer retreat after experiencing a period of depression and near exhaustion. They spent a day or two reading the Bible and talking about the ups and downs of their spiritual journeys. Finally, they simply started praying for God's Spirit to come and fill them with the power they needed to be effective in their ministries. Agnes shared how they immediately felt a sense of warmth and comfort, as though a great spiritual blanket was being laid over them. Then, one by one, they began praising God with words that they didn't know or understand. She thought I was ready for this same experience.

I awoke before six a.m. the next morning feeling like a kid on Christmas day. We gathered in the upper room. Agnes said the Holy Spirit was in all of us in our Baptism but we had to allow that Spirit to fill us. She invited me to sit as the others gathered around and laid their hands on me. Agnes began praying quietly. I could feel a tingling around my mouth as her hands trembled slightly on my head. Then, I found myself uttering syllables I did not know. As I spoke these strange words, the tingling moved throughout my body like a mild electric current. I felt an unspeakable joy flowing through me and out through my mouth with this new language.

Agnes was also praying in tongues. We did this together for about five minutes until she gradually brought it to an end, thanking God and praying that my life be used for the work of Jesus. This began a period of spiritual life for me that has shaped me ever since. For the next decade, I would get up before 5:30 every morning to spend an hour reading the Bible and praying in tongues.

Beginning a Ministry of Healing

I returned home and enthusiastically announced from the pulpit that I would start a series of Prayer and Bible Study meetings. A few women showed up for the first gathering, plus the lay leader, a retired man with time on his hands. I started by sharing some of the highlights of my experience in Massachusetts. We discussed problems the group had experienced with prayer, and I suggested we begin experimenting by praying for people they knew needed help.

Within a few weeks, the group grew to about a dozen, all women, plus our faithful lay leader. We had developed a list of 25 names of persons/situations we all agreed we would pray for daily. We would keep each person/situation on the list for four weeks.

The list contained people with heart problems, cancer, financial problems, marital problems, substance abuse problems, and others. We spent the first hour of each meeting studying the Bible, focusing on Jesus' ministry. After a period of quiet spent focusing on the presence of God's Spirit, we would pray by name for each person/situation on the list, visualizing the healing light of God's Spirit touching and surrounding each one.

Bill Mann

At the end of a Sunday service in early Spring 1958, I saw a man standing off to one side of the church. He needed a shave and looked like he'd slept in his clothes. After greeting the worshippers at the door, I asked if I could help him. I invited him into my office. He was clearly uncomfortable and nervous. He said he didn't know if I could help him. It was the first time he'd ever been in a church. His wife had thrown him out and said she was going to divorce him. He had no money and didn't know what to do. Being 24 years old and a not-yet-graduate of a seminary, I realized I needed to buy myself some time. So, I asked for his name.

"Bill Mann," he said.

"I don't have any money to give you," I said, "but if you can come back tomorrow at seven p.m., I will have some to help you hang on for a while."

Then, I handed him a copy of J.B. Phillips' modern translation of the Gospels and suggested he read it. He thanked me and left. The next evening, I was in my office at six-thirty, wondering if Bill would show up. A little after seven, I heard someone come into the church. There was Bill, dressed in a cleanly pressed suit, with his head held high and a smile on his face.

"Bill, what happened to you?" I couldn't help asking.

"I don't really know," he said. "When I left here yesterday, I went home and begged my wife to let me stay there overnight. I started reading that book you gave me. Then I got to the part where Jesus was telling the story of the man who had two sons, and how one of them took his inheritance and blew it all on drink and women and ended up in a pig pen. So he went home and begged his father to hire him to work on the farm. I realized that was *me.* Suddenly, I felt surrounded by a bright light that loved me. I knew I was going to be okay. Since then, I haven't had any desire to drink. I took a shower, shaved, and put on my best clothes, and here I am."

"Bill, you met the Holy Spirit of Jesus," I said. "You have been surrounded by the Love of Christ."

Bill stopped drinking altogether. He convinced his best friend, Harvey, to quit drinking. I got the two of them into an AA group. They both started coming to church. I discovered they were roofers. I asked if they knew anything about slate roofs, as the church's roof urgently needed some attention, and slate roofers were hard to find. They did, so we hired them to fix our roof. They did a splendid job. Bill's wife also started coming to our church. Though she professed to be Catholic, she was nearly overwhelmed by her "new" husband. My part in this healing was minimal. I just handed Bill a copy of the Gospels. But the same Spirit of God that had touched my life reached out to Bill—and his wife—in what I can only call a miraculous way.

Elsie Kraus

Elsie Kraus was a longtime Methodist. Her husband, Joe, was a non-practicing Jew but attended church faithfully every Sunday with Elsie. On Palm Sunday, they were not in church. Later that day, Joe called and asked me to come to their home. In hushed tones, Joe met me at the door and informed me that Elsie's doctor had just left. She was extremely ill with heart disease. Elsie was in her early 60s. Her heart was seriously enlarged, and the valves were leaking. The doctor said it was just a matter of days before her heart would simply stop.

I went upstairs to Elsie's bedroom. She was half awake, pale, and looked very weak. I greeted her, and she perked up a bit. We chatted briefly. I said I had missed them in church that morning and came by to see how she was doing. We didn't talk about her condition. Joe had told me the doctor had not informed Elsie of the seriousness of her situation. I asked her if I could pray for her. I put my left hand on her forehead, held her right hand in mine, and gave a brief prayer. I asked God's Spirit to flow through me and my hands into her body to heal and restore every part. I spoke slowly, feeling a vibration in my hands as I prayed. I concluded by thanking God for being with us and hearing our prayers.

Drew Seminary, in its wisdom, scheduled mid-term exams during Holy Week. That meant I had to spend every day of that week until Good Friday at Drew, either in the library, studying, or taking an exam. I also had to prepare for our Maundy Thursday service with Holy Communion. I was so frazzled by exams and other pastoral duties that Elsie completely slipped my mind. Joe had not called, so I assumed she had not died, but I was embarrassed about not following up on my Sunday visit.

I jumped in my ancient British Austin that got about 15 miles on a quart of oil, left clouds of smoke behind, and drove across town to the Krause residence. With fear and trembling, I rang the doorbell. After a brief wait, the door opened, and Elsie stood, fully dressed and looking better than I'd ever seen her. Their doctor had come by on Monday to check on her, expecting the worst. After about ten minutes, he asked Joe, "What has been happening here?"

"Nothing," Joe said, "except our pastor came over and prayed with Elsie." The doctor said her heart appeared normal, and the valves were no longer leaking. It sounded like a perfectly normal heart. That kind of thing just simply doesn't happen, he said.

My Missionary Calling

I graduated from Drew with a Master's of Divinity degree, *cum laude,* in June of 1959. We decided to stay at Franklin for another year as I wanted to do additional study at Union Theological Seminary in New York City that fall. My friend Gil Dawes had talked about becoming a missionary in Bolivia, and his enthusiasm was contagious. I was intrigued by stories of missionary pilots who traveled to share the Good News of Jesus. I contacted the Board of Missions of the Methodist Church in New York City. After much conversation, Carol and I contacted the personnel office of the Board, and they sent us many documents to fill out to become candidates for missionary work.

After a few interviews, we were invited to take psychological tests to see if we were suitable for overseas work. Things didn't work out as we had anticipated. We were invited for another interview, and, with considerable gentleness, informed that we were not accepted. The psychological exams indicated a certain rigidity of personality in Carol that they felt would not allow her to adapt well to the demands of a new culture. They offered to pay for some psychological counseling to see if she could make the necessary adjustments to be a candidate in the future.

We began seeing Dr. James Ranck, a professor of pastoral counseling at Drew and a clinical psychologist. We both liked him a great deal. Even after the Board stopped paying, we continued to see him. It helped me deal with my frustrations and the emptiness in our marriage. Carol and I were excellent friends and shared many common interests, but our relationship had yet to develop as desired by both of us.

Good Samaritan Methodist Church

In early March 1960, I got a call from the Rev. Weldon Gatlin, District Superintendent of the Western District of the Northern

Illinois Annual Conference. Rev. Gatlin was part of the "Oklahoma mafia" that had followed my dad to Garrett from Oklahoma in the early 1940s. He asked if I would accept an appointment to a new church in Addison, Illinois, a suburb of Chicago. He said the Rev. Ralph Miller had been "swarming the bees" in Addison, and they urgently needed someone to take over as founding pastor.

I called my dad for his opinion. Bishop Charles Wesley Brashares had appointed him to the District from Rochelle at the age of 39, making him the youngest person ever to serve as a D.S. in the conference's history. He loved the work as a D.S. He said, "A church can survive a bad pastor, but a pastor may not survive a bad church."

In his first year, my father got a salary raise for all of his 90 pastors. Every time he arrived for the fourth quarterly conference, his first question was, "How much of a raise are you giving your pastor this year?" He would be met with blank stares. Dad would then say, "Well, if you can't afford to give your pastor a raise, I may have to transfer him to a church that can. And, I need to tell you that I'm facing a shortage of pastors (a pious lie) and may not be able to supply your pulpit."

He also got every church in the District to pay its conference apportionments. Sometimes, a pastor would start crying poor in the middle of the year, warning that his congregation was having a hard time and might be unable to pay its apportionment in full. So my dad would say, "Well, if you can't get your congregation to pay its fair share, I may have to transfer you to a church with a smaller apportionment." That would also mean a smaller salary, motivating the pastors to ensure the apportionment was paid in full.

My paternal grandfather, the Rev. Dr. Otho Birten Morris, had been a D.S. in the Tulsa District in the Oklahoma Conference in the early 1930s. He fell in love with Eva, one of the few women preachers of that time. As my dad recalled his childhood, his mother, Wynemah Hunt Morris, had been a nearly-total shrew throughout her marriage to my grandfather, who also had to deal with the constant presence of his mother-in-law. So, when he found Eva, who could give him love, he finally got a divorce and remarried. This was nearly unheard of in 1935. Forced to leave the Methodist ministry, he became a pastor in the Christian Church. He died while I was in college.

My mom was in a panic when my dad became a D.S. Even as a child, I was required to ride with my father to meetings if he had to take a woman with him. He never wanted to be seen alone in a car with a woman who wasn't my mom. When the Arlington Heights church opened three years later, my dad volunteered to take that appointment. With 1,300 members, the church was already considered a good one. When he left after nine years, it was the largest in the Annual Conference, with more than 3,500 members and a new sanctuary.

My dad had mixed feelings about me taking the appointment to Addison. "It could be a good stepping-stone for your career," he said. However, he disagreed with the conference policy of appointing entry-level pastors to start new churches. "It's like putting someone who has never ridden a horse on a horse that has never been ridden so they can learn together," he said.

The day after Easter in 1960, we packed our belongings and drove back to Chicago. The 150-member congregation met at Fullerton Grade School in Addison with a choir and booming Sunday School. The new houses in this exploding suburb were starter homes, and the town was filled with young couples. Shortly after settling into Addison, we applied to adopt a baby. After several meetings, filling out many forms, and months of waiting, we got a call in March 1961. We drove to Chicago on March 10 to receive our daughter, Jennifer Ruth, who was born only five days earlier. It was a time of overwhelming joy for us and the congregation.

Gordon Davis, a super-salesman for Taylor Instruments, organized what the Methodists called a Fishermen's Club, about a dozen men who would gather once a week for supper and then go out two-by-two and ring doorbells inviting people to come to visit the church the following Sunday. I formed Get-Acquainted Classes to introduce people to the Methodist Church and Good Samaritan. The first class dealt with an overview of Christian doctrine, in which I emphasized the fundamental premise that God loves us all unconditionally. I pointed out that in the history of the church, it wasn't until the year 451, at the Council of Chalcedon, when 520 Bishops from all over the collapsing Roman Empire met, that it was decided by a vote of the Bishops that "Jesus was divine." The Bishops were divided over that issue, and the vote was close. Next, I gave an overview of Church history, warts and all. I pointed out how the church's history is essentially the story of how, as my New Testament professor, Dr. Howard Kee, put it, men unsuccessfully tried to "domesticate" the Holy Spirit.

The third Sunday was dedicated to the history of the Methodist Church. I traced the career of John Wesley, who, as a young student at Oxford, formed what he called the "Holy Club" of students willing to accept a rigid discipline of Bible study and prayer. The other students criticized them and called them "Methodists" because of their methodical disciplines. Wesley adopted this name wholeheartedly. Finally, I talked about the Disciplines of the Christian Life, sharing something of the importance of worship and prayer, service and sharing in the ministry of the church in our communities, finishing with an invitation to join the people of the Good Samaritan Methodist Church in following the leadership of Jesus.

I also began a Prayer/Healing Study group. About 10 women showed up for the first session. We bought copies of *The Healing Light* and used it as our study guide. We soon had a list of more than 20 we prayed for each day. There was great excitement in the group each week as people brought progress reports. The group nearly doubled in size.

Good Samaritan received 88 new members in the first year, over half of whom had never belonged to any church. The Annual Conference had given us a four-acre plot of land, and we started planning our church building. We got bids for the project, and by December 1960, we had hired a contractor and put together the financing through a mortgage from a local Savings and Loan for $100,000. On January 1, 1961, we had the ground-breaking ceremony. In the spring of 1962, we had the dedication of the new building, complete with the presence of our Bishop, Charles Wesley Brashares. The residential neighborhood being built next to our property named three streets in the new subdivision after the Methodists: one was Wesley Drive, another was Brashares Avenue, and the third was Morris Avenue.

Karen Campbell

The prayer group had been meeting for about a year when we were presented with the name Karen Campbell. Just nine years old, Karen was having trouble walking. A series of X-rays and blood tests confirmed she had tuberculosis of the hip joint and would need an operation. Even then, she might end up in a wheelchair permanently. The prayer group spent about 15 minutes visualizing the healing light of God's Spirit reaching out to Karen and flowing throughout her body, into every cell, purging away darkness and renewing and restoring any damaged tissues.

The next day, Karen's mother took her to the doctor to schedule the surgery. The doctor took more X-rays to better orient himself for the procedure. On Friday, after studying the new X-rays, the doctor called Karen's mother and said they didn't need to do any surgery. Karen's hip joint was perfectly normal. Whatever had been there in the first X-rays was gone. The bones were entirely normal! He offered no explanation, but really, none was needed.

Confronting Prejudice in Addison

The US Army had a Nike missile site just outside of Addison, where a battery of anti-missile-missiles was kept at the ready to defend us all from a possible attack from the Soviet Union. One day, a new army family moved in—a white sergeant with a Black wife and two brown children. It didn't take long for Addison's "good citizens" to begin putting up For Sale signs in the area near the army homes.

The Mayor of Addison called the commanding officer at the Nike site into town for a meeting. At two p.m. on the agreed-upon afternoon, Colonel Green arrived at the mayor's office. To the surprise—no, shock—of the mayor's secretary, Colonel Green was Black. She invited them to sit in the anteroom and rushed in to tell the mayor about this new development. The mayor didn't hesitate to leave out the back door. No meeting took place.

Bud Loftus, my Catholic Kiwanian friend and city attorney, let it be known he would issue arrest warrants for anyone responsible for any ugliness toward the sergeant and his family. I went to call on the sergeant and invited the family to our church. Knowing they would unlikely come to the church by themselves, I asked Ralph and Dottie Berg, leaders at Good Samaritan Methodist Church and near neighbors to the newly arrived army family, to bring them to our church the following Sunday.

The sergeant was on duty that day, but his wife and two daughters came with Ralph and Dottie. The superintendent of our Sunday School, Olin Heflin, was from Mississippi and had played tackle for Old Miss. When he saw this Black woman and her two children enter his Sunday School, he couldn't handle it. He didn't say anything or do anything ugly, but after church service, he came to me and said he'd have to resign as superintendent of the Sunday School.

"Fred, I'm sorry," he said. "I just can't do it."

"I can't accept your resignation," I said, "but I'll give you a six-month leave of absence so you can get your head and heart on straight."

He did. Three months later, on World Communion Sunday, Olin knelt at the altar and found himself next to the sergeant's wife. After that, he was all right and resumed his post as superintendent of the Sunday School.

Missionary Training

At the end of our three years at Good Samaritan, it had grown to a congregation of 227, making it the fastest growing church in the Conference. However, we were still interested in mission work. I invited a missionary couple on furlough in Brazil, Bob and Ella Jean Davis, to speak to our congregation. They introduced us to Gerson and Alicia Veiga, a young Brazilian couple living in Evanston. Gerson was getting his Ph.D. in Biblical Studies at Garrett, and Alicia worked as a bilingual secretary at the International Headquarters of Rotary International in Evanston. They encouraged us to go to Brazil. We reapplied to the Board of Global Ministries and were accepted after a few months of more paperwork and psychological exams. In June 1963, we said tearful goodbyes to the wonderful people at Good Samaritan and sailed off into the sunrise, as it were.

"I always suspected you were a drifter," said Ralph Berg, one of the church leaders, when we announced we were going to Brazil.

The first stage of our missionary career took us back to Drew University for a six-week course in linguistics with a couple hundred other missionary candidates. To our surprise, our dear friends Gil and Miriam Dawes were there, preparing to go to Argentina. Next, we went to Stony Point, New York, for a five-month orientation course. There were mini-courses in anthropology, sociology, theology, and politics. We were encouraged to think of ourselves as collaborators with the churches in the countries we were going to rather than "great-white-father-figures" going to "save" the natives. I was simply excited to be allowed to go to Brazil. I had been greatly influenced by Roland Allen, an English missionary and author. One of his books, *Missionary Methods: St. Paul's or Ours?* (1912) was exciting to me. Allen's conviction was that the success of St. Paul was due to his trusting in the Holy Spirit to work in and through the new converts. He entrusted the new churches he founded to the converts right from the beginning rather than keeping them "under supervision" for years and years.

A significant part of the Stony Point experience was with the 120 other missionary candidates: Methodists, Presbyterians, United Church of Christ missionaries, Episcopalians, and others. It was the richest ecumenical experience I'd had up to then. During that time, a large group of us took a chartered bus to Washington, D.C., to participate in the March on Washington organized by the Southern Christian Leadership Conference, the NAACP, the Congress on Racial Equality, and the National Urban League. A. Phillip Randolph, the president of the Brotherhood of Sleeping Car Porters, president of the Negro American Labor Council, and vice president of the AFL-CIO, initiated the march which was soon supported by all the other groups.

They'd hoped to get 100,000 persons to attend, but more than 250,000 arrived on more than 2,000 chartered buses, 21 special trains, and 10 chartered airplanes. Six prominent African-American leaders gave speeches, and Joan Baez and Bob Dylan performed. And, of course, the *I Have a Dream* speech by the Rev. Dr. Martin Luther King, Jr. electrified the participants and the entire nation. Carol and I were standing not more than 50 feet from the podium where Dr. King spoke in front of the Lincoln Memorial. It was one of the most exciting moments of my life.

On November 22, 1963, Carol and I went to New York City to pick up our passports at the Brazilian Consulate. We decided to splurge a bit and have lunch in Manhattan. While waiting for our food, the waiter came rushing into the dining room and announced to everyone that President John F. Kennedy had been assassinated. We spent the next few days glued to the television. On Sunday afternoon, we were watching *live* TV when Lee Harvey Oswald, the alleged killer, was shot by Jack Ruby as he was being transferred to another jail in Dallas.

Language School in Brazil

On January 12, 1964, our plane from Lima approached Rio de Janeiro. Our pilot swept around Sugar Loaf Mountain and gave us a magnificent view of the Cidade Maravilhosa (the Marvelous City) before landing at the Galeão International Airport. Marion Way, a Methodist missionary posted at the People's Central Institute, received us. He drove us to the Institute, where his wife, Anita, the daughter of Methodist missionaries to Brazil, graciously received us.

The next morning we flew to São Paulo, where Bob Davis, now the Field Treasurer for the Board, met us and took us to their home. Bob and his wife, EJ (Ella Jean), were most gracious. They had been part of the process leading to our decision to go to Brazil as missionaries and felt somewhat responsible for us. Bob took us to Campinas, about 60 miles away, where we were to spend the rest of the year studying Portuguese.

A week after arriving in Campinas, we began a new life. The director of the school was Parke Renshaw, a Methodist missionary who had been in Brazil for more than 10 years. He was a linguistic marvel and spoke perfect Brazilian Portuguese with no detectable accent. Classes were divided by sex: men in the morning for four hours and women in the afternoon for another four hours. That way, each partner could share childcare as needed.

Our lovely Jennifer was almost three. We found a delightful childcare center and she would spend half-days there, where she picked up Portuguese before we did. Men spent the first half hour every morning in chapel, with some scripture reading, a brief meditation, and sometimes music from fellow students. The Southern

Baptists, when it was their turn to lead chapel, felt obligated to point out to the Methodists and Presbyterians that we were damned to Hell because we had not been baptized by immersion.

In class, we were put in groups of four or five students. My group comprised Vernon Walter, a United Church of Canada missionary; Harry MacDonald, a Young Life missionary with a Presbyterian background; Jim Gravely, a fellow Methodist; Buddy Hughes, a Southern Presbyterian; and me. Each class was the same: we had a notebook with a series of one-page lessons. On one side were 10 sentences in Portuguese. The same sentences were in English on the back, though we were forbidden to look at that side during class. The teacher would read each sentence in Portuguese four times. Then, the five of us repeated it in unison four times. Then, we were to say it individually.

At first, it was totally impossible. It sounded like one long word. By the end of the first morning, we were all exhausted and had made very little progress. Our teachers were equally exhausted and frustrated. We'd spend the afternoon with our tape recorders, listening to the same sentences and cheating by looking at the English on the back. The next day was the same. The following week, we had a new set of sentences.

In the second quarter, we got some grammar drills where we had to say the sentence correctly with the change of one word. *A casa é verde* (the house is green). Then the teacher would say "branca," and we had to say, "The house is white." Then "red," and so on. We were required to make the changes without hesitation.

Along the way, we were introduced to irregular verbs. In Portuguese, each verb is conjugated six times in each tense. I, you, he/she/it, and then we, you, they. Six changes for each verb in each tense. When you add the present, past, imperfect, future, subjunctive, and future subjunctive, you end up with 100 different forms for every single verb in the entire language. And the irregular verbs are just that: irregular. Portuguese is the most complicated of all the

Latin languages. It is also more complex in terms of pronunciation. For instance, in Spanish, there are only five vowel sounds: a, e, i, o, and u. But in Portuguese, there are 11 vowel sounds, diphthongs, and nasal sounds.

We went to the Central Methodist Church every Sunday. The pastor, Rev. Dr. Bettencourt, had a PhD from Boston University and only preached in Portuguese. The Sunday School class we attended was often led by a young Seminary student, Eliezer, who spoke beautiful Portuguese.

On April 1, 1964, the Brazilian Army, led and urged on by the US Central Intelligence Agency (CIA), overthrew the elected president, João Goulart, accusing him of being a Communist. It was later shown that he was the largest landowner in Brazil. Goulart fled to Uruguay, where he spent the rest of his days in exile. Immediately, USAID, the US "development" agency, moved into the Brazilian ministries and restructured the country. The education ministry created a two-tiered public school system: creative, thinking education for the upper-class children destined to run the corporations and popular, technical education to prepare factory workers.

A repressive apparatus was put in place to deal with resistance. Hundreds of labor leaders, students, and community leaders simply disappeared. Many were tortured in army and air force establishments. Near-total censorship of newspapers, radio, and TV was put in place. We didn't have a clue what was going on. In May, Brady Tyson, a Methodist missionary who was teaching Political Science at the University of São Paulo (USP) while serving as chaplain to the Methodist students at that university and as pastor to a small Methodist church, came over to Campinas and met with me, Carol, and Jim and Ila Gravely. He spent a couple of hours explaining what had happened and warned us not to have *any* opinions about anything in the foreseeable future. He said that 12 of the Methodist students at USP had simply disappeared, never to be seen again.

❋ ❋ ❋

Back in Campinas, we were in the last lap of our Portuguese studies. Carol and I were the two best students in the school. The teachers called us the "new Parke and Eunice Renshaw." In October, we were told we'd be in the First Region, including Rio de Janeiro and the surrounding state. We celebrated our first Christmas in the tropics. A 25-foot-tall poinsettia grew in our backyard and bloomed at Christmas. We missed family back home but were entirely enthralled by our new country and its new-to-us customs.

After Christmas, we drove to the Annual Conference at Colegio Bennett, the Methodist school in the heart of Rio de Janeiro. We were warmly welcomed by the missionaries who were already there: Bob and Jane Spencer, George and June Megill, Ed and Nancy Tims, Anita and Marion Way, and Sarah Dawsey, the head of Colegio Bennett. At the end of the Annual Conference, we discovered we'd been assigned to the parishes in Teresópolis, Itaipava, and Cuiabá, up in the mountains about two hours' drive from Rio.

Before the General Conference of the Brazilian Methodist Church a year prior, Reverend Natanael Inocência de Nascimiento, a prominent pastor in São Paulo, who was the Rector of the Seminary in Rudge Ramos, put in place what he called "The Scheme" *(El Esquema)*. Reverend Natanael bragged he built the main buildings at the seminary with powdered milk from the Food for Peace program of the US government. The milk was allegedly for the poor in São Paulo, but he sold it on the black market to buy building materials. The Scheme was simply a political movement to give him total control of the church in Brazil. He aimed to "reform" the church to be more faithful to the Gospel.

Natanael was counting on the support of a young pastor in Petrópolis, Gessé Teixeira de Carvalho. In addition to being the pastor of a local church, Gessé was also the D.S. Regarding the crucial vote that would have given Natanael near-total control of the entire church, Gessé voted the other way, and the Scheme collapsed. However, Natanael was elected Bishop of the First Region, which made him Gessé's superior.[2]

There were elections for officers during the Annual Conference in January of 1965. Suddenly, I heard my name put forth as Secretary for Christian Education for the conference. I immediately requested my name be removed, but at the coffee break, Gessé and some of his friends asked me to reconsider. The other candidate was Natanael's son-in-law. If he were elected, it would give the new Bishop total control of the conference. I kept my name in the running, and to my surprise, I was elected Conference Secretary of Christian Education on the first ballot.

So that the Bishop would not see me as his enemy right out of the gate, once my appointment was announced to Teresópolis, I made it a point to invite him to our church to preach a series of evangelistic services. I now had to learn the responsibilities of the new role and how to carry them out. I was a member of the Bishop's cabinet with voice and vote on all subjects except for pastoral appointments. The plot would thicken over the next couple of years.

CHAPTER 3

Our Move to Teresópolis

We went to Teresópolis the Sunday after the Annual Conference where I preached my first sermon. We stayed at the home of *dona* Cecilia, one of the leading laywomen of the church. Her husband, *senhor* Alencar, was a gruff old timer with a story for everything but was not very active in the church. In his usual money-saving mode for the Board, Bob Davis hired an open truck to haul our goods from Campinas to Teresópolis. It wasn't good for our furniture, as it rained most of the ten-hour trip.

The parsonage was an apartment over the Sunday School rooms in the back of the church. The rooms were small, almost all of them precisely 9 x 9 feet. We had difficulty getting our dining room furniture into the dining room. The bedrooms had no closets.

The congregation in Teresópolis was enthusiastic. Jeny, who was now three and a half, was the star of the show with her golden curls and sweet smile. On Tuesdays, I drove over the mountains to Itaipava, a small town on the outskirts of Petrópolis. A new church building was almost finished. One of the first people I met was *dona* Esmerelda, with whom I stayed on the days I went to Itaipava. Her husband, *senhor* Juca, never darkened the church doors but was nice, and we had some interesting conversations. One time at the supper table, he confided in me that he was a *crente* (believer).

"Oh, good," I said. "Tell me about it."

"Well," he continued, "I don't smoke, drink or dance."

That was it. He picked up on the central core of what the missionaries had taught in Brazil: to be a believer, you didn't smoke, drink, or dance. To be a *crente* was to be different from the rest. Reuben Alves, a renowned Presbyterian theologian, said in one of his books that the missionaries taught their new followers that they should not do anything "life-affirming" like dance, go to the beach, or drink beer.

The church in Itaipava had Tuesday and Sunday evening services. On Thursdays, the Cuiabá church had an evening service. On Wednesdays, there was an evening service in Teresópolis. That meant I was to lead worship and preach six times weekly at three congregations.

We discovered we couldn't understand most of the people in our congregations. The majority of them spoke with a *Mineiro* accent. About half of them were missing a good portion of their teeth, which made for mumbling pronunciation. They had no trouble understanding us, were very loving, and forgave our gaffes.

I found a man who was the head of the National Park in Teresópolis who wanted to learn English. We met once a week, and I would present my Sunday sermon in Portuguese, and he would correct it for me. Then we would spend another hour conversing in English to improve his abilities.

I began by making home visits to the members of the congregations. On Mondays, Wednesdays, and Fridays, I would make calls in Teresópolis. On Tuesdays, I would be in Itaipava, making calls during the afternoon then leading the evening service. On Thursdays, I would make calls in Cuiabá in the afternoon then lead the evening service. I was invited to join the local Rotary Club, which gave me contact with the movers and shakers in Teresópolis.

All three of the churches grew slowly but steadily. The great majority of the members were lower-class workers. Many of the people in Itaipava and Cuiabá were caretakers of properties of the wealthy in Rio, who had weekend and summer places in the mountains. The Itaipava church had a retired army general and a retired air force general as members.

At times, I wondered what the hell I was doing in Brazil. Why hadn't the Bishop appointed me to be chaplain at Colegio Bennett, where I could relate to young people with an education? What should I do in these three parishes besides mark time? I gradually realized I was paying what my dear friend Brady Tyson called my "boonie dues." By living in the boonies and working with the lower-class people, I was learning about Brazil in a way I never could have if I'd simply been sent to Colegio Bennett to be chaplain for the rich girls there.

Carlos Colla

For Christmas, I gave Carol a Brazilian guitar. When we were settled in Teresópolis, we met a young man, just 21, who was selling mutual funds to people in town with money. He was reputed to be a great guitar player, belonging to a popular band in the area. I invited him to our home to talk about giving lessons to Carol. He soon agreed that if we provided him with lunch every Tuesday, he'd give guitar lessons.

His first lesson was teaching a popular folk song, *Eu tinha uma andorinha*. It only required three chord changes, and the melody was easy and catchy. He said Carol should practice an hour a day and he would be back the following Tuesday. Carol didn't get into this project and didn't practice the hour a day. I secretly dreamed about learning to play and began practicing the new song. I strummed away on her guitar for more than an hour a day.

When Carlos returned the following Tuesday, Carol fumbled through the song. Then, I took the guitar and flailed away with considerable success with the Andorinha. "Wow!" Carlos exclaimed, "I've got a student!" That was all the encouragement I needed, and I began to work on learning to play.

I looked Carlos up years later to discover he was a "figure" in the Brazilian music world, having written dozens of songs made famous by him and other musicians. He wrote several pieces for Roberto Carlos, among many other well-known musicians. Sadly, he died just a year ago with more than 100 songs under his name.

O Bate Papo

I immediately began to study the community of Teresópolis to see their needs and opportunities. Nestled in the hills outside Rio, it is partly a resort town. The town has about 50,000 inhabitants but grows to more than 120,000 during the summer months. There are several Roman Catholic churches and about 15 evangelical churches.

It became apparent that none of the local churches was coming anywhere near the crowd of vacationers. One of the main reasons was the significant cultural difference between the people of the local churches and those up from Rio. The tourists were primarily middle-class and upper-class and did not feel comfortable in the cultural environment of the churches. Also, in general, the people of the churches were suspicious of the "rich."

Knowing that including the middle and upper classes was crucial to the strategy of the Church in Brazil, I began to seek ways to reach across the abyss. I developed the idea of trying an experimental ministry of evangelization during the summer. The plan was to open a Coffee House. I recruited a team of four seminarians from our Methodist Seminary in Rudge Ramos (São Paulo) to spend the summer with us. I rented a shop in the city's main square where we set up a bar called the *Bate Papo,* which is Brazilian slang for "Chew the Fat." The Bishop of the First Region was so frightened by the experiment of the *Bate Papo* that I was transferred to a parish in the North Zone of Rio the next year to not allow a repetition of this kind of nonsense.

The seminary students and I met to define the goals of the experiment. First, we nurtured the hope of giving the seminarians a new vision of the church's role in the modern world. We hoped they could understand that evangelism is much broader than a simple series of preaching conferences. I hoped they could understand the difficulties in presenting the Gospel message in terms intelligible to modern urbanized people. Second, I wanted to explore the possibility of building a bridge of understanding between the people of the local church and the people outside. Third, I was hoping that some young people spending the summer in Teresópolis would gain a new understanding of the Evangelical Church and its message, through contact with intelligent young people like themselves.

We opened *Bate Papo* on January 3. The decorations were attractive, with the help of an artist friend from Rio. I recorded a loop of Beatles music mixed in with the current "Bossa Nova" samba music that had become popular in the Western world. I hired the church's Youth Society president to be the bar manager. Some other church members gave a range of services to the experiment. We sold soft drinks and sandwiches and played chess, checkers, and dominoes. Our bar was open from noon until midnight. We discovered that chess drew the group we wanted and installed six chessboards, removing the remaining games. We promoted several chess tournaments during the summer and included some local and regional champions. With games, music, and a group of youth, our bar became the most popular hangout in the whole city.

We decided not to discuss our connection with the church during the first three weeks to not scare the young people we wanted to attract. We feared that young folks would steer away if they knew the *Bate Papo* was sponsored by a church. But, by the end of three weeks, the whole town knew the Methodist Church had a "bar" on the square. To our surprise, no one turned away after discovering this. As the team mingled with young people in the square, there were many opportunities to discuss any subject, from economics to politics to faith. I believe that the significant impact resided in the personal testimony of the team, their care, and willingness to listen to others and not just talk.

Jonathan

Carol and I had wanted another child for some time. We met a couple from Rio who bought a hi-fi record player from us. We spent some time together and mentioned our hope of adopting a baby. About a month later, they called us from Rio and said a friend of theirs, a nun in a hospital in the State of Santa Catarina, said the hospital had a baby boy, about 25 days old, and that with the recommendation of our new friends, they would deliver him to us.

We decided I should fly down, hoping to bring back our new son. I caught a plane to São Paulo, carrying a diaper bag full of supplies. I transferred to a flight to Blumenau, Santa Catarina, and from there, a jumper flight to Rio do Sul, a small city in the state's interior. Then, I took a two-hour taxi ride on dirt roads to a small village where the Catholic Hospital was. This part of Brazil had been colonized at the end of the 19th century by primarily poor farmers from Germany.

I asked the taxi driver to wait for me and went into the hospital to ask for the sister who'd called our friends. She came to the front desk and asked for my ID. She immediately went into the nursery and returned with a 30-day-old boy, who was very long (he grew to be 6'5"), blonde, and blue-eyed. She told me his mother worked on a farm, and they assumed the farm owner was the father. She had me sign a book indicating I had received this baby boy, born February 16, 1966.

I returned to the taxi with Jonathan Blake Morris in my arms, much to the shock of my driver, who could not imagine a man taking care of an infant. We returned to Rio do Sul, where I checked into a hotel. At the reception desk, the people there asked me where the baby's mother was. They sent a woman, one of the hotel maids, to "take care of the baby." I thanked her, but I was giving Jonathan his first formula bottle when she arrived and said everything was okay. We went to the airport to catch our flight on a DC-3 back to Blumenau the following day. The flight attendants were nearly beside themselves to see a man with an infant, but Jonathan fell asleep promptly when the engines started.

While waiting for the continuing flight to Rio, I had to change his diaper. The only place to do that was on the Varig counter. The woman behind the desk had never seen a man change a diaper. Carol and Jennifer were anxiously waiting for me when I got to Rio, both deliriously happy with the new member of our family. The following week, I got one of my Rotarian friends, an attorney, to help me with what I thought would be the adoption papers. He had a better idea. He simply registered Jonathan as having been born to Carol in Teresópolis. Later, I took his new birth certificate to the US Consulate in Rio and got his US birth certificate. Jonathan was quite thin, but he filled out quickly under his new parents' careful watch, then grew like a weed.

From Teresópolis to Chicago

Being in Teresópolis complicated my new tasks as Secretary. I was given a small office at Colegio Bennett, but it was a two-hour drive, which meant it was not convenient for me to go to Bennett very often. I made a point of going down at least once a month for cabinet meetings. An interesting situation occurred when the Board of Global Ministries sent out a questionnaire about the role and place of women to be answered by every Annual Conference in the region. At the next regular meeting of the cabinet, I presented the questionnaire for their consideration. The whole idea was met with laughter on the part of the members of the cabinet and the Bishop, and that was the end of that.

I managed to put together a youth conference for the First Region. I arranged for us to meet at a nice campground on a beach near Cabo Frio. I invited one of my colleagues from language school, Harry MacDonald, who was in Brazil to start work for Young Life. They were successful in the United States, and Harry pioneered the organization in Brazil. He was charismatic, and I thought he'd be a good person to serve as keynote for the youth conference. We gathered around 100 young people for a four-day event on the beach. I also worked with the Women's Society of the Brazilian Methodist Church to put together a conference for women.

However, some storm clouds developed. One of the first things Bishop Natanael did after assuming the leadership of the First Region was to intervene in Colegio Bennett. The former director, Sarah Dawsey, who'd been head of the Colegio for more than 20 years, retired, and the man who took her position was not agreeable to the Bishop. Natanael used an episcopal prerogative to intervene and take over the school's administration. He fired many people and hired his own for the important positions in the school. He took charge of the finances, and there was much questioning about where the money was going. It was the most prestigious Colegio for girls in Rio, with a long waiting list. The wealthy and powerful families of Rio wanted their daughters to graduate from Bennett.

It became evident that Bishop Natanael planned to move me out of Teresópolis because of the *bate papo* experiment. Following a hallowed tradition, all the clergy entered the auditorium stage at Colegio Bennett. They sang one verse of "I'll go where you want me to, dear Lord," assuming there was some relationship between what God wanted and the Bishop's will. Then, the Bishop began reading the pastoral appointments. No one knew what their assignment would be. This was considered a spiritual exercise, but I saw it as a power play by the Bishop and his team of District Superintendents.

There was a tremendous discrepancy between appointments. The Bishop's decisions had life-shaking implications. If he disliked a pastor, that person could be sent far away, never to return. Thankfully, the salaries were socialized, so a pastor's income was the same regardless of his assignment. It took a while for nearly 150 appointments to be read. I finally heard I would be assigned to Pilares, but I didn't even know where that was.

I sought out Ed Tims, a fellow missionary who was also a D.S., to learn about Pilares. In the North Zone of Rio, the area is mainly working and lower class. The church had a nice parsonage built by a missionary, Ken Traxler. The current pastor was Sebastião Dornellas, father of my friend, and occasional tennis partner, Wesley Dornellas. Wesley was an active layperson in the conference who worked in marketing for some pharmaceutical companies and lived very well.

When I sought Wesley to get more info on Pilares, he said his father had a difficult time there. Traxler had been of the "great white father" school of missions and raised thousands of dollars in the States during his time at Pilares. The church and parsonage were built with US funds. He had a lot of money left over and built some houses for some of the poorer parishioners. He would always pay a bill for anyone a bit tight at the end of the month. Needless to say, he was greatly loved by the church members. However, when Rev. Dornellas arrived, he had no funds, as is typical of Brazilian pastors. Thus, he was resented by the congregation and delighted to be moving on.

We were expected to move by February 15. However, the road between Teresópolis and Rio was blocked by mudslides for several days, completely isolating the city and region. Rio itself was hit with torrential rains, more than 12 inches in 24 hours. Over half of the generators were filled with mud, leaving the entire metropolitan area without power for several days and then on rationed blackouts of nearly 18 hours per day for several months. When we finally moved into the parsonage, we found ourselves amid the worst heat wave in over 30 years. The first thing I did was buy a room air conditioner for our bedroom.

We were very well received at the church. Folks were excited that the golden days of having a missionary had returned. They didn't know I wasn't carrying suitcases full of money from the US One of the things they bragged about when I arrived was that we'd have a phone in the parsonage. We didn't know that the phone company would take an entire year to make the transfer. In the meantime, neighbors generously offered to allow me to use their phone when I needed to.

Fred Maitland, another missionary colleague, was the chaplain at Bennett and the Dean of the Seminario Cesar Dacourso Filho, a seminary the conference maintained at Bennett in the evenings for persons who wanted to study theology in preparation for ministry. Fred recruited me to teach Systematic Theology two nights a week. I had to correct my Brazilian students' Portuguese, which embarrassed me. It was also a challenge to water down Systematic Theology so that people who did not have a college education could grasp its concepts.

We also had an "outpost" Sunday School in a *favela* (slum)called Coca-Cola. It was led and anchored by a wonderful *mineira* (a person from the state of Minas Gerais) named *dona* Cecilia. *Dona* Cecilia lived on the top of this little mountain in the North Zone for several years and had become the community's unofficial "Den Mother." She started a school in her home for some of the children. She'd become a member of a Methodist church years before, so it seemed natural to her to start a Sunday School. She gathered between 20 and 30 neighborhood children every Sunday in her home.

I began visiting at least once a month. When *dona* Cecilia told me about the food shortages experienced in her community, I made arrangements with Diaconia. This ecumenical organization handled the distribution of the Food for Peace goods the US sent to

Rio. They offered us a dozen 100-pound bags of powdered milk. I packed about 1,200 pounds of powdered milk in my mini-station wagon and headed to the Coca-Cola *favela.*

When I got about a quarter of the way up the dirt road, my little car began scraping bottom until I couldn't move. I started unloading some of the bags, and a young man came over and helped me. I was able to drive ahead to a place where there were fewer ruts. We carried the bags across the ruts and re-loaded them into the car. Then he said he'd accompany me to *dona* Cecilia's to help unload them.

When we got to Cecilia's house, before I could get out of the car, I became aware of a shadow to my left. When I turned my head, I saw a revolver pointed at my ear. A police officer ordered me to get out of the car. The young man was hauled out of the car and pushed up against the wall of Cecilia's house with a revolver stuck in his back by another policeman.

I was wearing a suit and tie. I showed the policeman my passport and Brazilian ID and asked what this was all about. They said the young man was wanted for a series of crimes. I immediately said they must be mistaken, as he didn't live there and had only come up with me to help deliver the powdered milk. *Dona* Cecilia came out and said that he wasn't from there and she did not know him. After about 15 minutes of arguing, I convinced them he was not the man they sought, and they left. We unloaded the milk.

"You know you saved that boy's life," Cecilia said.

"What do you mean?" I asked.

"They would have killed him and left his body in a ditch. They were just on the hunt and didn't care who he was. If you hadn't been an American missionary, they would have killed him."

Sometime toward the end of 1967, Dr. Colin Williams, an Australian Methodist and scholar who was the Dean of the Divinity School of the University of Chicago, visited Brazil for a series of lectures on Wesleyan theology at our Methodist Seminary in São

Paulo. He came to Rio for a visit on his way. He expressed interest in the Umbanda religion, one of the African spiritualist religions that enslaved Africans brought to Brazil. There was a major Umbanda Center near our church, so I offered to go with him to one of their meetings.

From the outside, the Center looked a lot like a Baptist church. We got there a bit early, and one of their leaders came to welcome the two obvious *gringos.* I introduced myself as the pastor of the Pilares Methodist church and my companion as Dean of a major theological school in the USA. We were warmly welcomed. About a half dozen drummers began rhythmically beating their instruments when things started. The leaders got up and walked around in a circle, marching to the beat of the drums. The drummers gradually sped up their rhythm. The marchers did too, starting a dance-like march, gradually going faster and faster. This went on for about 15 minutes. The marchers were clearly getting tired when the man who had received us so cordially came to us and said, almost apologetically, "I'm sorry, but we are going to have to ask that you leave. You see, you have the Spirit of Jesus, and the other spirits won't come while you are here." So we left.

Meeting Colin firmed up my desire to go to graduate school. I applied to the University of Chicago Divinity School, seeking a PhD in Social Ethics. I got permission to return to the States to start my studies. We'd been somewhat frustrated during our two years in Pilares. The people there had never really forgiven me for not having money to hand out.

Shortly before our return to the States, a number of the pastors of the conference said that Bishop Natanael's intervention in Colegio Bennett had to be ended. The Discipline of the Brazilian Methodist Church—the rule book for all things Methodist—gave the Bishop the authority to intervene in conference institutions. However, the intervention had a two-year time limit. As the Secretary of Christian Education, it befell on me to enforce that. So,

I sent a letter to all of the Board members stating that the intervention would end in January 1968 and they were called to meet to reestablish the order of the Colegio and elect a new director the first week in February. I copied the Bishop.

There was nothing he could do. I was simply following the rules outlined in the Discipline. None of the Brazilian pastors would have had the courage to take the Colegio away from the Bishop, as they would be subject to severe reprisals. So was I, as he notified the Board of Global Ministries I would not be welcome back to Brazil. I was effectively being expelled.

The trip back took 11 days by boat. When we got to New York, we sailed under the Narrows Bridge, which was just being finished. It all seemed unreal. We were debriefed by Board members, had physical exams, then flew to Chicago to visit our families. My mother had died of a heart attack at age 55, two and a half years before. My dad remarried the year before our return, so we met a new family when we got to Elmhurst. My mother's death had not seemed real when we were in Brazil. But when I saw my dad's new wife, Ellen, in the parsonage, it hit me that my mom was *gone.* Seeing Ellen with him finalized that Ruth Morris was no longer with us.

My dad was pastor of the First United Methodist Church in Elmhurst, Illinois. That church's "good folks" had not accepted him—a new experience for him in his ministry. The Elmhurst congregation had not handled my mom's illness well, was uncomfortable with a widower pastor, and many didn't accept his remarriage. Dad transferred to the First United Methodist Church in North Platte, Nebraska, a year later.

After a few days in Elmhurst, we all drove to Estes Park, Colorado, the favorite vacation spot for our family growing up. We rented a couple of cabins at the YMCA campground and, on our way home, visited my brother, his wife, Janet, and their kids in Sheldon, Nebraska, where he was pastor. We returned to Chicago and rented a house in Harvey, Illinois, a lower-middle-class suburb on the train line to the University of Chicago. Carol made arrangements for a teaching position nearby.

It was August 1968, just in time for the infamous Democratic National Convention in Chicago that guaranteed the election of Richard Nixon. We watched the proceedings on TV along with the Chicago police riot in the streets, bashing peaceful protesters with their batons. A few months before, we had watched the riots in Rio on Brazilian TV as thousands of students protested the murder of a student, Edson Luis, by the military police. It came to a head when over a hundred students took refuge in the cathedral at the end of Avenida Rio Branco, which was immediately surrounded by mounted police. Several dozen priests and monks gathered around the cathedral, holding hands, forming a sacred barrier. The net result was the passing of the infamous Institutional Act V, which literally abolished any civil and human rights in Brazil.

The University of Chicago

In mid-August, I contacted Dr. George Playe, the head of the Romance Language Department at the University of Chicago, and asked if he needed anyone to teach Portuguese. He hired me on the spot and paid me the tuition for my graduate studies.

I finalized my registration at the Divinity School and was told to take entrance exams to prove that I was up to Chicago's standards. I didn't plan to fulfill this requirement. I reminded the people I was dealing with that I was a graduate *cum laude* of Drew Theological Seminary, which had been accredited by the Association of Theological Seminaries (ATS), the same organization that accredited the Divinity School of the University of Chicago. I suggested they had no right to pass judgment on people who had degrees from schools also approved by the ATS, and I would not honor their arrogance by taking their exams. They said I couldn't get credit for my courses without the entrance exams. I said I did not care—I was there to learn something, not to jump through a bunch of academic hoops. So, I started classes in September without taking the exams.[3]

At first, I was delighted with my classes. I kept asking my advisor about the requirements for my doctoral degree in Christian Social Ethics. He kept dancing around, and I realized they didn't have a program. I was expected to design my own Master's program. He said that might take a couple of years, then I'd have to *do* the program. After that came the designing of the doctoral program, which might take another year or two. After a ten-year lapse in higher education, I found the reading for my courses keeping me up till two or three in the morning. I had no desire to spend five or ten years there, so I began scouring the University catalog to see if there was another way to get a degree and get out. I discovered I could transfer my credits from the Divinity School to the University and get a Master's Degree in Social Studies with one more year. So that's what I did.

Phyllis Kirian, a beautiful young Black woman who worked in an office just down the hall from mine, began visiting me nearly every time I was in my office. She was a secretary at the University and was studying to be an opera singer. She gave a recital in the spring, and Carol and I attended. She had a fantastic soprano voice. She kept dropping by for a chat, eventually sharing that she was not happily married to her white husband. I didn't respond much to Phyllis except to listen to her. My relationship with Carol continued as it had for years, with mutual respect, deep friendship, and our two children.

In the summer of 1969, we took a brief vacation to northern Wisconsin, staying at the lakefront cabin of Dr. Fauser, a retired dentist and an old friend of my dad's. That was where we were when Neil Armstrong and his companions made their landing on the moon, which we, like millions of others, watched on TV.

In the fall, I moved into the Urban Studies program and started researching the development of Rio de Janeiro from 1565 to 1965.

I read everything I could find about Brazil and Rio de Janeiro: sociological studies on racism in Brazil, the history of the *favelas* in Rio, even some material on the urban renewal (removal) projects that were carried out at the beginning of the 20th century, forcing thousands of former residents up into the hillsides, expanding the *favelas.*

As the University's professor of Portuguese, I was asked to prepare qualifying exams for graduate students wanting to substitute Portuguese for French or German in their studies. I would administer the test, grade it, and so on. I petitioned the University to allow me to substitute Portuguese for French in my program. After a couple of months, I got a letter approving my petition. But then I got a phone call from Eleanor, who'd asked me to examine the two graduate students earlier.

"Mr. Morris, I believe the University has made an unfortunate mistake," she said, shaking her head.

"And what would that be?" I asked.

"Well," she said, "they approved your petition to substitute Portuguese for French in your program."

"And why is that a mistake?"

"Well, who will give you the exam?"

Totally dumbfounded, I replied, "Well, Eleanor, you might be able to decide that since the University saw fit to hire me to be its Portuguese professor, I don't need to take an exam."

"Oh, no, that won't do. I will ask the professor of Portuguese at Northwestern to give you the exam."

By this time, I was totally exasperated. I said, "Like hell, you will."

I hung up and searched for Dr. George Playe, my boss in the Romance Language Department. When he heard about my conversation with Eleanor, he did a facepalm, saying, "Sweet Jesus." He then picked up his phone and called Eleanor, asking, "If I write you a letter on my letterhead stating that Mr. Morris is qualified to receive a 'High Pass' in Portuguese, would that be okay?"

"Oh, yes," she replied. "That would be fine." So much for higher education at the much-esteemed University of Chicago. Not much teaching went on as most professors were already famous and into the Publish or Perish syndrome. Their classes consisted of 300–500 students who listened to them read the latest chapter in their new book.

In September, we moved to Lansing, Illinois, where I took the part-time position of Assistant Pastor at the First United Methodist Church. It included a worthwhile stipend and a lovely parsonage in Lansing. On the outside, everything looked good for the Morris family.

CHAPTER 4

Our Return to Brazil

In April 1970, I was contacted by Mac McCoy of the Board of Global Ministries, informing me that Bishop Natanael, my Bishop in Rio, had been caught in a major financial scandal and been forced to resign. A mutual friend, the Rev. João Daronch da Silva, the secretary of the Board of Social Action of the Brazilian Methodist Church, would be in St. Louis in a couple of weeks, attending the General Conference of the United Methodist Church. João had expressed an interest in my returning to Brazil and going to Recife as a missionary to direct a new Community Center his Board was sponsoring. Mac invited me to St. Louis to meet with him and Rev. da Silva.

When I met with João and Mac, I was thrilled to hear what João wanted me to do. I was to be the director of the Methodist Community Center in an impoverished area of Olinda (sister city to Recife). He also wanted me to work with the Roman Catholic Archbishop in Recife, Dom Hélder Câmara, to improve relations between protestants and catholics. We would attend the New and Returning Missionary Conference at Greencastle, Indiana, in July and then spend the month of August in Cuernavaca, Mexico, to learn about the region from Francisco Julião, former leader of the Peasant Leagues of Northeast Brazil, who was living in exile. Then, we'd travel through South America, visiting some of the more creative United Methodist projects in Bolivia, Chile, and Argentina.

Back at the university, I did a "factorial analysis" of Rio de Janeiro based on census data from 1965. I had to key-punch onto IBM computer cards all the data on the *bairros* of Rio and the 265 *favelas* that had been surveyed, including the number of toilets, radios, TVs, people per room, etc. Then, I took those cards to a computer that occupied a huge room. In about 15 minutes, it analyzed the data and spit out how all the different items "clustered" around certain factors.

Three factors determined the human ecology of Rio de Janeiro. One was the most obvious: income; the second was stage-in-life cycle: young, middle, or older; and the third factor was race: the whiter a person, the greater the likelihood they would live in one of the nicer areas of the city; the darker, the greater chance of living in a *favela* or at least a lower-class neighborhood. There were no earthshaking revelations, just evidence of what was happening.

I only had to write my thesis, which included chapters on the history of Rio and race in Brazil and concluded with generalized predictions of Rio's developmental trends. I handed it to Dr. Brian Berry, the head of the Urban Studies Center, and in June 1970, I was awarded my MA in Sociology from the University of Chicago. We began packing for the move back to Brazil.

The Trip Back Home

From the missionary gathering, we went to Cuernavaca, where we stayed for a month at CIDOC (the Intercultural Documentation Center), which Ivan Illich was running. Illich operated a Spanish language school to finance his operation. We were amazed to discover that over half of his local-hire language teachers had quit and moved across town to open their own school. They claimed that

Illich paid low wages and kept the money for himself, which was not a very "revolutionary" thing to do.

We met Francisco Julião, the exiled former leader of the Peasant Leagues in the Northeast of Brazil. Julião was a lawyer hired by the peasants to defend their interests against the onslaughts of the Northeastern landowners. After the military coup on April 1, 1964, he and other figures, such as Paulo Freire and the Governor of Pernambuco, Miguel Arraes, were given the choice of exile or prison. Wisely, they chose exile. Julião went to Mexico.

Illich had an excellent documentation center, so I spent much time in the library and participating in the center's life with the dozens of language students. Burt Lancaster was there with a beautiful starlet. He was outspoken on civil rights issues and other justice matters.

The most important contact I made in Cuernavaca was with a vacationing *Time* correspondent, Bill Marmon, who was there studying Spanish. Bill suggested I become a stringer for *Time* in Recife. He gave me the name and phone number of the bureau chief for South America. I contacted the bureau chief in Buenos Aires, who was delighted at the thought of having a genuinely bilingual stringer in Recife. If Kay Huff approved, he was okay with the idea. From Buenos Aires, we flew to São Paulo, where I paid a visit to the Central Methodist Church, also the headquarters for the Brazilian Methodist Church.

A young man showed up looking frail and weak. He was Anivaldo Padilha, a Methodist student leader who had just been released after nine months in Operação Bandeirantes, the principal torture center of the Brazilian army in São Paulo. He'd been denounced to the secret police by the Brazilian Methodist Bishop Sucasas. Shortly after, Anivaldo escaped to the US, where the National Council of Churches, under its Latin American director, the Rev. Bill Wipfler, took him under its wing. He'd fled from

Brazil to Uruguay, leaving his pregnant wife behind. He would not meet his son until he was eight years old. That son later became the Minister of Health under the Lula administration and a candidate for mayor of São Paulo. We then flew to Rio, where we stayed with our friends Wally and Isabel Williams. Wally was the pastor of the Union Church in Copacabana. Then, finally, off to Recife.

Meeting Dom Hélder

Recife, the largest city in the Brazilian Northeast—an area twice the size of France—is located on the Atlantic coast. In 1970, it had a population of just over a million. Near many beautiful beaches, it sits at the confluence of two major rivers that drain the interior of the State of Pernambuco: the Beberibe and the Capiberibe. The city enjoys a beautiful climate and cumulus clouds that provide a marvelous show every afternoon as the sun sets.

We worked in Caixa d'Agua, a poor neighborhood in Olinda, Recife's sister city to the north. Jennifer, 9, and Jonathan, 4, studied at the American School in Boa Viagem, an upscale beach neighborhood on the south side of Recife. We were contacted by the Presbyterians in Recife, who had a major seminary there. Before we arrived, the Methodists only had one missionary in Recife, a woman named Gladys Oberlin.

The Presbyterians had a lovely home that had belonged to a missionary professor at the seminary who'd returned to the US They offered us his home in the Madalena neighborhood. The house was only a few blocks from a private club with a dozen tennis courts, three swimming pools, and a professional soccer field. We purchased a Ford Cortina station wagon. Carol was hired as a teacher at the American School in Boa Viagem.

Like all of the Northeast, the income inequality was dramatic. Caixa d'Agua was one of the poorest *bairros* in the metropolitan area. The local funeral director told me he had an average of seven infant funerals every week. There was a fairly large property the Methodist Church had purchased. It contained a large wooden edifice that could only be called a shack, which housed the congregation on Sundays and the programs Gladys had put together. Funds were raised to build a larger and more permanent structure. I oversaw that project.

Gladys became a missionary like many women who felt a call to ministry but were not allowed to become pastors. She had a girls club, where neighborhood girls were brought together to play and learn. She taught the girls and their mothers how to prepare better meals on the meager resources they had.

I ran into John Buyers, the son of Methodist missionaries who had been born in Brazil. He was a businessman and had started the first supermarket in Recife. He was putting together a project to manufacture concrete products. I recruited his help in building our new structure, a large aluminum roof over an auditorium. The bottom four feet of the walls were concrete blocks with the top left open to provide plenty of ventilation. Several enclosed rooms were at the back, destined for a family planning clinic. We built a large water tank that enabled us to operate even when the city water supply was cut off. I insisted on installing three outdoor showers so the children who played in our playground could rinse off before going home.

I began forming some ecumenical ministries and made contact with the two Episcopalian priests, one Brazilian (Father Paulo Medeiros) and one American (Father Phil Getchel). Through them, I met Dom Hélder Câmara, the Catholic Archbishop of Recife/Olinda. He was already world-famous for his writings, poetry, and activities in the Second Vatican Council under Pope John XXIII. Behind the scenes, he was responsible for most of the Council's progressive actions. In 1968, he was the clear leader of the Catholic Conference of Latin American Bishops at Medellin, Colombia, which interpreted decisions of the Second Vatican Council for the churches of Latin America. He famously made the "preferential option for the poor," declaring that the church is the People of God, who are the poor masses, and *not* the Bishops, which had been the position of the Catholic Church since the First Vatican Council in 1868.

When Dom Hélder came to Recife, the first thing he did was sell his predecessor's Cadillac. He converted the Episcopal Palace into a social service center. He moved into the sacristy of the ancient Church of the Frontiers, *Igreja das Fronteiras,* where he said Mass every morning when he wasn't traveling away from Recife. He was unpopular with the military dictatorship. The censored media in Brazil was forbidden from mentioning his name. He became famous for his calls for nonviolent social change. He became known as the "Voice of those who have no voice" and received invitations to speak worldwide.

Dom Hélder's home at the Igreja das Fronteiras was machine-gunned on two occasions while he was traveling abroad. In September 1969, just one year before we arrived in Recife, a young priest, Father Henrique Pereira Neto, who'd been assigned by Dom Hélder to work with students at the federal university in Recife, was kidnapped and tortured to death. His body was dismembered, and its pieces were left around the campus to remind the students of who was in charge of Brazil.

Father Paulo took me to meet Dom Hélder. I was in awe. He embraced me and treated me like his son. I explained that the Methodist Church of Brazil had sent me to open and direct a Community Center in Caixa d'Agua and to seek to improve relations between Protestants and Catholics. He was familiar with the Methodist Church, having been invited to be the commencement speaker at the Methodist Seminary in Rudge Ramos (São Paulo) in 1968. His invitation came from the graduating students and provoked the Methodist Bishops to expel all the students, fire the faculty, and close the seminary. He was delighted to see in me a gesture of goodwill by the Methodists and welcomed anything I could do to improve relations.

He appointed Father Marcelo Barros, a young Benedictine monk who'd just been ordained priest the previous year, to be his liaison with us. Marcelo was to become my very dearest friend. We invited the local Lutheran pastor, Alberigo Baeske (who was later elected Bishop of his church), and his wife, Cebila, a journalist at the leading newspaper in Recife, to join us. We found a Presbyterian seminary student who was interested, though his attendance had to be clandestine or he would have been expelled. I also rounded up the two Methodist pastors in Recife, Pastor Lauro Cruz and Pastor Adolpho. Adolpho, the most recent arrival, was anti-Catholic and dropped out as soon as he saw Father Marcelo and a couple of other Catholics in our new group.

Marcelo brought along Father Hinácio and Polycarpo, two other Benedictine monks. Father Mauricio, a French Jesuit who was working with the victims of prostitution in Recife, joined us, as did Sister Dolores, the Mother Superior of an order of nuns in Olinda, along with a former nun, Peggy, who'd been the director of a Catholic school for girls in Belo Horizonte until she left to marry a French worker priest, Henrique. Two representatives of the Taize community in France were living in Recife as an outreach of that community. The Taize Community is an ecumenical monastic group comprised of Protestants and Catholics. Its founder, Roger Schutz, was a Protestant theologian. The two Taize brothers in our Equipe were essential to our work toward "being God's people across historical boundaries."

Together, we formed the Equipe Fraterna (Brotherhood Team). We met every Tuesday morning in an old colonial home in Olinda, the Casa da Fraternidade, where Marcelo lived. The first hour was dedicated to Bible study. Then, we spent about 40 minutes examining and evaluating the ministry of one of the groups, to help us all avoid the kind of paternalistic and domineering tendencies all our churches had toward poor people. We spent the last 15 minutes celebrating Holy Communion. One week, I would lead a Methodist Communion service. The following week, Father Marcelo would celebrate a Catholic Mass, and so on. For all of us, this became our church, where we experienced the Body of Christ and the unity of the Holy Spirit.

Father Paulo, the Episcopalian, said he thought we should tell Dom Hélder what we were doing. Dom Hélder received us warmly. When we got to the part about sharing Holy Communion, he scratched his head and looked pensive. Finally, he said, "I don't know if Rome is ready for this." To which Father Paulo said, "No, no, Dom Hélder, you don't understand. We aren't asking your permission. We are just telling you what we are doing." To which the good Dom replied: "Wonderful!" and gave us his blessing.

The Universidade Federal de Pernambuco

Shortly after we settled in Recife, I visited the Federal University of Pernambuco, a significant educational institution with over 12,000 students. With my shiny new Master's degree in Urban Sociology from the University of Chicago, I offered my services. I was promptly hired to teach a graduate-level seminar in Urban Sociology. I had 12 students in the course, a mix of architecture, law, and sociology students working on their Master's degrees. We agreed on a class project to study the human ecology of Recife, modeling the course on the theme of my thesis at Chicago, the human ecology of Rio de Janeiro.

After the first class, I was approached by Nina, one of the students. "You realize, don't you," she said, "that one of your main responsibilities as professor of this seminar is to not let any of our discussions get out of hand."

"What do you mean?" I asked. "This is a graduate seminar. Discussion is our main tool for learning."

"Well, that may be, but if you let things get out of hand, someone will be in serious trouble. You see, at least one of our colleagues is an informer for the military. We don't know who it is, but we know at least one is. If the discussion is too freewheeling, someone will say something that might lead to their being 'disappeared.' You don't want to be responsible for that."

So much for higher education under the dictatorship in Brazil. Nina was elected Secretary of the University's Student Union two years later. A week after that, she and the president, VP, and one other member were kidnapped by agents of the army. They spent 21 days being tortured by the same people who, a year later, would kidnap and torture me.

When Nina was released, she was dumped on a road on the outskirts of Recife. She found her way to my home in Madalena and asked for help. With the assistance of Father Phil Getchel of the Equipe Fraterna, I found her a place to stay. About three months later, the Equipe got Nina a scholarship for a doctoral program in Germany, where she fled into self-exile for six years. To get her out of the country, I called on Bruce Porter, one of our friends at the US Consulate, and told him Nina needed to leave Brazil to study but was afraid to ask the Federal Police for a visa after her torture experience. He took her personally to the Federal Police. Intimidated by an official of the US Consulate, they stamped her passport on the spot. She returned to Brazil after the military proclaimed a general amnesty in 1985.

The Drought

Time asked me to get some info about the impact of the four-year drought on the Northeast. In an average year, it only rained for a few months. When it did, the farmers raised cattle and grew sugar cane, beans, rice, and other vegetables. Sugar cane had been a source of great wealth in the 18th century. The State of Pernambuco was the wealthiest place in the world per capita during that period if you didn't count the slaves producing the wealth.

For millennia, the interior region of the Northeast had suffered periodic droughts. Our arrival in 1970 was at the end of four years with no rain. The government opened up several "work fronts" throughout the area where sharecroppers and day laborers were put to work building roads. I told Kay Huff I'd drive to the worst area and do a story.

I invited Father Paulo, my new-found friend and cohort in the Equipe Fraterna, to go with me to the State of Ceará. We traveled as cheaply as possible as I was only going to be paid something like $5 per hour for the time it took me to write the article—if *Time* decided to use it. We left Recife in my Ford station wagon, driving up to Mossoró in the State of Rio Grande do Norte the first day, spending the night in a *pensão,* a fleabag hotel. We continued to Fortaleza, the capital of Ceará, spending another night in a *pensão.* The drought completely burned the landscape, with nothing green to be seen anywhere. We got pictures of bag-of-bones cows eating paper sacks that had blown into their paths.

From Fortaleza, we drove to Canindé, where there had been reports of violence on a *fazenda* (plantation) nearby. We visited the work front where some 6,000 men housed in tents were working in the tropical sun daily for a salary of CR$2 (two *cruzeiros,* worth about US $0.40). We visited the Japuara Fazenda, the site of the conflict, where I interviewed *senhor* Pio, the key figure in the struggle. We returned to Fortaleza, where I interviewed the rural union's attorney, Dr. Lindolfo Cordeiro, who had defended *senhor* Pio in the aftermath of the conflict.

After about a week in the interior, I wrote the story and sent it to Kay Huff, who told me it was too long for Time and New York wasn't interested. So I sent it to Rev. James Wall, a fellow Methodist and longtime friend in Chicago. Wall was also the editor of the ecumenical magazine *The Christian Century,* which published the article titled "A Trickle of Justice in Brazil."

The Methodist Community Center

The new building at the Methodist Community Center in Caixa d'Agua was inaugurated with Dom Hélder, who preached a sermon emphasizing the importance of Protestants and Catholics working together. The people of Caixa d'Agua came out en masse to welcome the Archbishop joyfully. I told Dom Hélder we were installing a family planning center to assist all women seeking to control their fertility. We had a gynecologist, a nurse, and a social worker. By word of mouth, we assisted 2,000 women in the first year.

One morning, our social worker, Maria, came in laughing so hard she was crying. *Dona* Raymunda had filled out the intake form, which asked the usual questions: name, address, marital status, number of children, religion, etc. If the woman was Catholic, she had to answer another question: Do you understand that the service you are requesting is forbidden by your church? This was to protect us from any accusation that we were deceiving people into using birth control. To this, *dona* Raymunda, who already had six children, said: "Listen, if the Pope wants me to have any more babies, let that sonofabitch come over here and take care of them."

In addition to classes for mothers, Gladys organized a girls' club. We had GED courses, with 90 people working toward their high school diplomas. The city provided Arthur Paula as their teacher. The Brazilian Methodist pastor, Rev. Lauro Cruz, who was part of the Equipe Fraterna, held worship services to a growing congregation every Sunday evening.

Carol and I discovered Tamandaré, a beautiful beach, about a two-hour drive south of Recife. A fishing village, it had no paved streets, just a few stores and home-style restaurants. It also had a fishermen's school. Fishermen went to sea on the traditional *jangadas,* a raft of six to eight balsa-wood logs held together by ropes, with a rudimentary mast holding a sail that propelled them out to sea. The fishermen *(jangaderos)* would sail as far as 200 miles, often spending four to five days at sea before returning home.

We found a plot of land for sale in the second row from the beach. I designed a split-level house with three bedrooms and two baths above, a living/dining area and kitchen at the mid-level, and another bedroom and bath below. I found an architecture student in Recife who converted my sketches into construction plans. The house was entirely of exposed brick, with the typical clay tile roof. We used decorative porcelain tile in the kitchen and bathrooms to give some color. We borrowed $5,000 from my life insurance policy and built the house, which, including the lot, cost us $7,500.

We spent every other weekend at the beach. Being the early 1970s, we spent a lot of time sunbathing, doused with baby oil, getting lovely tans, which resulted in my dealing with skin cancer in my 80s. Sunscreen was unknown, and it was considered healthy to have a good tan in those days.

Professional Photo-Journalism for USAID

Carol resigned from her teaching position at the American School and became secretary to a division head at USAID (US Agency for International Development). There were 250 US families stationed in Recife, the second-largest USAID operation in the world. In the five to six years before we arrived, the United States had invested more than $1 billion in development projects in the Northeast. The five divisions in USAID were primarily staffed with US university professors on sabbatical.

Carol was hired as Administrative Secretary to the head of the Engineering Division. This got us invited to the social life of the Consulate/USAID people. Most had signed up for two to three years with great idealism and enthusiasm, but the majority finished utterly disillusioned. They realized the projects they were engaged in were not accomplishing the stated goals of helping the local people. The head of USAID discovered that I did some photography and asked if I would do some stories for their *War on Hunger* magazine. They wanted me to do five articles, one on each division, about the most successful project the division had carried out over the past 10 years. I accepted a contract to write five illustrated articles for their magazine.

I visited the heads of each division and asked them to point me toward their most successful projects. I was authorized to travel throughout the region at USAID's expense to get pictures and interview people about the project. To my surprise, no one felt they had anything to brag about their projects.

The education division had just finished building a "land-grant type" university in Fortaleza, Ceará. The University of Arizona was contracted for that project. When I interviewed the professor heading up the project, he said, "We did what they requested and built a great 'dry land agriculture university.'" However, he added, "It's not going to help the people because all we know how to do is capital-intensive, and what they need is labor-intensive. For instance, we teach them how to use tractors and cultivators. But one tractor un-employs 40 laborers. And only the rich landowners can afford to buy a tractor anyway. So, we are helping the rich get richer and throwing people out of their jobs. We succeeded in doing what they asked us to do, but it's not what was needed here." So, no photos and no story.

The engineering and agriculture divisions had a joint project in Ceará: fish farms. When the engineers built new highways at intersections where they had to make overpasses, they had to dig holes in the ground to get dirt for the ramps leading to the overpass. They filled those holes with water, making small ponds where they sowed Tilapia fish. Then, they produced food for the fish by taking alfalfa and turning it into pellets to feed the fish. I got some great pictures of men pulling fish from those ponds. But, again, it didn't work out as well as hoped, as the wealthy landowners took over the ponds, controlled the fishing, and sold the fish in the local markets.

The one project that was a success was bootlegged into USAID by a Brazilian engineer, Dr. Paulo Sá Campos. He told me about a project he'd put together without the knowledge of his superiors at USAID. He'd been studying the socio-economic problems of the Northeast since his university days. He examined hydrographic maps of the region and discovered there were numerous underground rivers under the surface of this drought-prone region. Paulo designed a project to drill an artesian well in one of the driest parts of the area near Piriprí, Piauí, called Morro dos Cavalos.

Paulo put his project into the USAID forms, among other projects. It was signed off by his boss, who didn't even look at it. The project provided $50,000.00 to buy a plot of land in Morro dos Cavalos and drill a well. That was it. Then Paulo purchased a plot of about 12 acres for practically nothing. About six months later, he showed up with the well-digging machinery, putting down about 3,000 feet of pipe and hitting it big. Water spouted out of the 10" pipe about 12 feet into the air. Paulo didn't do anything with the water, just let it flow.

He returned about four months later and discovered that most of his 12 acres were now a vast green spot with native grasses growing up to three feet high. Some people there asked, "Dr. Paulo, would it be all right if we let some of our cattle into your plot to eat some of that grass since you're not doing anything with it?"

"Let me think about it," replied Paulo, who eventually said it would be okay. He returned three months later and put in an irrigation system, channeling the well water into shallow ditches around his acreage. Then he planted vegetables, returning three months later to find huge onions, carrots, green beans, squash, black beans, and beets. He told his men they could sell the veggies in the local market—which they did—except for the beets. He told his employees they should be careful not to allow anyone to eat the beets, as they might cause "social problems" in the community, subtly implying that beets had aphrodisiac properties. When he returned the next time, there was not a beet in sight.

Next, he organized the men grazing their cattle on his grass into a cooperative and helped them put a formal structure into using the water. It became the property of the coop, and the green spot became a public commons. This $50,000 project that Dr. Paulo Sá Campos bootlegged into USAID became the most successful project of the entity during its 10 years of existence—and more than a billion dollars.

A Surprise Invitation

We'd been in Recife just a few months when I got a phone call from the head of the IBGE, the Brazilian Census Bureau. I met him when he visited the University of Chicago. My lead professor, Dr. Brian Berry, was known as one of the leading academics in urban sociology and geography. The Brazilian was there to consult with him. Knowing I was fluent in Portuguese, Dr. Berry asked me to interpret. The head of the IBGE became aware of my thesis as Dr. Berry had gotten me to publish a summary of my thesis in the *International Geographers* magazine. In that article, I had put not only my name as the author but also the name of Gerald Pyle, a fellow student studying to be a geographer. Gerry produced half a dozen maps and graphs for my thesis. The IBGE had invited me to present my thesis at a three-day conference of the International Geographers Union. Mine would be the only "Brazilian" paper to be given. My plane fare and hotel would be paid. I was highly flattered and quickly accepted the invitation.

On arrival in Rio, I was nervous, as the members of the conference were all professional geographers. I was introduced as a Methodist missionary in Recife who had completed my study of the human ecology of Rio de Janeiro at the University of Chicago. I summarized my methodology, the work done, and the conclusions drawn. I spoke for nearly an hour, and spent another 45 minutes answering questions. At lunch, some professors said they'd heard the same story presented by Dr. Gerald Pyle of Ball State University in Ohio. I told them Gerry had nothing to do with the study except that I had hired him to do some maps and graphs. They had an *aha!* moment because that explained why Dr. Pyle could not answer any questions about the study.

Resistance

After we'd been in Recife for about a year, the young man, Zé Gaucho, who lived in the Casa de Fraternidade with Marcelo, began talking to some of us about *Ação Popular*. This movement had begun among Catholic youth around 1962 in the pre-revolutionary days of the Goulart regime. Former President Goulart rambled on about reforms, though he did very little to enact any of them. Zé met with Marcelo, Peggy, Sister Dolores, the Mother Superior of a convent in Olinda, and me. He eloquently described how Catholic students, mainly in São Paulo and Rio Grande do Sul, inspired by Pope John XXIII and the Second Vatican Council, had formed *Ação Popular*, hoping to participate in the coming social revolution.

In the Northeast, this was encouraged by the formation of SUDENE, the government entity that promotes the region's development. Its head, Celso Furtado, was a progressive intellectual who'd written several books on the structural problems faced by the area. Without significant land reform, he argued, there was no possibility of change. Since the political structures were controlled by the same people who owned all the land, he designed SUDENE to encourage development in the area without the necessary land reform. This resulted in a corrupt and inefficient bureaucracy located primarily in Recife. Millions of dollars of tax monies were channeled into the Northeast. Most of it built miles of beach condos, making the rich richer.

Zé also told us how *Ação Popular* and the leaders of the Communist Party of Brazil (PC do B) came together. The Brazilian Communist Party, PCB, has a long history. Some of the more noted Brazilian intellectuals, like Jorge Amado and the architect Oscar Niemeyer, were openly members of the Brazilian Communist Party. The party had not been outlawed in Brazil except for part of the Getulio Vargas dictatorship in the 1930s and early 1940s and, more recently, under the military dictatorship. By 1970, it was considered the party of "little old ladies in tennis shoes" and not a significant threat to anyone. But in 1971, the PC do B was a different story. There were a dozen or more self-styled revolutionary groups, many of whom spent their time robbing banks, hoping to purchase enough weapons to launch a military movement against the Brazilian military. One pulled off the kidnapping of the US Ambassador in Rio. But nothing represented a real challenge to the dictatorship. The number of political prisoners and persons being tortured and disappeared kept growing.

One night in the fall of 1972, an American student arrived at my home. He was on a solo backpacking trip through South America. Someone in the States had said if he got to Recife, he should look me up. He said when he got off the bus in Altamira, Pará, he was immediately arrested by the military and accused of all sorts of things. The area was overrun with Brazilian soldiers, complete with tanks, armored cars, and machine guns. With his beard and Spanish accent, the Brazilian army personnel assumed the student was Cuban. After three days, they decided he was what he claimed, and he was released.

I sent a Telex to Bruce Handler, my *AP* contact in Rio, telling him what the student had reported. This was the first news about the budding guerilla warfare in Brazil, and the *AP* ran with the story. The PC do B had sent about 60 of their folks up into that area as early as 1968, mostly fleeing from the security forces in São Paulo and Rio, but also as part of a long-term Maoist strategy of launching a rural guerilla war against the military, taking advantage of the hostility that existed between the peasants in the states of Pará, Maranhão, and Goiás in the area known as Araguaia.

Members of the PC do B, mostly university students, moved into the area and took cover. As the TransAmazon Highway project of the military government began slashing its way through the jungles, it trampled over the peasants. By 1972, the PC do B militants were in a position to provide leadership for a guerilla resistance. By the time my American student got off the bus in Altamira, there were some 25,000 Brazilian troops deployed in the region, planning to smash the band of 60 guerillas. Even using napalm, they found their regular massive military efforts were not effective. Their troops couldn't find their enemy and came down with Yellow Fever and other jungle ailments. The army changed tactics and sent in some 400 trained infiltrators who looked like peasants and could gather the intelligence to locate and kill their enemy. By the end of 1974, they'd killed 60 of the guerillas and over 150 peasants who had allied themselves with the resistance, burying them in mass graves in the jungles with virtually no records kept.

Back in Recife, Zé had been replaced by a woman named Mará, who continued enlisting the support of Marcelo, me, and others for some of the political prisoners who were being tortured by the military. There wasn't much more we could do except be in solidarity. We found attorneys to provide some defense for some of these prisoners. Visits were made to the prison on the island of Itamaracá. Letters were written to Amnesty International. I took 35mm photos of the depositions then sent the negatives to my friend Brady Tyson at the American University in D.C. Brady got them to Senator Edward Kennedy, who read them into the Congressional Record. After being in Recife for about a year, Mará came to me and said she was "under the gun" and needed to leave. Mará was a striking redhead, so I gave her a brown, shoulder-length wig that belonged to Carol. She caught the bus and made it safely away from Recife.

Divorce

In 1973, Carol and I had a three-month furlough in the US. I'd come to the decision we couldn't continue with our 19-year marriage, and I told her I wanted to get a divorce. To some degree, Carol seemed relieved. There'd been many days and nights of tension, anger, and frustration. We both had periods making significant effort to deepen our relationship, but we didn't know how. We had spent several thousand dollars on psychologists and counselors, trying unsuccessfully to make our marriage what we both wanted. We had had a "friendship marriage" that fell short of what either of us wanted.

On our way home to the United States, we spent a few days in Manaus, taking a boat ride up the river to the confluence of the *Rio Negro* and the *Solimões,* which form the Amazon river. The Rio Negro is actually black, as its name suggests, and the Solimões a dirty brown, sort of like the Mississippi. They don't mix for many miles until they gradually blend. We visited the Opera House, which had been inaugurated in 1896, just eight years after the establishment of the Republic of Brazil. It was a monument to the inordinate wealth of the region created by the "rubber boom." During that period, the ladies of the region were famous for sending their elegant garments to Paris to be dry-cleaned.

Then, we flew to Atlanta, Georgia, where Carol's sister, Winifred, and her family lived. Carol and the children would stay with Winifred until Carol could find employment as a teacher and get her own place. After a few difficult days in Atlanta, I flew to Washington with Jennifer, who was 12. Then we took the train to New York. On that trip, I explained to her that her mother and I would be getting a divorce. It was an excruciating conversation, but Jennifer was a mature pre-teen and absorbed the shock as well as one could hope.

In July, I attended the annual New and Returning Missionary Conference. I was an emotional mess. I felt tremendous relief in ending the relationship with Carol, but I was saying goodbye to one of my best friends and two beloved children. Lewistine "Mac" McCoy was at the conference, and on the second evening, I told him my news. We'd been one of his favorite missionary couples. He had no idea of any problems. I told him I wanted to continue my work at the Methodist Community Center in Recife and suggested I could take a leave of absence from the Board. Neither of us knew how the Brazilian Methodist Church would respond to my divorce. Divorce was not legal in Catholic Brazil, and no missionary had ever divorced before.

Also present at the conference was a young university student, Minerva Carcaño[4], a sophomore at Southern Methodist University. A popular youth leader in the Methodist Church, she was there as a youth observer, being sponsored by the Board of Discipleship. One evening, a missionary couple from Angola shared how the people there revolted against the Portuguese colonists. They blathered on about having a ministry of reconciliation and building bridges between the downtrodden and Portuguese wielders of power. After listening for a while, I called bullshit.

"Because of the power discrepancy, there is no basis even for dialogue between those groups," I said. "When all the power is on one side, which is unwilling to give an inch, any talk of 'reconciliation' is nonsense. The church's role must be to support the people in their struggle for freedom and independence. That doesn't mean taking up arms, but it means being at the service of the people—to do whatever they ask of us."

That went over like the proverbial lead balloon. But it caught the attention of Minerva, who later asked me about the new movement called Liberation Theology. I was likely the only person among the 100 participants at the conference who had any idea what that meant. A Peruvian Catholic priest, Gustavo Gutiérrez, had written a book in 1969 with that title. It caused a storm among "progressive" elements in the churches. Minerva and I spent the rest of the week discussing the Christian base communities in Brazil and this "new" theological movement. I did not consider myself an expert on the subject. Still, I shared what we were doing in Recife with the Equipe Fraterna, our support for political prisoners, and our understanding that the Good News of Jesus of Nazareth required a movement toward freedom and independence of people in all places.

CHAPTER 5

The Beginning of the Beginning

After the Missionary Conference, I flew to Nebraska, where I spent a few days with my brother, his family, and my son Jonathan before flying to Rio to begin my new life. Upon arriving, I needed to go to Colegio Bennett, the Methodist school in the Flamengo district. That week, the Board of Global Ministries held a major international meeting with Methodist leaders from all over South America. I had been conscripted as a translator.

While at Bennett, I stopped by the office of my Bishop, Almir dos Santos. I told him about the divorce and suggested I would ask for a leave of absence status with the Annual Conference. He cited an old Brazilian saying: "The one who knows the temperature at the bottom of the pan is the spoon that stirs." He asked to pray with me, for me, and for Carol and the children, then said he wished the best for all of us and thanked me for sharing this news with him.

The following Sunday, I invited the family that had provided me temporary hospitality to a *churrascaria* restaurant to show my appreciation. When we returned home, we discovered someone had broken into the apartment. Nothing was missing except for my two Nikon cameras. They'd been in my suitcase, and it was clear this was an inside job, probably done by one of the sons of the host family. Of course, I could not make any accusations, but the sense of betrayal was great. Added to the loss of my two beloved children, it left me in a sorry state. There was nothing to do except get in my car and head back to Recife and my "new life."

It was a four-day trip, and I was alone, listening to music on my 8-track player in the car. On the third day, just as dusk was arriving, a burro galloped off the side of the road into the right front of my car. I was going about 50 mph, so it was a significant crash. Thankfully, I was not injured, but the vehicle was damaged, and the burro died on the spot.

I called my friend Jim Gravely, who was living in Salvador and told him about my situation. I then called my insurance company. Jimmy came out from his home in the city, and the insurance agent also arrived. I turned the car over to the insurance company and went with Jimmy to his house. When I shared the news of my impending divorce from Carol, Jimmy and his wife were sorrowful but showed real solidarity with me. The following day, I took a bus to Recife. It was a 12-hour trip. As I arrived after such a difficult ten days, I was buoyed by a spirit of joy and enthusiasm that had no real explanation. I'd lost my family, cameras, and car, and didn't know what I would be doing in Recife after the end of the year, but I felt great.

The next day, I took the bus to Caixa d'Agua and was delighted to find that all was well at the Center. The family planning clinic was rolling along, Gladys was fine, and her programs were going well. Pastor Lauro was taking care of the church. I found an ad for an apartment in Espinheiros, a nice neighborhood in Recife. The price was right, and I had my new home within a week.

John Buyers had shown me a street in downtown Recife with several auction houses. One Saturday, I found a white wicker dining set, a bed, and a couple of side chairs. While at the auction house, I ran into John and shared my news and that I was looking for a new job. He said he was seeking a manager for his concrete block manufacturing plant. I started to work with ConcretoBlocos do Nordeste on September 1. I told John I knew nothing about concrete, but he said he would teach me what I needed to know. What he wanted was someone he could trust.

The Transition

I went to the Central Methodist Church on the first Sunday back in Recife. At the end of the service, I told the congregation that Carol and I would be getting a divorce and I planned to stay in Brazil and continue to work at the Community Center as long as the Board of directors wanted. I had no idea how they'd respond. Much to my surprise, the entire congregation embraced me, one by one, wishing me well and welcoming me home.

That evening, I went out to Caixa d'Agua and shared the same message with the congregation there, with the same result. These wonderful people loved Carol and felt empathy for her and the children. But they also felt and showed solidarity with me. I was nearly overwhelmed by the outpourings of love from those two congregations.

My brothers and sisters of the Equipe received the news of our divorce with the same kind of solidarity. I helped Ricardo and Malú Alessio, who had come to Recife from Paraná, become engaged in the Equipe. They were educators and began their careers at the Federal University of Pernambuco. I introduced them to the beach at Tamandaré, and they bought a lot and built their own beach house there.

I started my new job at ConcretoBlocos. John Buyers was a wonderful person to work for. He wanted someone to watch his back and help him walk through the minefields of SUDENE, the Northeast Development Corporation. In October, Bishop Omar Daibert, the Bishop in charge of the Brazilian mission field, told me he was flying to Recife to discuss my new status. He arrived, accompanied by a Methodist pastor from Minas Gerais, the Rev. José Feo. A longtime close associate of Bishop Daibert, Rev. Feo was a major wheeler-dealer in the Methodist Church.

After a couple of words of greeting, Bishop Omar began to explain what I could and could not do regarding the Community Center and the Methodist Church. First of all, I couldn't continue as director. It would not be fitting for a divorced man to lead a Methodist institution. He said I could never have any kind of relationship with a woman in Recife.

With remarkable calm in the light of the outrage I felt, I said, "Bishop Omar, in the first place, the Community Center is a non-profit corporation duly inscribed in the public registry under the laws of Brazil. It is not an ecclesiastical entity, so it is not your business. In the second place, if you think I will determine my private life by your pietistic and moralistic wishes, you are very much mistaken. My wife and I came to a mutual decision to terminate our marriage. There is no scandal involved. And that is none of your business. So, if I find a female I want to associate with, I will do so, and that is also none of your business. Do we have anything else to discuss here?"

He didn't know what to say. Men who get to be Bishop in Brazil assume they are God's personal representative on earth—like the Popes—and since the clergy under their supervision are usually intimidated by them and thus totally subservient, he'd never had anyone challenge his positions. Rev. José Feo, a traditional boot-licker, likewise maintained total silence. I never saw either of them again. The Board of Directors of the Center met in November and unanimously elected me to continue as director of the Center—without salary, which I was happy to do.

Tereza Cristina de Assis Carvalho

A few weeks after I returned to Recife, I went downtown to CitiBank. The Center had some funds we didn't need for a while, so I stopped by the CD (Certificates of Deposit) desk to see if putting some of our funds into a CD or two was worthwhile. The young woman who handled CDs was attractive and charming. She promptly gave me the information I needed, and as we chatted, I decided to try out my new status of being single for the first time in more than 20 years. I mentioned I had a beach house at Tamandaré and asked if she'd ever been. She said no, but had heard it was a wonderful place. I wondered if she would like to go for a weekend. Much to my surprise, she said yes, adding that she'd have to ask her mother for permission.

I had known her as Tereza, but now I had her full name: Tereza Cristina de Assis Carvalho. She was 22 and a third-year law student at the Faculdade de Direito of Recife. Two days later, I returned to the bank, and she said she could go, but her brother, Enrique, who was 15, would also have to go along. In middle-class Brazilian society in 1973, that was typical.

When we went to Tamandaré, Carol and I always took our maid (Leó). The following weekend, Leó and I picked up Tereza and her brother and drove to the beach. They were awed. We arrived just before noon, quickly changed into swim gear, and went to the beach. The sand looked like refined sugar and squeaked under foot. The water was amazingly clear, and its average temperature was 88 degrees. We returned to the house for lunch, followed by naps in hammocks on the upper-level porch.

We went for another dip in the ocean before supper and spent the evening chatting on the porch. Sunday morning was breakfast, beach time, packing, and driving back to Recife. A few days later, I invited Tereza to a movie. She agreed, but her sister, Maria Elena, had to accompany us as a chaperon. So there I was, almost 40, going out with a beautiful, charming, and intelligent 22-year-old university student, always chaperoned by another member of her family. But I was flattered she would go out with me, so I continued.

Over the following months, I introduced Tereza to the Equipe Fraterna. Her mother, Francisquinha, was a devoted fan of Dom

Hélder. Knowing I was his friend helped overcome her initial reluctance to have her daughter date an older divorced man who was also a Protestant pastor and a businessman.

During this period, I especially enjoyed being the lay director of the Community Center. While I was a paid missionary, I always had to deal with the unspoken jealousy of my Brazilian colleagues because my salary was about three times what the Brazilian Methodist Church paid. But now, even though I had nearly tripled my salary in my new job, they no longer resented it because it was secular work.

The Center continued to prosper. During the first 12 months, we served 2,000 women through the family planning clinic through word of mouth. The average number of children those women had when they came to us was 5.2. They were desperate not to bring any more babies into the world to die of starvation, dysentery, or parasites. The GED course we offered had more than 90 students.

Pastor Lauro was a bit more problematic. He resented that I was the director of the Center. One day, he came to me to denounce some of the boys. Lauro said they were "stealing showers." We encouraged them to use the large open yard in front of the Center to play soccer, and when they finished a sweaty game, they would go to one of the three showers I had installed outdoors under our big water tank and rinse off before going home, where they didn't have running water. Lauro also expressed his disagreement with the family planning clinic. He said he didn't believe in family planning. I suggested it was just a way of helping poor people deal with a significant problem. I asked if he and his wife didn't use family planning, to which he replied, "Of course." So, I asked why if it was okay for him, it wasn't for those people. He had no answer.

In April, João, the young man that the city of Olinda had sent to the Center to be the teacher of the GED course, informed me he needed to resign. His wife just had a baby, and he lived in Jaboatão, clear on the other side of Recife. It took him two hours on buses to get to the Center. Almost the next day, I came down with the flu and spent 10 days in bed with a fever. As a result, I could not pay João his last salary and the severance pay he was entitled to under Brazilian Labor Law.

When I got well enough, I got in my car on a Sunday morning, after preparing two checks for João and the receipts for the Center's bookkeeping, and drove out to Jaboatão to give João the payments he was due. I'd been to his house the month before for a *pipa,* a typical celebration of the birth of a new child in the family, so I knew how to find it. When I got to his house, I clapped my hands (the way Brazilians knock on doors when visiting), and a voice from inside said, "Enter."

The house was a simple, lower-class home in an urban residential development. Six steps led up to a porch, and the front door was partially open. Thinking it was João who'd responded, I opened the gate and went up the stairs to the door. When I stepped in, I was confronted by two soldiers armed with machine guns. They put me against the wall and searched me, just like in all the B-movies. I protested, identifying myself as the Rev. Fred Morris, Director of the Methodist Community Center in Caixa d'Agua, saying I had come to give João his salary and severance pay. I asked them why they were in João's house and where João, his wife, and baby were. They didn't answer my questions but allowed me to show them the checks and receipts I had brought. Then, they held me at gunpoint for two hours until an army lieutenant arrived. He spent another hour questioning me, took a "deposition," and finally let me go.

Thoroughly frightened, I returned home and searched my apartment for anything the army might find suspicious. João was an excellent teacher of the GED program, but I knew nothing about his private life. The next day, I went to the Federal Police, told the sergeant what had happened, and asked about João's whereabouts. They professed total ignorance and referred me to the Political Police (DOPS). I went to DOPS headquarters and told my story again, this time to a plain-clothed inspector, but got the same answer.

By this time, Tereza and I had become very close. She was intelligent, and we had stimulating conversations. Her father, José Antão de Carvalho, had been a Major in the army, a graduate of Brazil's West Point, the Agulhas Negras academy. In 1964, when the military overthrew the elected government of João Goulart, José had been the military attaché of the Governor of the State of Pernambuco, Miguel Arraes, and he was outspoken in his opposition to the *coup*. As a result, he was imprisoned in the military hospital in Recife for nine months and forcibly retired from the army. I had no problem in letting Tereza know of my opposition to the dictatorship, which, of course, she shared with her mother, who then told José that I was not the "typical *gringo.*"

At the same time, Tereza was quite frank in describing herself as being *fútil,* which in Portuguese means superficial and materialistic. She was in law school but showed no interest in the profession. She didn't buy any required textbooks and attended classes mainly for social contact with the other students. She didn't take notes and periodically purchased notes from another enterprising student. Then, the night before exams, she would meet with a half dozen of her colleagues and do an all-nighter, reviewing the notes taken and preparing for the exam. She would leave the exam with a 10, the highest mark.

The Beginning of the End

In June 1974, John Buyers sent me to Alpina, Michigan, where the Besser Corporation manufactured concrete block machinery. I was to spend a week learning about how to run the million-dollar machine that ConcretoBlocos had purchased. One afternoon, I bought the latest copy of *Time* magazine, where I discovered an excellent article about my Archbishop, Dom Hélder Câmara, titled

"Pastor of the Poor." The article was excellent, though thoroughly critical of the military dictatorship for their treatment of the poor masses and their censorship of Dom Hélder. I vaguely wondered if that detail might not create a problem for me. It did.

I'd convinced Carol to allow me to take Jennifer and Jonathan to Brazil with me on my return for a month in Recife. I discovered some years later that this created a major problem for the dictatorship, as they assumed that I was the author of the article that was unflattering to them. They had decided simply to deport me back to the States on my arrival back in Brazil, but when I showed up with two children, aged 7 and 12, they simply didn't know what to do and let me in without any problem.

We arrived in Recife the last week of June. I got an invitation to the Fourth of July celebration at the home of the US Consul out on Boa Viagem beach. Shortly after arriving, I was approached by my friend Paulo Sá Campos, the engineer at USAID who'd done the project at Morro dos Cavalos in Piauí state. He said, forcefully though quietly, that I needed to go to the Consulate the next day. I had no idea what it was about, but Paulo was insistent. The next morning, I went to the Consulate for the first time.

The Consulate was headed up by Carl Schultz, Interim-Consul, as the former Consul had left in June. I was immediately taken into Mr. Schultz's office, where he and a few other staff members were waiting. Schultz said I was being looked at askance by the Brazilian military and I needed to go to the Fourth Army Headquarters the next day, July 6, and meet with Colonel Meziat, head of the G-2 section. I asked why, and he said he had no idea, but I needed to be there at four p.m. "And if I don't return, what will you do?" I asked.

He replied, "Nothing. There is nothing I could do." Not very reassuring.

After a nearly sleepless night, I presented myself promptly at the Fourth Army Headquarters in the center of Recife at four p.m. I waited over 40 minutes to be received into the office of Colonel Meziat, who was accompanied by another Colonel. They were sitting on one side of a coffee table that held a couple of tape recorders. I was asked to be seated with absolutely no cordiality. Both men were stone-faced.

After a few moments of silence, I asked why they'd asked me to come. Meziat responded, "I'm sure you know." I didn't. We sat in silence for a few more moments, then Meziat said they were not happy with some of my associations. More silence. They were clearly waiting for me to say something that would incriminate me, which I had no intention of doing. I asked what he meant, and again, he said, "I'm sure you know." He said that my changing from being a missionary to a journalist to a businessman was strange. I responded by saying that my divorce from my wife had upended a lot, but now I was primarily the manager of ConcretoBlocos.

Finally, Meziat said they wanted me to write a detailed report on my past ten years in Brazil, describing my work, friendships, and activities. He said it looked like I was "messing around in things that weren't my business," and I needed to report back in one week. With that, they terminated the meeting and ushered me out.

I was terrified. The consul said he wouldn't help me in any way, so there was no point in returning to him. It was clear that I was on my own in dealing with these representatives of the dictatorship. I was reluctant to tell Tereza about this turn of events. So I entertained Jennifer and Jonathan while they were with me, and at night, I worked on the declaration for the Colonel. I wrote my "report" out in longhand, running onto page after page of history. I started with our arrival in Brazil on January 12, 1964, going through the year at language school, the transition to the pastorate in Teresópolis, Itaipava, and Cuiabá. Then to Pilares, the University of Chicago, Recife, and my work at the Caixa d'Agua Community Center. I deliberately made it all as dull as possible.

The week passed, and I was back in the waiting room at the Colonel's office. Finally, I was allowed into his office again and simply handed him the manuscript. The document was about 12 pages of handwriting on ruled paper. They told me to return the following Thursday and ushered me out. By this time, we were at the end of July, and my two beloved children were returning to the US. They didn't want to go, as they loved being in Brazil, their home country. With a great deal of anguish and tears all around, I took them to the Recife airport and bid them farewell, hoping I could have them back again in another year. Tereza was helpful at this time, showing empathy for my suffering over the kids. Simultaneously, I began to see some problems in our relationship. Her being *fútil* was obvious. And I had become aware of her mother's total dominance over her.

Thursday came, and I returned to Meziat's office. This time, the atmosphere was different. They served me the traditional *cafezinho*, which is almost obligatory in any encounter in Brazil. The two colonels even allowed themselves to smile a bit as we started our conversation.

Colonel Meziat began by saying he appreciated my report. They had decided if I stopped fooling around with journalism and avoided "bad company," by which he clearly meant Dom Hélder, I could continue my life in Brazil. But I needed to be careful with my contacts and activities. They decided I was not a real danger to the country and let me go. The sense of relief I felt was overwhelming.

A Truly Subversive Act

At one of our weekly meetings of the Equipe, Marcelo said that Dom Hélder needed someone to drive him up to Campina Grande in the State of Rio Grande do Norte, as he was to address a meeting of university students. The meeting was to be semi-clandestine, as the dictatorship was suspicious of students and would not want Dom Hélder to be speaking to them. I was sure that if we were discovered, the worst that would happen would be my expulsion from Brazil, as we were all confident they would not imprison and torture an American citizen.

On the following Wednesday, at two-thirty p.m. I drove behind the Catholic Church of Espinheiros, where Dom Hélder stood behind a large palm tree. He got into my car, and we drove to Campina Grande for three hours. When we arrived, more than 350 university students from all over Brazil were there for a meeting of the National Student Movement, which was no longer officially allowed. Dom Hélder spoke for about an hour. Then we drove back to Recife, arriving shortly after midnight. Dom Hélder slept the whole way home. The military was informed that the Archbishop had spoken at the meeting, but they didn't know how he got there.

We were busy preparing the factory to install the Besser machinery at the plant. We bought a dump truck and hired some new workers. Having spent the week in Alpina learning all about the machine, I was in an important role and felt engaged in my job. The Community Center was cruising on automatic pilot, and Tereza and I spent every other weekend at Tamandaré. Life was good.

Tereza was very affectionate—with the lines carefully drawn. She was exuberant, warm, and delightful. During our courtship, I never saw her perturbed. She was always calm, relaxed, and collected. On the second Sunday in September, I held a little spiritual retreat, spending several hours alone, reading the Bible, meditating, and reflecting on what was happening in my life. I was more than a little gun-shy about a new marriage. And despite all the charm and delight she brought me, I had seen some warning flags. So I made a decision. We'd exchange engagement rings, and I'd invest another six months in my relationship with Tereza. I'd work on pushing the limits regarding the aspects that concerned me, primarily her dependence on her mother.

I felt a lot of relief and began working more on developing our relationship. But it was not to be. On Saturday, September 28, Dom Hélder flew to Rome for a convocation of Bishops. He was to be gone a month. I spent the following day with Tereza, ending it in her living room playing chess. She was good, and we were evenly matched. We both clobbered José whenever he got up the nerve to play us. We usually played sitting on the carpeted floor, so I took my wallet out of my tight pants. At about eleven p.m. I went home, forgetting to grab my wallet.

On Monday morning, I drove to the factory in Camaragibe and got to my office at seven-thirty a.m. We had serious cashflow problems, and our telephone was suspended for lack of payment. A little after nine, I used my home phone to order sand, gravel, and other materials for the plant.

I had an appointment with Tereza's father at ten a.m. in downtown Recife to sign a contract for some work my new little company was to do. Not wanting to be a salaried employee for the rest of my life, I'd formed a roofing and waterproofing company. Some months before, a man representing SWEPCO (Southwest Petroleum Company) had appeared in Recife looking for a representative. Someone at the US Consulate had referred him to me. I talked with John Buyers, and he had no problem if I wanted to take on the distributorship of SWEPCO for Recife. I placed an order with SWEPCO for $10,000 worth of materials, and José became my salesperson in his retired status.

As I was heading toward Recife, I had to pass a fiscal barrier, where the State of Pernambuco checked the loads of trucks coming and going. That's when I saw Luis Soares de Lima, a young man I'd gotten to know when I had an exhibition of photographs in Olinda. A friend of mine had a booth there and allowed me to sell some of my pictures there, pictures of a *jangadeiro* on the beach with his raft; a Black girl in a *favela* in Recife; a worker cultivating pineapple in Piauí; a boy holding a machete; an old woman smoking a pipe; a couple of pictures of Dom Hélder, the Archbishop. Luis had seen the pictures and inquired about the photographer. The owner of the booth gave him my phone number. He called me and said he would love to learn to do photography. That began our friendship.

Our Time Had Come

Luis never talked much about his past. As we worked in my darkroom, we would talk about this and that, and before long, we discovered we shared a dislike for the dictatorship and a love for Dom Hélder.

When we got to my apartment, I made the necessary phone calls then left to meet with José. Luis came along to run some errands. That's when we passed the man with a beard dressed in a business suit. As I unlocked the car, I saw the bearded man run out of the building toward us with a pistol in his hand, yelling something. At the same time, three vehicles roared up, GMC Suburbans, the vehicle of choice of the army security forces. A dozen men appeared, all dressed in Levi's and T-shirts, armed with .45 pistols or machine guns. We were told to put our hands on the car's roof and spread our legs.

Luis and I looked at each other over the car. We knew our time had come. When we heard that Nina, one of my former students, had been kidnapped just a year before, Luis and I went to a quiet bar near the river and agonized over Nina's plight. We were sure she was being tortured. I remember saying to Luis that I wouldn't last five minutes under torture. He responded with some wisdom that was impressive for one so young. "If you understand that these people are the enemy of the people you love and all that you believe in," he said, "and they are going to torture you no matter what you do, you can resist more than you think. If they want "A," and you give them "A," they will want "B"; if you give them "B," they will ask for "C," and so on. There is no escaping. So there is no benefit in giving them anything. They will keep on torturing you to get more info. If you don't give them anything, they will torture you. They will promise to stop, but they won't."

By then, the leader of the gang had them put hoods over our heads, handcuffs on our wrists, and pushed us into one of the

Suburbans. I was put on the floor in the middle, and Luis on the floor in the back. I could feel the barrel of a machine gun pressed against my ribs. The car took off with a flourish. I heard someone on a walkie-talkie, saying they were returning to the "hospital."

I knew Recife quite well and could follow our path by keeping track of the right/left turns. In about 10 minutes, we were in downtown Recife at the Fourth Army Headquarters. We heard the metal gate being opened. We were then told to get out. With our heads still hooded, the handcuffs were removed, and we were told to take off our clothes, keeping only our shorts on. My watch and engagement ring were taken.

The End of my Years in Brazil

I was taken down a long hall and pushed into a cell, and the door was slammed shut. I took the hood off as there was no one to prevent me from doing so. The cell was about seven feet long and four feet wide. There was no window, the only ventilation being an opening at the bottom of the door to pass food trays. The door was made of iron bars with a half-inch plywood panel placed outside to cut off any view. At eye level, a four-by-twelve-inch sliding panel served as a peephole. The roof was clay tile, with one glass tile in the middle that gave some illumination. About seven feet off the floor, a grate of iron bars was embedded in the walls, creating a cage-like effect to the cell and preventing any athletic prisoner from escaping by removing the tiles. The walls were blood red and flat white. The floor was alternating yellow and black concrete tile slabs. I was naked except for my shorts.

I realized I could be tortured; I'd already heard Luis scream from somewhere not too far away. But the kind of fear I would have expected to feel was absent. I found myself repeating, for the first of dozens of times, *The Lord is my shepherd; I shall not want.* After about fifteen or twenty minutes, they came for me.

Before opening the door, they ordered me to replace the cloth hood. I saw my torturers only once in the days to come. They handcuffed my hands behind my back and pushed, shoved, and dragged me down the corridor, through a door, up another short passageway, and into a room that was to be, for me, a torture chamber. The questions began.

"I am an American citizen," I said immediately. "I want to see my Consul."

"Here is your Consul," one of them cried as he hit me in the abdomen.

"Where were you taking Alanir?" someone demanded.

"Who?" I had never heard that name before. More blows.

"Luis. Where were you taking Luis?"

"Nowhere. I was going to the Bank of Brazil. He was going to get off on the way somewhere. He hadn't said where." Now, the blows came to the groin. I fell to the floor in agony.

"Get up, you son of a bitch," someone cried as I was kicked in the back. There were more questions and blows in rapid succession, with people constantly coming in and out of the room.

Then, a voice I recognized later as Luis Miranda Filho, a notoriously sadistic Recife policeman, said, "We've already sent a car for your fiancée. Tereza will be here soon. We'll strip her and work on her till you decide to talk."

There were more questions and blows. "Who are your Commie friends? Why does an s.o.b. American like you come down here to subvert our country? Your own country's gone to hell. Can't even keep your President. We'll teach you!"

Then it all stopped. I heard the man who would be my principal interrogator in the days ahead humming quietly. Water ran into a bucket, then splashed at my feet. Still humming cheerily to himself, the man walked to the other end of the room and returned with a wire, which he fastened to the second toe of my right foot. He returned with another electrode, which he attached to the nipple of my right breast with a spring clip that cut into the flesh. I heard my inquisitor pull up a chair and sit down. In a very calm voice, he started the questions again.

"Where were you taking Alanir?"

"Nowhere," I replied. "I was going to the Bank of Brazil, and he was going to get off on the way."

The first jolt was a light one, a sort of tickling and pulling at my breast. My interrogator increased the current. I began to jump around on the wet floor. I clamped my mouth shut as hard as I could, not wanting to scream and give him any satisfaction, but as the current increased, my mouth flew open with a great bellow of rage and pain. The current kept increasing, and I fell to the floor. Then it stopped.

"Get up," he yelled.

As soon as I was on my feet again, the same questions were repeated, accompanied by more shocks. Again, I fell to the floor. Up again. More questions, more shocks, falling once more. Finally, the shocks stopped. My inquisitor took the electrode from my breast and began pushing down my shorts, the only clothing I had left. *Oh, no!* I groaned to myself. *This I can't bear. I know I can't.*

"Nervous, huh?" he inquired. "Now we can have some real fun. And if you don't talk, we'll shock it right off you." With this, he fastened the spring clip to the base of my penis and returned to his chair.

I fell with all my weight on my back and my hands, which were still manacled behind me. The current continued as I squirmed and wriggled on the floor. The room filled with laughter.

Once again, the command came to get up. It was harder than before, as I'd sprained my left wrist in the fall. After a few more rounds, they stopped. The electrodes were removed from my penis and foot, and I was led back to my cell. The handcuffs were removed from one wrist, brought around in front of my face, passed through a bar of the cell door at eye level, and refastened. Still hooded and trembling, I was left alone, hanging from the door of my cell.

It couldn't have been more than fifteen minutes before they came for me again. The hood was pulled down over my face, and I started the short walk to the torture chamber. Once more, I repeated the Shepherd's Psalm, *The Lord is my shepherd; I shall not want....* Again, I found myself calmed by those ancient words. I wondered how many people had used that Psalm at similar moments through the centuries. I was also curiously surprised at how it helped. I knew that no one, not even God, was going to save me from the hands of these men. But the Psalm confirmed their limited capacity to touch me where it mattered most.

I was questioned with electric shocks and more beatings for about another hour, then hung up again in my cell. This was repeated two or three times before I was taken into a different room. I was made to sit, the handcuffs were removed, and my arms and legs were tied to the chair with leather straps. One electrode was placed on my breast and the other on my right ear. These were the worst shocks of all. I felt like my head was actually going to burst. I screamed, jumped in the chair, tried to break the straps, and finally, on at least two occasions, was rendered unconscious.

At one point, my chief inquisitor launched off on a long and emotional tirade against Dom Hélder, saying he was a shameless traitor to his country. At another point, one of my torturers got down on the floor in front of me, lifted my hood, and yelled, *"Eu sou foda! Se voce não cooperar, eu vou lhe matar!"* The face, I learned later, was that of Luis Miranda Filho, a man clearly proud of his role as a defender of Christian culture in Brazil, willing to kill for the cause. He returned shortly afterward with Major Maia, the chief of the Fourth Army torture operation. Miranda announced they would now bring in Luis. They wanted me to ask him for his address to round up the rest of his group. They declared that he was a rotten, no-good, Communist son of a bitch. If I cooperated, they would let me go; if not, they would keep torturing me until he gave in.

I recalled my late-night talks with Luis about the futility of cooperating with the enemy. It was better to remain silent from the outset. I didn't know if Luis was involved in anything subversive. I hoped he was; if so, I didn't want to cause him to betray himself. Amid my confusion, the door opened, and I heard them drag Luis in. He was breathing with apparent difficulty as they shoved him over to stand near me.

"Tell Fred your name," someone ordered.

There was a pause, and I heard Luis take a deep breath. "My name is Alanir Cardoso." He spoke with a defiance that startled me but also made me proud of him. Like hundreds of others of his age, I imagined he'd probably been in some sort of student trouble in 1968–69 and changed his identity to avoid imprisonment. He'd never spoken to me of his past. In Brazil, I learned not to ask questions. People told you what you needed to know. I was truly glad at that moment. Knowing nothing, I had no secrets to tell.

"Fred," Luis (or Alanir) continued, "I'm sorry that our friendship has led to this. I really didn't think it would happen." He was interrupted by a violent body blow. I wanted to reach out and help him.

"Fred," he started again, "I'm sorry."

"I know, Luis," I said. "I understand." They gave me a heavy jolt that forced another bellow from me.

"Alanir," someone said, "Fred wants you to give us your address. We know he is innocent, but if necessary, we will torture him to death if you don't give us your address."

"Fred, do you want me to give them my address?"

"If you can," I said weakly, hoping he would understand that I didn't want him to. "You know what you have to do." With that, I received another violent shock, and as soon as it was over, I was struck violently on the side of the head two or three times.

"This son of a bitch isn't going to tell us," one of our tormentors said. "Give it to Fred." They turned on the current again, and as they dragged Luis out, I heard him say, "I'm sorry, Fred," once more.

I was unstrapped, handcuffed, and dragged back to be hung on my cell door.

The routine was established and went on. Hood on the head, handcuffs behind my back, half-shoved, half-dragged down the corridor, repeating the Twenty-third Psalm to myself, once more feeling an inner poise that the circumstances didn't in any way warrant. Luis was there again.

"Alanir," one of them said, "Fred wants to ask you something. He wants to know your address."

"Beg him," a voice whispered in my ear. "Beg him!" With that, I received a blow on the side of the head.

"Luis," I started. "How are you doing?"

"Mais ou menos," he replied, noticeably weaker than in our earlier encounter. "How are you?"

"I don't know, Luis. They want me to ask you to give them your address. Can you?"

"Do you want me to, Fred?" he asked.

"Beg him!" insisted the tempter's voice at my side. "Beg him, or we'll kill you right now!"

"If you can," I mumbled, hoping Luis would understand. Then came another shock and another bellow from me.

"Okay," Luis said. "I'll give the address." *No, don't,* I cried inwardly. They stopped all the rough stuff with anxious expectations, waiting for Luis to speak. But he merely repeated, "Okay, I'll give the address."

"All right, what is it?" someone yelled.

"My address is . . . " Then he didn't say anything more.

"My address is . . . " Then came another shock and a scream from me.

"Wait!" cried Luis. "I'm giving the address." Another pause. "My address is . . . " Incredibly, I found myself laughing inside.

"I live in a *pensão,*" he offered. "I live in a *pensão* downtown." Another pause. I could feel he was trying to buy time before giving up the information. "I live in a *pensão.*"

"Where, goddamn it? Tell us now, or we're going to kill Fred." Another violent shock went through me.

"I'm giving it. I'm in a *pensão* downtown in Recife." It must have been nearly an hour later when Luis finally gave them the address of a cheap hotel in downtown Recife. There was a scuffle as some of them rushed out, obviously to raid the hotel. Then, as Luis was being led out, he finally said, "I gave it to them, Fred."

I was unstrapped, handcuffed, and then dragged off again to be hung on the cell door for the rest of the night. My left wrist was quite swollen, and the handcuff was cutting into the flesh. My body was aching all over, my head was throbbing, I was thirsty and exhausted, but I had a strange feeling of exhilaration. I had made it through the day! I had made it through this day, and I could make it through the next.

I began fantasizing that they'd release me. I knew prisoners were often dumped on the street at night when the army was through with them. I started to think about arriving at my fiancée's house, our embrace, and the joy I would have in reassuring her that I'd survived. It was an image I was to nourish often during the days ahead.

I knelt to relieve my aching legs. I prayed. I didn't pray for deliverance; my idea of God didn't include the Lone Ranger. I gave thanks for having survived and prayed for strength. They came again a couple of hours after daylight. I was ordered to replace my hood, the door was opened, the handcuffs were removed and refastened behind my back, and I was led off for more questioning. I could still hear Luis. His cries were more varied now, mostly weaker. Occasionally, he burst forth with sounds of barking.

I was taken to another room. My arms and legs were strapped as before, but this time, no wires. A new voice quietly asked, "Fred, how are you feeling?" This must be the "good guy" of the team, I immediately thought to myself. The next session was with the "bad guy."

Sometime in the evening, I was surprised by the jailer opening the peephole and wordlessly offering me a piece of bread and a glass of water. The jailer asked me if it was true that I was a pastor, and I said it was. He shook his head in obvious confusion and closed the peephole again.

I was taken back for another hour or so of questioning and then returned to the cell. Now, however, for the first time, I was not hung on the door but simply shoved into the cell, the handcuffs removed. There was no bedding. I removed the hood, folded it for a pillow, lay on the bare concrete, and fell asleep.

At about six-thirty, the jailer woke me by opening the peephole to ask if I wanted some bread and coffee. I was hopeful that we were reaching an end. In the chamber, my hopes were dashed. Instead of being strapped to the chair, I was hung by the handcuffs from a hook high over my head and close to the wall. My chief tormentor began by saying they were tired of my lying and that today I was going to confess my sins. He started by asking when I had introduced Luis to Dom Hélder. When I said never, he struck me in the back with his fist, then slapped me on the back of the head. These blows were followed by a rapid-fire series of questions and more beatings. I could hear them questioning Luis in the next room. He sounded only semiconscious; his answers to their questions were only moans and grunts.

My inquisitor produced a new gadget. He began rolling what must have been a spiked wheel over my back, scratching the skin. As I flinched, he laughed and pushed down harder, closing some sort of electric circuit and giving me a shock. This was to be the procedure: the wheel was passed back and forth, and each time I refused to answer, he pressed the device down into my naked back.

After what seemed like forever, he stopped and walked away, leaving me semiconscious and dangling by the handcuffs on the wall. Suddenly, a voice said quietly, "It's all right. I'm not going to hurt you." I perceived the cold metal of a doctor's stethoscope.

That evening, I dozed off, only to be awakened when Major Maia opened the peephole about an inch and said, "Fred, we're beginning to have second thoughts about you. We're beginning to think maybe you're connected to official organs."

"Uh," was my only response.

"Yes, we know you're guilty, or we wouldn't have brought you here," he said, "but we think now you might be working for the CIA. How about it?"

"No, thank you," I said. "I've got enough trouble already." With that, he shut the peephole. They must really be confused by now, I thought. They bring me in for being a Communist and want to send me out as a CIA agent.

It must have been around midnight when they came for me again. I was made to sit down and was greeted by the major and one of his colleagues. "Fred," began the major, "to be or not to be, *zat* is the question." Obviously, he had been practicing that little bit in English for a while.

He continued in English, "Are you a Communist, or are you a CIA agent?"

"Did it occur to you that I might not be either?" I replied in Portuguese. "Can you imagine that I might be just what I am, a former missionary trying to make an honest living in business here in Recife and who happens to have some friends you don't like?"

"Fred, we wouldn't have brought you here if we weren't sure you were guilty. We suffered much more trying to decide if we should bring you in or not than you have suffered here."

"I doubt that very much," I answered. "But if you were so sure of my guilt, then why all the questions? If you have any real evidence, why not just take me to court rather than torturing me?"

"Look, you are here to answer questions, not ask them." He then proceeded to rehearse the string of coincidences and circumstantial evidence that they had against me, most of it based on depositions made by people I'd never met who had implicated me while being tortured. My friendship with Dom Hélder and Luis, which I had never denied, were the only concrete things on the list.

That night was the worst. My feet ached mercilessly, and I longed to sleep—impossible while shackled in a standing position. I began thinking again about what I'd do when and if I finally got out. Would I be allowed to stay in Brazil? What would I do if I went back to the States? At that moment, I resolved to tell my story to as many people as would hear me. I rehearsed everything verbally from Monday morning to that moment. I went over every session of torture, remembering every word said and every barbarity practiced. Even if it took months or years, I decided to do that at least once daily until I got to a typewriter or tape recorder. I knew that was the only way to keep the story straight. Dawn finally came, and a new jailer arrived with coffee and a piece of bread. I was allowed to bathe in the wretched bathroom beside my cell.

It must have been about eight-thirty when they came again. One of my interrogators explained that the reason I was always hooded was so I would then be unable to recognize them on the streets and so could not try to kill them.

In the afternoon, the major returned. "Fred, how do you feel? Everything okay?" he asked cheerfully.

"Just great," I responded. "Never better."

"Well," he continued, "as you know, Brazil belongs to the community of nations. We have treaties with many countries, including the United States. One of those treaties gives you the right to see your Consul, so, of course, we will let you do that. We will have you take a bath, shave, put on your clothes, and take you to see your Consul. You are to speak only in Portuguese. Afterward, you will be coming back here, so be careful not to exaggerate anything that has happened to you."

I was standing in front of him, my head hooded, naked except for my shorts, my hands manacled behind my back. My wrists were cut and bruised, the left one sprained, no feeling in either hand, and my back and buttocks were scratched and bruised. I'd spent two of the past three nights standing up, had eaten only one meal in four days, and had been threatened, beaten, cajoled, kicked, and shocked into unconsciousness. So, at the end of his little speech, I burst out laughing.

"What in hell are you laughing about? There's nothing funny about your situation."

"I'm sorry, but I just thought of a joke."

"Jesus Christ! How can you think of jokes? What is it?"

I told him I had remembered the old story about President Eisenhower's visit to Moscow. The Russians, wanting to show that theirs is an open and free society in which everyone is happy, brought in a peasant from the interior, put him on TV, and told him he could say anything he wanted as the American President was there. People all over the world were watching him on TV. The peasant, thoroughly intimidated, remained silent. They insisted repeatedly that he should say anything he wanted until finally he took courage, looked straight at the TV camera, and said, "Help!"

After returning my clothes, watch, and ring, they put me in a Volkswagen microbus. I was handcuffed, as usual, but allowed to remove the hood, though the windows of the vehicle were painted over. However, I knew Recife very well and figured out that they were taking me to Jaboatão, an area out by the International Airport. We finally arrived at a military base, where I was escorted into a room by the Colonel, who appeared to be in charge, and left by myself. Before leaving, he said the American Consul would be arriving shortly. It was about four p.m.—I was delighted to have my watch back.

I was in a guest room probably used for visiting officers. It wasn't fancy, but it had a bunk bed, a couple of easy chairs, and a table with a straight chair. Two windows looked out onto a garden area. A pitcher of ice water and a couple of glasses were on the table.

After a few minutes, I lay down on the lower bunk. A real mattress! Too wound up to rest, I got up again and returned to the easy chair. Some movement outside the window caught my attention. I saw a soldier dressed in military camouflage drop down from a tree in the garden. Puzzled, I watched closely as he snake-crawled across the lawn, pushing a large rifle before him. Then he pointed it at my head.

What is this all about? Suddenly, it occurred to me that perhaps the Consul wasn't coming after all. It was getting dark, so I got up and turned off the lights; I could make the marksman's task a bit more difficult. I sat in the other chair, and sure enough, his rifle followed me. Suddenly, the door opened, and a corporal came in, turned on the lights, and went out, locking the door behind him!

The more I thought about it, the more logical it seemed that this was a setup. They were going to shoot me. I knew of more than one case of someone who'd been kidnapped and tortured and later appeared by the side of some road, shot to death. The explanation given was always that they had tried to escape and were shot in the process. I suddenly realized that October 3, 1974, would be my last day on earth.

I didn't want to die. Then, suddenly, like a warm cloud, a feeling of peace settled over me. *I don't want to die,* I said to myself, *but I can do it. It's okay.* The only thing I could think of was what St. Paul had described as the Gift of Faith in 1 Corinthians. It wasn't physical courage but a sense of peace and acceptance.

At about five p.m., the door opened and the Colonel came in, accompanied by the American Consul, Mr. Richard Brown. I was never so happy to see anyone in my life. I'd only briefly met Mr. Brown when he assumed his post in Recife and asked me to meet him at the Consulate. He knew about my interviews in July and August with Colonel Meziat and wanted to meet me. I hadn't seen him since.

He began the conversation by saying it had taken a lot of diplomatic pressure from the embassy in Brasília to get him in to see me. He wanted to know if I was all right and being well treated. I said I had been instructed to speak only in Portuguese, to which he replied, "We are US citizens, and our language is English."

Recalling Major Maia's threats, I told him I was fine but winked at him so the Colonel could not see what I was doing. Mr. Brown got the message immediately and said: "Mr. Morris, I am here representing the government of the United States of America. If you have been mistreated in any way, there will be hell to pay. Please tell me what has been happening to you."

I repeated all the details I had rehearsed every day of my imprisonment. He pulled out a notebook and took extensive notes. The Colonel, who was in charge of a communications battalion and had nothing to do with "security" matters, sat there with his mouth open most of the time, stunned by my report.

After about 90 minutes, Mr. Brown asked if I had any physical signs to corroborate my story. I took off my shirt and showed them the scratches on my back and the scabs on my wrists, then lowered my pants to show the deep purple bruises on my buttocks. Then, the door opened and Mr. Brown was informed his time was up. Before leaving, he offered me the strongest assurances the highest authorities would see to it I be tortured no more. Mr. Brown also said he'd return to see me the next day. He could do nothing about any charges that might be brought against me, and I would, of course, have to return to my cell. He also said my fiancée's parents had hired a lawyer for me.

After he left, the Colonel returned with his personal Bible, offering it to me, saying he'd been a student at a Baptist high school in Rio. Later, he brought me a marvelous chicken dinner with mashed potatoes and gravy. Unfortunately, I couldn't eat it, not having eaten anything since Monday except a couple of pieces of bread given to me by the turnkey of my cell.

Back at Fourth Army headquarters, I was required to give up my clothes, and once more, I found myself sitting on the floor of my cell in my shorts, wondering if that interlude of quasi-reality had been only an hallucination. It was about seven-thirty when they sent for me again. Hooded and handcuffed, I was led off to the chamber where my principal torturer was waiting for me. He told me I was to make a formal statement about my ten-and-one-half years in Brazil. He would take it all down; it would then be typed, and I would be asked to sign it the next day.

I awoke on Friday certain that the worst was over. This was to become a pattern. Each day began with the promise it would be my last one in prison. After my morning coffee, I did some exercises in my cell—push-ups, sit-ups, running in place. A bath, dressing, then off for a ride, head covered, through the streets of Recife for about fifteen minutes, only to return to Fourth Army Headquarters for a fifteen-minute encounter with the Consul, Richard Brown, in Colonel Meziat's office. Mr. Brown brought news of Tereza and my friends and family. He inquired about my treatment and gradually secured a mattress and more edible food. He had no word ever about my possible release.

The questioning continued, but only sporadically. Sometimes, I wasn't questioned for an entire day, then I would be grilled for five or six hours at a stretch, once, even all night. My usual interrogator was replaced by a man with a powerful, pulpit-like voice. His questions concerned the World Council of Churches and its upcoming Assembly in Nairobi, Kenya. He obviously knew a lot more about it than I did. Then, he wanted to know the names of my friends in the Brazilian Methodist Church. I was totally evasive, pointing out that I'd lost touch with my former colleagues since I left the Rio area in

1968. He insisted, so I finally gave him the names of two Methodist pastors I said were my closest intimates in the Methodist Church: Rev. Antonio Baggio and Rev. Sebastião Dornellas. Both were in their late 70s and had been retired and inactive for several years.

Brown was clear he could do nothing about getting me out of prison. They hadn't charged me with any crime, so there was no way to know how this might end. And if they did charge me with something, the US government could only insist that I be treated well and guaranteed "due process" under Brazilian law, which didn't ensure due process to anyone in the aftermath of Institutional Act No. V, which had been decreed in December 1968.

On the 15th, I was taken from my cell in the late afternoon, given my clothes, ring, and watch, and driven to another military installation in the neighboring city of Olinda. There, they made forty sets of my fingerprints and insulted me continually while making gross remarks about the character and families of the members of the *Equipe Fraterna,* the ecumenical group I had started when I went to Recife, whom they said was holding a prayer vigil on my behalf at the Benedictine monastery in Olinda. The following day, some of the other prisoners told me in loud whispers it had been announced on the radio that I was to be expelled from the country as an *undesirable,* though they did not know when.

In the afternoon of the 16th, they came for me again. This time, Major Maia himself, the chief of the torture chamber and a self-avowed graduate of the School of the Americas and proud defender of democracy and Christian values, put me in the middle seat of a Suburban and started out of town. I asked the major where we were going, and he said "to Tamandaré." He added that they needed me to check out my beach house at Tamandaré and sign a document stating that they had not damaged it while occupying it during my imprisonment. I said I would happily sign their document without the trip, which seemed to please him, so we drove directly to the Federal Police headquarters in Recife.

I loved Brazil and its people and beautiful beaches, but I was anxious to get out. The Federal Police had a bunch of papers for me to sign. Then Richard Brown showed up, and they took me to my apartment in Espinheiros so I could pack a bag for my trip to the US.

At my apartment, which they had also been occupying since my kidnapping in the hopes of capturing other "subversive" elements who might drop by to see me, I made a quick inspection to see what was missing. My Smith-Corona portable electric typewriter and several books from my library were gone.

While packing a suitcase for my trip to the US, Richard Brown started speaking to me very softly. At first, I didn't understand him. Then I realized he was speaking pig-Latin. He told me that he and Ambassador John Crimmins were under much pressure from the Brazilian regime and Secretary of State Henry Kissinger. Kissinger was upset that this little event was affecting the most cordial relations he enjoyed with the Brazilian military, as he did with the Chilean, Argentinian, Uruguayan, and Paraguayan military. Brown asked me to go to Washington, D.C., as soon as possible and visit as many of the members of Congress, both senators and representatives, who had been involved in my case. It turned out there were ten senators and nine representatives who'd been active in seeking my release. He wanted me to thank them for their help, then ask them to write letters of commendation of Brown and Crimmins and send them to the Department of State, requesting that their letters be placed in their personnel files. I agreed to do so, and, as it turned out later, this was a wise move on behalf of Brown and Crimmins, as Kissinger sought to sack them both for their defense of an insignificant US citizen in a foreign land.

I was taken back to Federal Police headquarters and given a two-inch foam mattress for a bed on the floor of one of the offices. I was told that my fiancé's father, José Antão de Carvalho, a former Major in the Brazilian Army who had been forcibly retired in the aftermath of the *coup* in 1964, as he had opposed the extra-legal actions, would be coming by in the morning for me to sign a Power of Attorney for him to be able to settle my affairs. They also wanted me to sign a check on my account at Citibank in Recife to pay for my plane fare to New York. I flatly refused this, saying that the trip was their idea and they could pay for it. They did.

Before drifting off to a somewhat fitful sleep, as I anticipated the beginning of a totally new life back in the US, I was visited by two or three Federal Police officers who simply wanted to talk with me about what sort of things I had been doing to get into such trouble. They did not seem surprised when I told them that I was a pastor who had not been doing anything subversive except being a friend of Archbishop Dom Hélder Câmara.

In the morning, I was abruptly awakened sometime after six a.m. and told to get ready as I was catching a nine a.m. flight to Rio. I asked about the meeting with José but was simply told that I had to hurry to avoid missing the flight. Reconciled to the impossibility of my staying in Brazil and certainly not anxious to spend any more time in the hands of the Brazilian authorities than necessary, I hurriedly got everything together, deliberately dressing in an all-black outfit for my travels.

Once in the Suburban, as we were heading toward the airport, I asked if they could take the route by the beach at Boa Viagem so that I could say my goodbyes to that part of my life. Much to my surprise, they acquiesced, and we made the trip by the beach route, arriving at the airport about 30 minutes before the scheduled nine a.m. flight.

As I was being escorted out of the Suburban, I saw some members of the *Equipe Fraterna* down the sidewalk at the entrance to the terminal. They were hurrying in my direction for a goodbye, so I dawdled around, fussing with my suitcase and my shoelaces. Finally, my friends were there, and we had a few moments of embraces and well-wishing until the police agents took me by the arms and led me to the plane.

Richard Brown had promised me that I would have some time with Tereza before leaving, but she was nowhere to be seen. I was rushed through the terminal, onto the tarmac, and up the stairway to the waiting 737. I was accompanied by a police agent who was armed with a .38, which he made a point of showing to me. We were given the two front seats on the right-hand side of the plane.

Shortly after sitting down and buckling my seat belt, I was startled to see Major Maia coming on board. He approached me, and after I got up from my seat, he extended his hand for me to shake in front of all the passengers on the plane and said, in Portuguese, "I hope there are no hard feelings."

CHAPTER 6

Now What?

THERE WAS A COMMOTION outside the plane through the still-open door. Tereza ran across the tarmac, accompanied by Richard Brown. As she ran up the stairs, I leaped over my guard (I had been given the window seat) and met her at the door for a dramatic Hollywood-type embrace, complete with passionate kisses. In between the kisses, she said she would go to the States to marry me as soon as possible.

Then the poor, baffled police agent got his wits about him and forcibly separated us and dragged me back into the plane and into my seat. The door was immediately closed, and the aircraft taxied out to the runway and took off. My emotions on this flight were a kaleidoscope. On the one hand, I rejoiced that I had made it. I had not only survived unspeakable torture by unspeakable torturers, but I had not betrayed myself or my friends. My final embrace with Tereza and her whispered words gave me hope for our future. At the same time, I had no idea what would be waiting for me in the US. And I was agonizing over what fate might await Luis, who had no Consul to rescue him.

When we arrived in Rio de Janeiro, a Volkswagen Beetle squad car awaited us. I was whisked away from the airport to the Federal Police headquarters in Rio, where I was deposited in a cell for the rest of the day. Compared to the bare-bones cell in Recife, this was a Sheraton. There was actually a bed with a relatively clean mattress. There was a chair to sit on.

As the afternoon passed, two police agents chatted with me. They had been following my story in the Brazilian press, which, despite the censorship, had been printing whatever crumbs of information they could get about an American missionary being tortured in Recife, and wanted to know from me what was really going on. I told them. And, strangely enough, they believed me. It should be noted that during much of the military dictatorship, many Federal Police agents operated strictly as police agents. In the evening, at about nine-thirty p.m., they came for me again and put me into the Volkswagen squad car. Those same two agents were charged with getting me to the airport and onto the eleven p.m. Varig flight to New York.

The press was out in force as word had circulated that I was being expelled from the country. Our Volkswagen drove up to the boarding stairway, and my two police escorts took me out of the car with their .38s drawn and took me up the stairs, holding my arms. At the jet's door, they holstered their guns. Each of them gave me a Brazilian embrace and wished me "all the best" and *"desculpe qualquer coisa"* ("please overlook any inconvenience"—a typical Brazilian goodbye). They then handed me off to the flight attendant standing at the door.

When the "fasten seat belt" sign was off, I tested my new freedom by going to the restroom without asking for permission. As I worked my way toward the back of the 707 with an exhilarating sense of being free, I was shocked to see a Brazilian friend seated as a passenger: the Rev. Aarão Sapzezian, an Armenian pastor from São Paulo who was now working for the World Council of Churches in Geneva. He was as surprised to see me as I was to encounter him.

When I returned from the restroom, responding to his invitation, I sat in an empty seat beside him. He had been at a WCC gathering in Buenos Aires for the past 10 days and was returning to Geneva through New York. We'd met some years before at the Methodist Seminary in São Paulo, where he was a professor when I had visited the seminary. Though our contacts had been few, we knew we were kindred spirits. He said my escapades had been in the Argentine press throughout his time in Buenos Aires. He wanted to know what had happened to me in great detail, so we spent most of the flight to New York whispering as I related, for the first time, the events of the previous 17 days.

I'm that Poor Son of a Bitch

Early in the morning, I returned to my seat for some sleep and awoke as the plane descended into JFK. I noticed a copy of the *Brazil Times* newspaper (an English language paper) on the seat next to me and quickly browsed through it. My eye was caught by a headline: "American 'subversive' to be deported." My American seatmate saw what I was reading and said, "I wonder what happened to that poor son of a bitch."

"I'm that poor son of a bitch," I said. He was stunned into total silence. I thought I was being clever rather than prophetic. But I was wrong.

After the plane landed, the flight attendant asked me to remain seated while the other passengers disembarked. She then gave me a packet of my documents, including my new passport with a full-page stamp stating "*Expulsado.*" I got in line behind the other passengers and went through immigration. When the agent saw the stamp, he asked, "What did you do?"

"I was the friend of a Catholic Archbishop," I replied.

Shaking his head, he passed me on, saying, "They do strange things down there."

After the usual wait for baggage, where I finally picked up my suitcase that contained the remnants of my life in Brazil, I went out into the free world. I happily found my brother waiting for me. He'd flown in from Nebraska the day before. With him were two long-time friends and associates, the Revs. Paul McCleary, a former United Methodist missionary to Bolivia who was now the head of the Latin American division of the Board of Global Ministries, and Lewistine McCoy (Mac), a missionary in China until 1950 when all missionaries were required to leave. I was delighted to see them both, as I had kept my head "above water" for long hours in prison by thinking about how the Board of Global Ministries would receive me and provide me with new service opportunities and support for my new life.

After the initial embraces, we got into a taxi. We went to "Heaven on the Hudson," the Interchurch Center built by Rockefeller at 475 Riverside Drive to accommodate all church boards and agencies that wanted to establish their offices there. It was right next to Riverside Church, which Rockefeller built in the 1930s for the ministry of the Rev. Harry Emerson Fosdick, one of the ecumenical giants of that time. They took me to a conference room where we spent an hour or so in what would properly be called a "debriefing." McCoy and McCleary expressed their concerns for me and their satisfaction that I was home again, relatively safe and sound. They asked myriad questions about what I had undergone, which I answered as directly as possible. During this conversation, a call came from Methodist Bishop Jim Armstrong of South Dakota. Jim had been a friend since his Episcopal visit to Brazil in 1970 when he went to Recife to meet Dom Hélder, and I served as his contact and interpreter. He expressed deep concern for me and offered his support.

As the conversation wound down, a bit of awkwardness crept into the room when Mac asked me what I intended to do now. I was somewhat taken aback by the question, as I'd been nurturing the idea they would have a program lined up for me. I had assumed that as the Board had been one of the most outspoken critics of torture in Latin America, they'd want to have me itinerate to a bunch of churches throughout the country to tell my story and garner support for human rights. But the question made it clear they had nothing in line for me and were not interested in an ongoing relationship.

I said I'd like to re-activate my status as a UM missionary. My first wife and I had separated in June of 1973 after 19 years of difficult marriage. So, I asked the Board and the Bishop of the First Region of the Brazilian Methodist Church for a leave of absence to deal with personal matters. Both entities allowed for a two-year leave of absence under that category, with the option to return to active service at any time before the end of the two years. After two years, re-applying for missionary status would have been necessary. However, I'd been on leave of absence for less than 10 months, so I assumed I could request reactivation and they'd find something for me to do.

But it was not to be. Mac responded immediately that I was not on leave of absence status. I had resigned. That simply was not true. I reminded him of our conversations in July and October of 1973 when it was agreed I take a leave of absence to see how the Brazilian Methodist Church handled my new status as a divorced person, as I was the first missionary ever to get a divorce. Divorce was yet to be permitted under Brazilian law. He excused himself to check the files to find my letter of resignation, which didn't exist. He returned and said it must have been misplaced, but he knew for sure that I'd resigned.

It became immediately apparent that the Board did not want to have anything further to do with me and that I'd become a painful embarrassment to them. Paul McCleary's silence during this was eloquent testimony that they were firmly prepared to finalize our relationship.

At that moment, I was in a fog. For 17 days and nights, I'd held on under sometimes agonizing torture and seemingly unending hours of solitude, held together in part by my conviction that the Board would stand with me. Since the fall of 1963, when I went into missionary training, a six-month period that included six weeks of linguistic training followed by four and a half months of intensive training with over a hundred other missionary candidates, I'd been a kind of "fair-haired" boy for the United Methodists in Brazil. The Board made it clear in the training program that for them, the days of the "great white father" kind of missionary, leader of missionary compounds, and ruler of paternalistic ventures, as had been the pattern since the mid-19th century around the world, were over. We were expected to collaborate and partner with the national churches wherever we went, no longer in charge of everything, as had been the pattern for so long.

That fit me very well, as my call to the mission field had been that I'd be privileged to share with the Brazilian Church what God was doing in that country. I had no thought I was taking the Gospel to the benighted Brazilians. I knew that the Holy Spirit had been at work there and was at work in ways I didn't understand but wanted to share in. However, when I got to Brazil, I discovered that most of the nearly 90 United Methodist missionaries were involved in the old-style missionary patterns: building up institutions like schools and seminaries, and "saving souls," which usually meant getting more people into the pews. There were some exceptions, like Brady Tyson, Bill Bigham, Wick Wofford, and Derrell Santee. Still, for the most part, the new ideas hadn't trickled down very far. At the same time, wonderful and great-hearted folk who clearly loved the Brazilian people were all too comfortable in the traditional role of being in charge. So, I found myself to be one of Mac's favorites as I was wholeheartedly engaged in the new pattern of missionary service.

Mac was proud, almost beyond words, of having a missionary associated with Dom Hélder. He never ceased to recount this detail to other mission colleagues. I sent depositions from political prisoners in a semi-clandestine manner. Brady Tyson translated them and got Senator Ted Kennedy to read them into the Congressional Record. He nearly got me into trouble—or perhaps he did—when he bragged that he had a missionary sending him that stuff, as that was like putting a signboard on me: I was the only United Methodist missionary for nearly 1,000 miles in any direction.

This warm and personal history of support and comradeship set me up for an incredible fall when it became clear that Mac and the Board had no further use for me. The lifeboat I'd been holding on to for the previous 17 days and nights suddenly went underwater, taking me with it. I felt like I was standing somewhere up on the wall of that conference room, watching the events unfold below. I could hardly breathe. I couldn't believe this was happening.

Looking at their cold, stony faces, I realized that Mac and Paul weren't going to change their position. I said, "Well, if I have *been resigned,* I want to ask for the separation benefits the Board put in place last January." After a couple of years of study and recommendations at the January 1974 Board of Global Ministries meeting, the Board passed a special provision for aiding missionaries returning from the field who might have difficulty finding gainful employment. The new agreement said that any missionary who'd spent more than one term in the field was entitled to one month's salary and benefits for every year with the Board or until he/she found gainful employment. As I'd more than 10 years with the Board, I would get as much as 10 months' salary and benefits to carry me into a new job.

My nearly overwhelming dismay only increased when Mac and McCleary said, almost stumbling over each other, that the particular provision had not passed. It had been recommended by the staff, but the Board had turned it down. There was nothing for me—no job, no benefits, no severance pay—nothing after 10 years with the Board of Global Ministries of the United Methodist Church.

Finally made uncomfortable by my total consternation, they excused themselves from the meeting, leaving me with my brother, who was also in shock. He knew nothing of the internal workings of the Board, though he'd been a Methodist pastor two years longer than I had. He later said he simply could not believe the cold way they treated me.

After about 10 minutes, they returned, and Mac said they'd arranged $1,000 as a kind of hardship gift to tide me over. They made it clear this was a special *charity* on their part and outside of their obligations to me, and I should be very grateful for the Board's generosity.

Another detail I didn't even think of at the time but shocked my brother, who commented on it after we left the building, was that they did not make any provisions for me to have a medical exam. I had lost 17 pounds in 17 days. After the beatings and electric shocks I had undergone, along with the stress and lack of food, it would have been expected for them to require a physical exam to see if I had any long-term effects of the torture. But once they had the ten $100 traveler's cheques in hand, they gave them to me and ushered us out the door, assuring me of their "prayers and best wishes."

It is not the slightest exaggeration to say that it took me years to get over this treatment. I had been Mac's fair-haired boy for 10 years in Brazil. I was one of the few missionaries who was on the same page with him about the role of missionaries in today's world. I thought he'd been totally supportive of me through the divorce, and I had been, without even thinking about it, counting on him to support me as I began my life again. I still have scars on my wrists, and I had no feeling in the backs of my hands for nearly six months, caused by nerves that were pinched by the same handcuffs. That feeling eventually returned.

However, I experienced an incredible sense of betrayal by the Board of Global Ministries and the church I had loved and sought to serve, which I suspect is still with me. These were my friends and colleagues, my companions in the fields of the Lord. And they simply ushered me out the door. On the way out, they did say they'd reserved a room for us at a hotel downtown at Penn Station for the next three nights. A couple of months later, they sent me a bill for that room, which I refused to pay. They also mentioned that *Time* magazine asked me to stop by their offices.

Before leaving the building, I went up to the 13th floor where Mac's office was and asked his secretary, Marilyn Sauer, who'd been a friend all these years, if I could see the minutes of the January 1974 Board meeting where the separation benefits provision had been voted on. She gave me a copy of the minutes, which I still have, and I quickly found that the benefits *had* passed. Mac and Paul had simply lied to get me out the door quickly and cheaply.

Many years later, in 1992, a friend of mine, Yvonne Dilling, the Latin American person for the Church of the Brethren, asked me if I'd go with her and the members of their Mission Board to Rio Verde, Brazil, where they had a small congregation. They'd never had any work in Brazil and had no one on staff or in the field who spoke Portuguese and knew much about the country. They were having some problems with that little church and its pastor, and she wanted me to be their interpreter for a 10-day visit to Rio Verde. The visit went splendidly, and she was most grateful for my participation. Some months later, she told me she'd attended a meeting of Latin American executives of the mainline denominations and encountered Joyce Hill, one of the principal executives of the United Methodist Board of Global Ministries for Latin America.

Yvonne told me she asked Joyce why they'd let me "get away," as she had been greatly impressed by my understanding of and love of the Brazilian people.

Joyce responded: "He's CIA." End of conversation.

Yvonne was incredulous. She'd been closely involved with a former CIA agent, who had come in out of the cold after more than 25 years with the agency because of what was happening in Central America under the Reagan administration. She said she'd asked him one time how one could tell if someone was an agent or not, as all too often, missionaries and journalists were accused of being CIA agents. He said, "It's easy. If someone enters your organization and it begins to go down the toilet, you can be sure they are ours. If your organization prospers, they aren't. We don't infiltrate organizations to get information. We usually know more about what's happening than the missionaries do. Our goal is to subvert their work."

Apparently, the Board had accepted the accusations made by the Brazilian army after I got away that I must have been a "double agent," a Communist CIA agent, working to subvert the work of Dom Hélder Câmara. So they wanted to get rid of me as quickly as possible, no questions asked. Also, the Board was under attack by a very conservative group of Methodists called Good News, funded by the Heritage Foundation and the Institute for Religion and Democracy (IRD), two agencies that served the purposes of the CIA without being identified with that agency. The IRD formed chapters to work in and on the United Methodist, Presbyterian, Lutheran, and Episcopal churches, primarily stirring up a spirit of division over the issue of homosexuality. They successfully divided those churches and undermined their ability to support the National Council of Churches of Jesus Christ, a powerful lobbying group for social justice.

The months after my return to the US were a blur. The shadow of Alanir still being in the torture chambers hovered over me. I also worried about Tereza as detailed threats had been made toward her. After my brother and I left the Board of Global Ministries offices, we took a taxi down to midtown New York to visit the offices of *Time*. We were received by Ben Cate, one of the editors who'd been following my trajectory and had published a note of support while I was still in prison in Recife. He was anxious to have me write an account of my experience. I told him Major Maia, the chief of the torture chamber, had warned me that if I made any unfortunate comments to the US press, they would grab Tereza and torture her. I knew that was not an idle threat. Cate understood my concern and suggested I still write up my story. Then they'd publish it as soon as I got word from Richard Brown, the US Consul in Recife, that Tereza would not be harmed.

I stopped at a store in Times Square to buy a tape recorder and some cassettes. I wanted to record all the details so I wouldn't forget them. We went to our hotel, and I spent hours telling my story to the tape recorder and my brother. Next, I took the train to Washington, D.C., to visit Kim and Carol Flower. Kim was with the State Department and had been stationed in Recife. He'd gotten into the State Department in an unconventional way. After graduation, they decided to take a year and backpack around Europe. On their way, they stopped off in Washington to visit some friends. One of them convinced Kim to take the exam for the Foreign Service while in town. He did it with no preparation, then forgot all about it.

After they got home nearly a year later, Kim said they were lying on the deck of a friend's boat in a marijuana fog when a telegram caught up with him. He'd been accepted for an appointment in the State Department and should start work in about a month. He and Carol looked at each other and said, "Why not? We like to travel."

Kim's first assignment was at the US Consulate in São Paulo. He took depositions from Brazilians asking for asylum. The US never gave asylum to any Brazilian. But Kim was assigned the task of writing down depositions of horror for nearly two years. He said he also went down to his office on some Saturday nights and stamped visas into the passports of some of those folks so they could leave Brazil and go to the United States.

In Recife, he was in the US Information Agency office, helping to write US propaganda to get into the Brazilian press. After two years, he was assigned to Nepal, where he worked directly with Caroline Clendening "Carol" Laise, the ambassador there. She was also the wife of Elsworth Bunker, the US ambassador in Vietnam at the time. When Carol Laise was transferred to Washington to become the first female Assistant Secretary of State under Henry Kissinger, she took Kim with her. After she retired, Kim was picked by Kissinger to be his frontman for his domestic travel.

I knew nothing of this transition, so my first choice for a place to stay in D.C. was with these folks. They were delighted to host me, though I found Kim had changed ideologically from the radical leftist pot-smoker I'd known in Recife. He'd become incredibly conservative with his constant association with one of the major war criminals of the 20th century.

Another friend, Brady Tyson, was also in Washington teaching political science at American University. He knew just about everyone in D.C. and got me in touch with Joe Eldridge, a former United Methodist missionary in Chile. Joe had been involved with some Catholic priests, promoting grassroots democracy. After a year of Pinochet's dictatorship, Joe had been advised to return to the States. He'd recently arrived in D.C. to be the founding director of the Washington Office on Latin America (WOLA), an organization sponsored by Protestants and Catholics that would become a major human rights defender. In December, with Brady's help, Joe got me an interview with a Congressional Committee about torture in Brazil.

Lobbying in Congress

I followed Richard Brown's request and went to Congress to thank all the members who'd helped me while I was in prison. Joe, who was destined to become one of the most effective lobbyists on human rights, went with me on those visits. We went to the State Department to meet with the man on the Brazil desk. I met Alex Watson, a young career officer who became the Undersecretary for Latin America some 30 years later. I introduced myself and said I would like to know the names of all the members of Congress who had been active on my behalf while I was in prison. He looked through some folders, then asked, "*Who are you?* These people have never been on the same list except at Roll Call."

He then gave me a list of ten senators and nine members of the house. Senators Ted Kennedy and George McGovern were there because of their long concern about human rights. Senator Sam Nunn of Georgia made the list because Carol was living in Atlanta and got a lot of Methodists and ex-Brazil missionaries there to contact his office. Senator Henry Bellmon (R) of Oklahoma was on the list because my dad's brother Warren was a prominent Republican player in that state; Senators Roman Hruska and Carl Curtis, two Republicans from Nebraska both got more than a thousand letters and phone calls generated by my brother and my dad; Senators Percy and Adlai Stevenson III from Illinois got more than a thousand calls and letters from the United Methodists in my home conference.

The Brazilian military had miscalculated. In 1974, the Methodist Church in Brazil had fewer than 40,000 members. The United Methodist Church in the United States had over *10 million* members. At the time, exactly 100 members of the entire 535 members of the US Congress professed to be members of the United Methodist Church. They'd been deeply disturbed to learn that a Methodist missionary was being tortured in Brazil.

Joe and I set out to visit those 19 offices. The visits were brief, as we were usually received by a staff member. But we did get to talk with some of the senators. I thanked them profusely for saving my life and their dedication to human rights. That usually got blank stares, as most of them didn't know what human rights were.

I requested they write letters to the State Department, commending Consul Richard Brown and Ambassador John Crimmins for their coming to the defense of a US citizen in trouble and that these letters of commendation be placed in their personnel files. This was at the request of Mr. Brown, who told me Kissinger was planning to sack both of them for jeopardizing his good relations with the Brazilian generals. The letters worked. Kissinger tried to punish both but ran into too much resistance.

One of the most remarkable encounters came in the office of Senator Carl Curtis, chair of the Senate Finance Committee. An extremely conservative Republican, Curtis was known as a shill for Mutual of Omaha. We were in his office for more than 30 minutes, during which I commended his courageous defense of human rights and encouraged him to keep up the good fight. Just as we were leaving, he asked, "Reverend, excuse me, but can you clear up one detail for me? Is Brazil in Africa or South America?"

After visiting as many members of Congress as we could, I said goodbye to Kim and Carol and flew off to Chicago. The Rev. Dr. Dow Kirkpatrick, who had been my friend since my days in Addison, had been hospitalized and invited me to fill his pulpit at First Methodist Church in Evanston. This was my first public appearance since arriving home.

I stayed with my dear friend Bill Campbell, a former parishioner in the Good Samaritan United Methodist Church in Addison, for a few days. Dom Hélder returned from the Synod meeting in Rome and was scheduled to speak at the University of Chicago on October 30, which happened to be my birthday. The Archbishop of Chicago had made it known he would not be welcoming nor receiving Dom Hélder because of his "red" tendencies. So, when he arrived at O'Hare Airport, I was the person waiting for him.

We had a warm embrace, and I accompanied him to his hotel in downtown Chicago. His lecture was titled *St. Thomas Aquinas and Karl Marx.* He learned to speak English after age 50 and could communicate fairly well, but his Brazilian accent was nearly unintelligible when speaking to a crowd. Fortunately, a printed copy of his speech was available for everyone in the packed Rockefeller Chapel. His address was followed by a reception in his honor, then a press conference. His criticism of the Brazilian dictatorship's use of torture, murder, and disappearances made him a popular international figure.

I told him of the threats made to Tereza. In the press conference, one of the journalists asked him about the Methodist missionary who had just been expelled from Brazil after being tortured. "Well, that's a very unusual situation," Dom Hélder replied. "The Brazilian army has accused my friend, Fred Morris, of being a Communist. Then they said he was a CIA agent. It looks like he may have been the very first Communist CIA agent in history." This brought down the house.

As we were parting, Dom Hélder said, "I only hope that now one of their own has suffered at the hands of the dictatorship, the people of the United States will take seriously what has happened in Brazil and what is still happening. If so, then your suffering will not have been in vain."

The *Time* Story

I spent the next two weeks working on my story for *Time* magazine. I finally got it down to about ten double-spaced pages when Richard Brown called me from the Consulate in Recife and said he had assurances that Tereza would not suffer any consequences if I went public with my story. As her father was a career officer in the army, it would be unthinkable for the military to attack his daughter for her bad taste in boyfriends.

So, I called Ben Cate and said I could give him my story. He told me to fly to New York on their dime as soon as possible. He said I needed to get my story into 600 words or less. I was stunned. I had closer to 10,000 words. I began cutting and cutting. After three days, I was down to 3,000 words, but it was still too long. I told Ben I needed help cutting it down. We were going over the material when I mentioned that I repeated the Psalm to myself, *The Lord is my shepherd.... Though I walk through the valley of the shadow of death*... he broke out in goosebumps, excused himself, and in five minutes came back and said we had another 1,000 words. He then helped me cut and slash and get it into the required format by the deadline.

The First Tourist to the World Trade Center

I had purchased a Pentax 35mm camera and several rolls of Kodachrome, so on Saturday morning I took the subway down to lower Manhattan and took some pictures of the Statue of Liberty. I wandered around the area where the World Trade Center Twin Towers were just being finished. I walked into one of the Towers and was told it wasn't open yet. As I walked out, I saw a group of about 20 women going into the other Tower. Without thinking, I simply joined their group. They went in and got on a couple of elevators and went up to the 70th floor. They were going to the Personnel Office, looking for employment.

I walked over to the other bank of elevators and pushed the button for 110, the top floor. When the door opened, I saw a huge open space, with no partitions, filled with hundreds of paint cans, sawhorses, ladders, etc. I pulled out my new camera and began taking pictures. The views from the 110th floor were amazing in all directions. I spent the next 90 minutes just looking and looking—and shooting three 36-exposure rolls of Kodachrome. I was overwhelmed by the fact that I was the very first tourist to visit the Twin Towers.

The next day I just wandered around the Times Square area, waiting for Monday morning, when *Time* would hit the newsstands.

At seven-thirty a.m., in the lobby of my hotel, I purchased three copies of the magazine and anxiously leafed through them to find my story. Two pages! With a picture of me, Dom Hélder, and a political cartoon poking fun at the Brazilian generals. It couldn't have been better.

The *Today* Show—and 25 others

The following day, I went to the NBC studios for an interview for the *Today* show. During my interview, Barbara Walters, the co-host, enjoyed a cigarette in the lounge. When she came back on camera, she said something like, "Wasn't that something?"

From there, I was taken to two radio talk shows. Then *Time* magazine flew me to Chicago for an interview on Kup's Show, a Sunday night program hosted by Chicago columnist Irv Kupcinet. Ben Cate said they'd put me up in a hotel in Chicago. I casually mentioned that I hoped it would be better than where I stayed in New York, as that hotel was too reminiscent of my cell in Recife. He was stunned and embarrassed. As a result, I was put in a suite in the Drake Hotel on Chicago's Gold Coast.

The interview with Kup went exceptionally well. He'd scheduled me for 30 minutes of his two-hour program with Michelle LeGrand, the famous pianist, scheduled to be a significant part of the program. After we got into the conversation, he stopped and rescheduled our part for the entire first hour, cutting into the piano music.

The *Chicago Tribune* had done a page one, "over the fold" story on me the same day the *Time* story appeared. The *Time* person handling it told me a woman named Amy Conger had asked me to call her. It turned out that Amy was an American who'd lived in Chile before the Allende election and the *coup* the CIA led against him, putting Pinochet in power. She'd been married to a Chilean for a while but had gotten a divorce.

After the *coup* on September 11, 1973, Amy was picked up by the Chilean army and held prisoner for more than two weeks. Though she wasn't physically tortured, she was kept naked the whole time and threatened repeatedly with rape. When she got out, she went to the US Embassy, where she was pretty much ignored. Her father was wealthy and paid for her plane fare home.

Amy came to the Drake Hotel and told me her story. When I got home, I contacted Les Whitten, partner of Jack Anderson, who wrote the most widely syndicated column on what was happening in Washington and worldwide. Les wrote about Amy's experience and how the embassy did nothing to help her. He had a lot of stuff on Kissinger and was eager to do a job on him if he could find a good peg to hang it on. *Time* then took me on a whirlwind tour of 25 other TV channels, ranging from Cedar Rapids, Iowa, to San Francisco, Los Angeles, Boston, and New Haven.

Testifying before Congress

I was scheduled to testify before a congressional committee with Father Bryan Hehir of the National Catholic Conference on December 11, 1974. Brady Tyson and Joe Eldridge arranged my testimony before the sub-committee led by Congressman Don Fraser of Minnesota. I was asked to write out my testimony so it could be distributed to all the committee members before the event. Father Hehir had just returned from a month-long trip around Latin America to see the human rights situation firsthand. His report was quite alarming.

I was quite impressed to be in the halls of Congress and a committee room. But I was put off by the detail that apart from Congressman Fraser, not one of the members of his sub-committee had bothered to show up, except for an ultra-right-wing Republican from Kansas, Representative Larry Winn, who came to criticize us after we had made our presentations. He mentioned he hadn't had time to read our testimony, nor had he arrived in time to hear us. He stated that I was probably interfering in Brazil's internal affairs and deserved to be chastised. I responded by saying that I was in Brazil to work with the poor masses of that country.

Brady told me afterward that the absence of the members was typical. The important detail was that everything said would become a part of the Congressional Record and could be used by human rights defenders worldwide. At the end of my testimony, I made these observations about torture:

> *Torture brutalizes and dehumanizes not only those who are tortured but those who torture, those who are intimidated by the torture of others, and those who try to ignore the fact that torture exists.*
>
> *It dehumanizes those who are tortured by treating them as less than human and, in many cases, by forcing them into less-than-human feelings and often into less-than-human acts. If one is forced to betray friends, companions, and family through torture, as many are, the psychological and spiritual damage may be irreparable, quite apart from the permanent physical damage that often results.*
>
> *It dehumanizes those who torture. In addition to the psychopathology induced and encouraged in those who practice torture, persons and governments who resort to torture, for whatever motives, betray their social contract with their fellow humans and effectively secede from the human community.*
>
> *It dehumanizes those who are intimidated. Churchmen who cease to proclaim the gospel in its fullness out of fear; students who cease to make the search for truth their vocation out of fear; journalists who give the public less than the truth for fear of reprisal; workers who, through fear of repression, are not allowed to organize to defend their interests; politicians who can only rubber-stamp authoritarian proposals from dictatorial regimes,*

for fear of the consequences of more independent, conscience-led actions—all these and in fact, the whole community of man share in the dehumanization caused by torture.

Torture dehumanizes those who try to ignore it, saying it is an "internal affair" or a passing phase. Such indifference dries up the wellsprings of human sympathy and compassion and breaks the social contract of the world community to be concerned for the whole family of man. Civilization and freedom are not built and cannot be maintained by those who assume the posture of indifference.

I concluded my remarks by quoting from the testimony of Senator Ted Kennedy before a committee the year before when he said, "We have to decide what kind of people we want to be. Are we going to stand for human rights or close our eyes to the barbarities carried out by authoritarian regimes around the world?"

Our Wedding

Tereza had been working night and day to finish her law degree ready to fly to the States for our marriage. Her willingness to leave her home and family and live in exile with me was impressive. I was delighted to make plans for our life together. Of course, one of the major problems was that I did not have a job.

Brady got Senator George McGovern, head of the Senate Committee on World Hunger and first director of the Food for Peace program that President Kennedy had begun in his first few months in office, to ask the Library of Congress to do a study on the impact of the first ten years of the Food for Peace program in Latin America. Then Brady had them focus more on northeastern Brazil as a case study. My name was dropped into the hopper as one who was exceptionally qualified to do the study. After a lot of screening, I was given a contract to write a book on the Food for

Peace program results. I would be paid $6,000, and the work would take about five months. That bought us some time. I also applied for a position at the Institute for Policy Studies.

Ellen, my stepmother, was delighted to organize our wedding at the First United Methodist Church of North Platte. We scheduled it for Sunday, December 28, 1974 and invited the entire congregation. On December 18, Tereza and I went to Orlando for a pre-honeymoon trip to Disney World. The wedding was lovely. Tereza was beautiful. My dad exuberantly performed our marriage. The next day, we drove to Estes Park, Colorado, for a few days before heading back to Washington, D.C.. On our way, we stayed in Chicago for a few days with my friend Bill Campbell. Bill had twin 12-year-old daughters who were delighted to meet Tereza. We drove up to Evanston to the home of Dow and Marjorie Kirkpatrick to pick up a color TV they no longer needed. It filled up half of the back seat of our large 1969 Chrysler. We drove across Indiana, Ohio, Pennsylvania, and into D.C.

We started apartment hunting and settled on a lovely new condo in Alexandria, Virginia, called Place One. About a week after moving into our new home, I got a call from the *Canadian Broadcasting Corporation* in Toronto, inviting me to do a show called *Man Alive.* They flew me up and put me in a five-star hotel so I could do the program on Monday—live!

The host was a significant figure in Canadian TV, and this show was one of the top programs in the country. It was set up like most talk shows, with us sitting on two sides of a coffee table, real coffee in hand. The host asked me to share why I was in Brazil and why the military became interested in me. Dom Hélder Câmara was well-known in Canada for his non-violent approach to social change. I explained it was primarily my close association with him that brought me to the army's attention. When I went into detail about the torture itself, my host was outraged.

Brady gave me the contact information for two Brazilian exiles living in Toronto. Betinho, a famous Brazilian sociologist/journalist, visited my hotel after the show on Monday. Betinho arrived around nine-thirty, and we talked until after two a.m. We discovered we had many friends in common and, of course, were united in our opposition to the horrendous military dictatorship.

A few days later, I got a call from the program host saying the audience had broken all records and the ambassador of Brazil had filed a formal protest with the Canadian government for showing this program. He demanded equal time to present the Brazilian government's point of view. The CBC told the ambassador they'd be pleased to give them equal time, provided they send a team to Recife to interview all of the parties involved, starting with Consul Richard Brown and including Colonel Meziat, the head of the Intelligence Section of the Fourth Army, and Major Maia, the head of the torture chamber where I'd been held. That ended the conversation and the protests from the Brazilian Embassy.

The Council on Foreign Relations

I started my contract with the Library of Congress at the end of January, working from our apartment in Alexandria. As an official consultant, I could access documents not readily available to the average citizen. My first task was reading about Public Law 480, which President Eisenhower had enacted to deal with agricultural surpluses.

I was surprised to learn that the law, which President Kennedy used to establish his Food for Peace program, was not primarily concerned with aiding the impoverished people in Latin America. Its first priority was finding an outlet for the ever-increasing surplus of foodstuffs produced by US farmers. The second purpose was to develop new markets for US agricultural surpluses. The third goal of the law was to aid needy people in Latin America.

I accepted an invitation to speak to the Council on Foreign Relations in New York in February. My talk was titled *The Human Cost of the Brazilian Economic Miracle*. I presented how the amazing growth figures came at the cost of repressing the labor movement. The economic model produced consumer goods that most people in Brazil could not afford to buy. They were making a short-term boom, and as soon as the upper middle and upper classes had a new car or two, there would be no way to expand the market. I shared with them my own experience of being tortured because of my sympathies with the poor masses.

The Council comprised the Trilateral Commission gang, like Henry Kissinger, the Rockefellers, and that sort of folks. Kissinger wasn't there that day, but David Rockefeller was. After my presentation, the president of Random House approached me and said, "I think they tortured the wrong person." He invited me to lunch with him and one of his editors, saying he wanted to do my "book." I happily met with him. However, the editor started out with a bucket of cold water, saying they would not be interested in my book because they didn't bother publishing books they weren't sure would sell at least 10,000 copies.

The next day, Tereza and I drove to Drew University, where I'd been invited to be the chapel speaker. I shared with the students my experience in Brazilian torture chambers and how my faith had enabled me to survive. At the end of that talk, two people were waiting at the door. They introduced themselves as Drs. David and Joan Weimer. She was a professor of literature at Drew; he was a professor of literature at Rutgers University. David had been a Rhodes Scholar in Brazil and fell in love with the country, but was agonizing over what had happened since the coup in 1964. They invited us for dinner at their home, and thus began a friendship we've nurtured to this day.

David came to Alexandria in the spring and spent a couple of days with us. Sometime later, he sent me a screenplay he'd written about my experience in Brazil. I carried it around for the next 30 years or so, not knowing how or where I might find someone interested in making a movie of it.

When I Met Robert Redford

While working on the book for the Library of Congress, I consulted with Mark Schneider, Senator Ted Kennedy's staff member on Latin America. Later, Mark became the head of USAID for Latin America during the Clinton administration. One day, I went to Kennedy's office to ask Mark for assistance in getting some research material. Sitting in a chair in the much-overcrowded office, I observed Senator Kennedy entering his private office. I asked Mark if he could introduce me as I wanted to thank him for his help.

We were completing our conversation when Senator Kennedy stuck his head into the office and said, "Anybody here want to meet Robert Redford? Come on out."

There was a stampede to the door as Redford was probably the hottest star in Hollywood at the time. He was in Washington to film *All the President's Men* with Dustin Hoffman. He'd dropped by to ask Kennedy for a tennis date.

Mark and I walked into the reception area of Kennedy's office, where the senator introduced his staff to Redford, who very graciously shook everyone's hand. Kennedy introduced me to Redford, saying, "This is the Rev. Fred Morris. We had quite a time getting him out of prison in Brazil last fall."

As I shook hands with Robert Redford, he pointed to my face and said, "I saw you on television," referring to my *Today* show appearance.

To which I responded, "I saw you in a movie."

Kennedy, Redford, and I briefly discussed the human rights situation in Latin America, especially in Brazil. I was surprised and delighted at how much Redford knew and how much he clearly cared. About a month later, I thought if I could get Redford to announce a trip to Brazil, then on the eve of his trip, which would be greatly ballyhooed in Brazil, he'd announce he was canceling after hearing about the human rights situation and the widespread use of torture by the military government. I knew that would be a significant blow to the prestige of Brazil—and to the generals.

I found out where Redford was staying and spoke to a young woman in his office, requesting that he call me. The next day, the receptionist at my condo handed me the messages she'd taken for me. With trembling hands and a shaky voice, she said, "R-r-r-r-obert R-r-r-edford called. Is that *the* Robert Redford?"

"I suppose so," I replied as I took the pink message slip and walked to the elevator nonchalantly.

I called the number Redford had left and spoke with him. I told him I'd like to meet and discuss how he could help with the human rights situation in Brazil. He graciously agreed, and we set the date for breakfast at his hotel. I was leaving town that day to drive to Nebraska with Jennifer and Jonathan, as my brother had set up a whirlwind tour of more than 30 United Methodist Churches. We'd be driving straight through to make that, but I figured we could leave after breakfast without any problem.

However, it was not to be. Early on Saturday, I got a call from Redford's secretary saying he'd been filming the underground garage scene with Deep Throat all night and would be sleeping until the afternoon. I couldn't delay my trip, so I missed my meal with Robert Redford.

Speaking in Nebraska

The speaking tour went very well. For 15 days I traveled all over the state, often speaking twice daily. Jennifer and Jonathan enjoyed time with their cousins in Beatrice, where Hughes was pastor. Speaking to the Rotary Club in Beatrice provided an important insight into how the people of Heartland USA felt about human rights. I had finished my brief presentation when the president of the club came up to me. He was at least 6' 5" tall and must have weighed at least 280, and wore a DeKalb Hybrid cap. He put his massive arm across my shoulders and said, "Reverend, I'm also the president of the John Birch Society here, and, God-damn it, we're going to put a stop to this." He proceeded to organize a letter-writing campaign among his Rotarians and Birchers to their members of Congress to cut off aid to Brazil because of their use of torture. "We aren't going to pay those bastards any more money to torture anyone," he said. "That's UnAmerican!!"

My presentations were well received by all of the United Methodist Churches. The good people were shocked and concerned to know that such things happen. I assured them that I was one of the fortunate ones who'd lived to tell the story, and that, unfortunately, our government was involved in training military officers from all over Latin America to carry out this kind of defense of democracy in our name.

Congressman Leo Ryan

In January 1976, I got a phone call from Congressman Leo Ryan, a Democrat from California. He was later murdered in Guiana by the Jim Jones cult when he went to investigate charges that some people from California had gone there under false pretenses. He said he'd read my *Harper's* piece and was outraged. He was writing to Kissinger, the UN General Secretary, U Thant, and the Brazilian Ambassador in D.C. He asked me to visit his office to see if I approved of his letters. I did.

Ryan was on the House Appropriations Committee. When they met to review the proposed budget and got to a line item of a few million dollars for military assistance to Brazil, Ryan stood up and read parts of my *Harper's* article for the whole committee and demanded they cut off all military aid for Brazil. He prevailed in the committee by a narrow margin. Military assistance for Brazil was cut off in June of 1976, once and for all. No more Brazilian military officers were trained in torture at the School of the Americas in Panama.

Religion and the Presidency '76

When the contract with the Library of Congress ended, I was unemployed. At the same time, a student at Wesley Seminary in Washington and a friend of Brady Tyson suggested I hold a conference to bring together candidates for the presidency to talk about their religious beliefs. Gerald Ford looked vulnerable, as there was an intense backlash against his pardoning of Richard Nixon. After some months of brainstorming, we devised the plan to hold a conference in January of 1976 called Religion and the Presidency—RAP-76. I was named Executive Director, and funds were raised to guarantee a salary of $1,500 a month while I put this event together.

RAP-76 resulted in some 200 religious leaders, including mainline denominations like the United Methodists, Presbyterians, Lutherans, and Episcopalians, plus Pentecostals and conservative Evangelicals; Roman Catholics; Jewish groups, Conservative, Orthodox, and Reformed; some Muslims; and some Christian Orthodox. Religious publications like *The Christian Century, Sojourners, Christianity Today, Pax Christi,* and *National Catholic Reporter* sent representatives. We held RAP-76 over two days at the New York Avenue Presbyterian Church in the heart of Washington, D.C.

Eight presidential candidates participated: Mo Udall, Henry Jackson, Terry Sanford, Sargent Shriver, Fred Harris, Milton Shapp, Birch Bayh, and Lloyd Bensen. The principal absence was Jimmy Carter, who was most openly religious. We sent out a questionnaire to the candidates, requesting that they respond in writing. The questions asked for their opinions on divorce, abortion, prayer in schools, the use of nuclear weapons, and other religion-related concerns.

Each candidate was given 45 minutes to make an opening statement, followed by 45 minutes of questioning by a panel of four religious leaders and 30 minutes of questions from the audience. The general consensus was that the event was well worth the effort. The candidates dealt with our questions thoughtfully. The religious leaders were enthused, and many suggested this kind of event should become a part of our regular pre-election series of debates and presentations by the candidates. It didn't.

CHAPTER 7

How We Got to Costa Rica

In February of 1976, I was invited to be one of the principal speakers at the annual retreat of 350 United Methodist pastors of the three Annual Conferences in New York State. I shared the honors with one of the most noted theologians of the United Methodist Church, Dr. L. Harold DeWolf, professor of Systematic Theology at Boston University. I was somewhat startled by my reception, especially from the younger pastors. They appeared to be in awe of my "heroic" exploits in Brazil. It took some effort to show them there was nothing heroic about being kidnapped and tortured. Among the clergy present was Rev. David Durham, chaplain at Cornell University.

In our conversations in the evening, David asked what I planned to do next. I had no idea. I'd received an inquiry from SWEPCO (Southwest Petroleum Corporation), the company I'd worked with in Recife just before my kidnapping. Buddy Thomas, the vice president for overseas sales, called and inquired if I'd be interested in taking over their distributorship in Costa Rica. I knew very little about Costa Rica and needed funds to get there and start a company, so I was stalling in giving Buddy an answer.

I had been looking for a job in Washington without success. I'd contracted with Haldane Associates, a group of headhunters that helped place executives in new positions. I met with a counselor at Haldane, who turned out to be a former Methodist pastor, every week for a couple of months. He showed me how to write a resume and "sell" myself. Their advice was to write to somewhat important people and ask for suggestions about the next steps in my career.

I did this for a few months with intriguing results, starting with Senator McGovern, Senator Kennedy, and Senator Clarke of Iowa, who was on a food committee with McGovern. All three were helpful and gave me three or four names of persons in various organizations and their permission to use their names as a reference. By dropping the names of the senators, I got interviews with the head of the World Bank and a dozen more organizations in D.C. But in every case, all I got was a few more names and an apology that no jobs were available. This was at the end of the recession of 1974–76, and most places were still letting middle-level people go. Within three months, I'd collected more than a hundred letters wishing me well but explaining I was overqualified for anything they had. I didn't get as far as a single job interview.

I shared this with David Durham, and he called me in Alexandria a few weeks after I visited Cornell, saying his wife had come into an inheritance and they'd be willing to "invest" in me by making $5,000 available to help get me to Costa Rica to start my business. That encouraged me to reach out to a few friends. Soon, my dear friend Bill Campbell offered us $2,500, expressing his interest in buying part of the company I'd be setting up. Then my former college roommate, Tom Wharton, came through with another $2,000.

I called Buddy Thomas and said we were interested in his proposal to go to Costa Rica. I told him I needed to do a market study to see if I could make a go with a roofing company there. He offered to pay the plane fare for Tereza and me to go down and check it out. I also attended a conference on human rights in Washington that spring. One of the speakers was Rodolfo Silva, ambassador from Costa Rica. I sought him out and briefly told him about my experience in Brazil. That conversation started a new friendship.

In June, Tereza and I flew to San José to explore what was to become our new home. Brady Tyson gave me the name of Javier Solis, a former Catholic priest who published *Pueblo,* a leftist newspaper in Costa Rica. Neither Tereza nor I spoke much Spanish, but Javier spoke excellent English. Javier was more than gracious and made several valuable contacts for me. He also contacted Cristina, the sister of the wife of the future president of Costa Rica, Rodrigo Carazo, who had a rancho on a beach at Puerto Limón. He got an invitation for us to spend the weekend at a Caribbean beach with her and some friends.

We took the train from San José to Puerto Limón, a beautiful 12-hour trip over the mountains and through the jungles. The following weekend, we flew down to the Pacific coast to visit the beach at Manuel Antonio. We stayed at a small hotel where we met a Costa Rican couple. He was the son of the owner of Tropigas, the primary seller of bottled gas in Costa Rica. They even gave us a ride back to San José in their Jeep and took us to their home, where they offered us marijuana in their living room. When we declined, they teased us about not being "with it."

I made contacts with people in the public sector and with construction companies. We were well-received everywhere we went. Costa Rica was the only country in the hemisphere to abolish its army in 1948. On our return home, I told Buddy Thomas I'd be delighted to be SWEPCO's distributor in Costa Rica if they could give me a line of credit to get me started.

In early June 1976, I went to Dulles for my flight to Dallas/Ft. Worth for a week-long training program at the SWEPCO headquarters. After checking in, I boarded a bus to take all the passengers to our plane. Once we were settled, I saw that sitting across from me was a major of the Chilean Air Force. I could tell from his uniform, insignias, and his ID badge. Knowing that the

Chilean military had overthrown the elected government of Salvador Allende just three years earlier on September 11, 1973, and had murdered some 30,000 of their own citizens in the aftermath, I found myself nearly overwhelmed with rage.

After a few minutes, even before the bus began to move away from the terminal, I called across to him, saying, "Torturador! Asasino!" He looked up at me with shock on his face. I repeated it: "Torturer! Murderer!" The US Army Colonel sitting next to him was equally startled. There were several other men in both US and Chilean uniforms. I was quite sure this was one of the regular junkets the US Army carried out for the Latin American military to win their allegiance and train them to obey our foreign policy goals. I knew from firsthand experience some of them were taught torture methods. My own Major Maia of the Brazilian Army bragged to me about his year at the School of the Americas.

When the bus arrived at our plane, and we began to move out, I spoke loudly to the elderly woman walking in front of me, "I really get tired of seeing our tax dollars spent taking a bunch of murdering military types from Latin America on tours of our country."

Much to my surprise, she responded, "Yeah! Me, too."

My seat was on the aisle in the plane's last row, just in front of the toilets. The anger I felt was overwhelming, and I was still raging inside.

When we got up to altitude, and the seat belt signs were turned off, the US Army colonel stood before me, clearly upset. "Who do you think you are to be insulting people who are our guests here in this country?" he asked.

"I am a US citizen who doesn't believe we have any business cultivating friendships with illegal governments and their military, governments that came to power by a military *coup*, overthrowing an elected president," I replied.

"But that doesn't give you the right to insult these people," he countered.

"Well, I have more than a right," I replied. "I have a *duty*. I was kidnapped by the Brazilian Army two years ago. I spent 17 days in their torture chambers, being tortured by a major, like the guy with you, who bragged to me about being a graduate of the School of the Americas, where he was a guest of the US Army. I have a duty to insult these thugs." I said all of this loudly so nearby passengers would hear. He disappeared up the aisle to his seat.

In another 10 minutes, he was back with the Chilean major. The colonel said, "I think you should apologize to this man for your remarks."

"Forget it," I said. "He knows his government is illegal and murderous. They murdered more than 30,000 of their own citizens three years ago."

To which the major replied, in English, "No, it was only 20,000." I couldn't believe he would confirm they had murdered their own citizens and was only quibbling about the number.

I repeated that I'd been tortured by the Brazilian military, who'd enjoyed the same kind of hospitality he was now enjoying, and there was no way I was going to apologize. I added that he should be ashamed to be in the Chilean Air Force, as it was known around the world for its torture and murder of its own citizens. "How can you wear that uniform and not expect to be insulted?" I asked.

They both returned to their seats. As I was getting off of the plane, one of the passengers, who'd heard the entire exchange, said he'd walk right behind me to be sure no one stuck a knife in me on the way out.

That week, I was part of a group of 10 people from around the world who were being trained to use SWEPCO products. Buddy entertained us well—good hotel breakfasts and Texas steaks at night. I needed to learn a lot. They covered the commercial advantages of their products and the various waterproofing systems we had available to us. At the end of the week, I began to feel like maybe I could actually do this.

On Sunday, I flew back to D.C., and we began to pack for Costa Rica. I contacted Rodolfo Silva at the Costa Rican Embassy and told him about our plans. He invited us to have dinner at his home before we left. We were surprised to find another couple at the dinner: Father Benjamin Nuñez, Founder and Rector of the National University in Heredia, accompanied by a lovely woman. Father Nuñez offered me a job teaching at the University, which I accepted, as it would give me a basis for residency in Costa Rica.

We were going to drive to Costa Rica, which was quite an adventure, as San José was about 3,000 miles from D.C. We planned to camp along the way and spend a few days at Stone Mountain National Park with Jennifer and Jonathan, who lived nearby in Atlanta. Our car was loaded up like Grapes of Wrath with all our belongings that we could get into it and/or on top of it, and my Yamaha 500 motorcycle followed along on a tow bar made for motorcycles.

While we were at Stone Mountain, one of the rangers came to me and said I had a phone call. It was Consul Richard Brown calling from Recife to inform me that Kissinger was planning to make a move on him and Ambassador Crimmins. Speaking in code, he said the "head bull" was working things out to send the smaller bulls (Brown and Crimmins) to the slaughter. He asked that I call him collect on my way to Costa Rica every 3–4 days to see how things were going. If the head bull made his move, Brown wanted me to get Les Whitten and Jack Anderson to unload their heavy artillery on "Big Hank." I contacted Les Whitten. He was chomping at the bit to attack Kissinger and said that this could be the peg he needed to hang all his stuff on.

We headed south, stopping a few days in New Orleans, driving into Texas, and down to Houston to say goodbye to my Aunt Lois and her family. Then, on to Mexico. As we neared the border, several signs said to "go this way," as it was shorter and quicker. So I did. But it also had no gas stations for the first 400 miles. At about

300 miles, I realized my '69 Chrysler, which got about 14 miles per gallon, wouldn't make it. But, along the way, some ingenious Mexicans had set up 50-gallon drums and were selling gas. At a premium price, of course. So I filled up the tank, and we made it to Guadalajara. Then, on to Mexico City.

I had the joy of showing Tereza the Anthropology Museum in Mexico City, which is, to me, one of the wonders of the world. The Pyramids of the Sun and Moon were also on our tourist list. Then, we continued to Guatemala. The highway was pretty smooth, but with three or four curves each and every mile, I started to get car sick. As we stopped at a gas station, I requested a can of STP, a gasoline additive. But the young teenager working at the station poured it into the power steering, not the oil reservoir. Before we got to Guatemala City, the power steering went out as the STP dissolved all the seals in the unit. Even before that, the radiator sprung a leak, and the engine overheated. I had to stop right in front of an army installation. I had heard horror stories about the Guatemalan army, but a couple of soldiers came out and brought me water and instructions on where I might find a mechanic.

The next day, I drove to the mechanic's shop, and he soldered the seam of the radiator. While I was waiting, I noticed white crosses painted on doors of the houses near the shop. In my limited Spanish, I asked the mechanic about it. He explained that each cross represented a family member who'd been shot down by unknown assailants while, in most cases, sitting on their front porch. I finally understood it was assumed that the victims had been murdered by unofficial death squads of the army. Most of the victims, said my informant, had been school teachers or members of unions. Welcome to Central America.

We were delayed five hours at the border to El Salvador while the customs inspectors went through all our stuff and demanded a $100 bribe to let us through. At the Honduras border, we were extorted again—a bit less money this time—but they required that one of their uniformed soldiers ride with us to the border to Nicaragua. The next day, we had to stop in Managua to wait for a procession of military vehicles. Somoza, the Nicaraguan dictator, was escorted by about 15 Jeeps and personnel carriers. All traffic was stopped until he had passed. I knew little about Nicaraguan history then, so I wasn't as fearful as I should have been. A false step could have been fatal.

Costa Rica at Last

When we finally got to San José, we drove to the home of Hugo Assman, a Brazilian former-priest theologian. Javier Solis had introduced us to Hugo, and he insisted that we stay with him and his lovely wife, Mel, until we found our own place. Hugo was part of the progressive wing of the Brazilian Catholic church and had been threatened by the military. He fled from Brazil to Chile in the early 1970s. Then, with the overthrow of the Allende government in 1973, Hugo's life was at risk, so he fled to Costa Rica. He and Mel had to get married to get out of the country, and a Methodist preacher had done them the favor. He had been in Costa Rica for three years and, with the help of funding from the World Council of Churches, had founded an ecumenical theological think tank called DEI (Department of Ecumenical Investigations). They published books on Liberation Theology and related themes.

Knowing of my experiences in Brazil and my friendship with Dom Hélder, Hugo was delighted to help us. Hugo and Mel provided us with a place to sleep and meals for nearly three weeks until we found an apartment. I was to discover later that this hospitality by Hugo was his way of controlling persons of particular interest who arrived in Costa Rica. He was considered to be one of the pioneer liberation theologians of Brazil.

During this time, I went to José Miguel Alfaro, the attorney Javier had recommended. He accepted all the paperwork we had brought to get our resident status and began legalizing our new company, M. y C. Servicios para la Construcción, Ltda. That was Morris and Carvalho, which came to be known within a year as simply M. y C. among the construction industry of Costa Rica.

The address of our new home was "from the Soda Rohrmoser, 200 meters north, 50 meters west and 25 meters north." San José didn't have street names and numbers, just landmark addresses. The Soda Rohrmoser had burned to the ground 20 years earlier but was still the landmark for our apartment. My favorite address in San José was "From the public urinal of Plaza Viques, 150 meters south and 50 meters west."

Sadly, things had been rocky with Tereza for quite some time. A major point of tension was her mother didn't want her to take the pill. Francisquinha had read that some women had heart attacks or strokes from it. I'd read pretty much everything available in medical journals before we opened the family planning clinic in Caixa d'Agua and pointed out that the risks of a normal birth were precisely twice the risks involved with the pill. About eight months after we arrived in Costa Rica, she got pregnant with our first child, Jessica Raquel Carvalho Morris, born on October 31, 1977. Two and a half years later, our son, Erick José Carvalho Morris, was born on March 20, 1980. Both Jessica and Erick were delightful children and have been a source of joy and pride throughout their lives.

The day after we moved into our apartment in San José, I visited some construction companies to sell my roofing and waterproofing products. I called nearly all the construction companies in the country and all the engineers and architects, one by one, and requested appointments to present SWEPCO's products and systems.

After about a month in Costa Rica, we visited the Union Church, an English-language church in Moravia, a suburb of San José. They had a reasonably stable congregation, mostly ex-patriot retirees from the US and Canada. The pastor was returning to the

US within a month, and I was invited to serve as interim pastor. When the new pastor arrived, they discovered he was a nice guy from Tennessee but not a very good preacher. So, as the unpaid associate pastor, I was asked to preach one Sunday each month. It became embarrassing when everyone noted that church attendance was up about 30% on the Sundays I preached.

We started a small prayer/healing group that met in our home every Tuesday evening for over five years. I shared what I'd learned about healing from Agnes Sanford, and the group became a source of spiritual strength for Union Church. However, in 1982, our relationship with Union Church came crashing down. I was enthused that the Sandinista revolution had been successful in Nicaragua. By then, the enthusiasm for the Sandinistas in Costa Rica had dwindled to just about zero. The public media and the government of President Monge became severe opponents of the Sandinistas. Some members of Union Church were influenced by those forces and became strongly opposed to the new Nicaraguan government.

As a pastor, I had a custom to invite the congregation to build the Pastoral Prayer. I suggested we start with large concerns about the world, then focus on local and national concerns in Costa Rica and any personal matters they were worried about. Jean, one of the members of Union Church, was a Dutch missionary with the Latin American Mission. The LA Mission was a conservative group based in the US with strong connections to Fuller Seminary. Jean's father had been the head of Shell Oil.

Jean started asking for prayers for the people of Nicaragua to resist the "Communists" who had "taken over" that country. This created a real problem for me in the pulpit, as I knew the government of Nicaragua was not Communist and was doing all it could to help the people of their country. Jean also shared that he went to Nicaragua once a month with $5,000 he got from the US Embassy in San José to hand out to pastors in Nicaragua to aid them in their resistance.

I needed to offer a word of correction, saying the Sandinistas were not Communists and, in fact, the Communist Party of Nicaragua was anti-Sandinista. This became an almost weekly contest. The tension persisted. The new pastor arrived and proved to be conservative both theologically and socially. He was not comfortable having me around. My monthly preaching assignments came to a halt. He announced he would preach on a new book of the Bible every Sunday, starting with Genesis.

After a few months, he had to be away and asked me to preach in his absence on the Book of Isaiah. I figured I wouldn't get many more chances, so I talked bluntly about Isaiah's concern for the poor, the widow, the orphan, and the marginalized people. The congregation seemed to love it. However, shortly before the annual assembly of the Union Church, a proposal was made that the associate pastor must be elected annually by a 67% vote. This was clearly aimed at me. When the election came up, it was pointed out that only full members could vote. Of the 110–120 persons who attended the church on Sundays, only around 35 were actually members. Many participants knew they would be in Costa Rica for only 2–3 years and so didn't transfer their membership from their home church in the States.

I missed the 67% number by one vote. My name was off the bulletin the following Sunday, so Tereza and I simply did not return to Union Church. To our surprise and dismay, not one member of Union Church called us to express support or thanks.

Competition, Legal Hurdles, and Faith Tests in Costa Rica

The engineers and architects I dealt with understood me well. I only had two competitors. One mainly got government contracts because he had supported the National Liberation Party of *don* Pepe Figueres, which had won the brief civil war in 1948. He did really shoddy work, and when he was called upon to honor one of his guarantees, he simply closed down his company and organized a new one, thus invalidating the warranties and giving the roofing business a bad name. The other competitor was honest, but his first love was cinema and theater, so he wasn't aggressive in the field.

The engineers were interested in this *gringo* who showed up representing SWEPCO. I was out every day meeting with potential clients. I started this process in mid-July, and by October, when my first order of materials from SWEPCO arrived, I signed my first contract for $1,500 to waterproof the indoor concrete planters in the new FERTICA office building.

This contract involved putting a layer of asphalt paste on the walls and floor of the permanent internal planters, then pushing down into the paste a fiberglass mesh, then putting another layer of the paste on top. As I had no workers yet, I did the job myself and became semi-famous for being the *gringo* who was actually on his hands and knees working.

A few months later, the company that hired me for that job contracted M. y C. to do a major roofing job on the new Justice building in San José. In between, the Firestone Company contracted us to do a $25,000 renewal of the flat roof on their offices and plant. But the big breakthrough came when Standard Fruit Company hired me to waterproof 10,000 square meters of roof on their box-making plant in Puerto Limón. That was a $90,000 contract and actually capitalized our company.

After we'd been in Costa Rica for a year, I got a visit from the local equivalent of the sheriff, saying that as I had yet to establish my residency, I had 30 days to leave the country. I'd contacted my lawyer, José Miguel Alfaro, at least twice a month, inquiring about my residency. I had asked at the embassy in Washington before we left and brought everything with me, including a certificate of good conduct from the local police and an original birth certificate. When I rushed to his office with my deportation order, he opened a drawer in his desk and pulled out all my documents. He'd done absolutely nothing up till then about my residence. Nothing.

I discovered that my principal competitor had called in some political favors to get rid of the *gringo*. I was, in effect, working illegally. As it turned out, José Miguel Alfaro was already in the campaign for being the country's next Vice President, so he had some political strings he could pull. Within a month, my residency was granted.

My life was one of constant stress during those years. I got up every day except Sundays at five a.m. and met my workers at six to take them to their place of work for the day. I always had a crew of three: the Bermudez brothers, José Antonio, Luis, and Guillermo. These young men were excellent and efficient workers. The only problem was that they were, like so many men in Costa Rica, functioning alcoholics and totally irresponsible fathers. I discovered that José Antonio had three women bearing him children, and he contributed nothing to their support. Luis, the same. Guillermo had two women and five children, to whom he contributed nothing.

After about my third year in business, I hired a salesperson. Javier was diligent and relatively effective. He made a pretty good salary on commission. But after five years, I discovered he'd broken into one of our filing cabinets and gotten the address of a Shell spin-off in Puerto Rico that manufactured a line of products similar to SWEPCO's. I'd purchased some materials from them, which were much cheaper than those from SWEPCO. But I knew they were not as good, so I stuck with SWEPCO's line for government contracts and top-of-the-line construction companies. Javier wrote to the Shell company and sought to buy materials to open up his own company.

Fortunately for me, the export manager in San Juan let me know Javier was seeking to set himself up as my competition. I fired him for being disloyal. Disloyalty was one of the actions that permitted an employer to fire an employee without paying any kind of severance. Javier took me to the Labor Court, demanding five months of pay and benefits, but the judge threw out his case.

Sometimes, I had to hire additional workers, especially for a large contract. My experience with these men was not positive. Without exception, during my 12 years in business, every man who worked for me stole from me in one fashion or another. Usually, they stole asphalt roofing materials to do small jobs on the side. That was grounds for termination but very hard to prove. So I just had to build into my business plan a percentage of loss to theft by my workers. Another problem was they nearly all failed to show up for work on Monday mornings, sleeping off their weekend drink. I soon became accustomed to a four-day work week.

I had an entirely different experience with my female employees. I could leave my wallet on my desk while I went out and never miss anything. They showed up on time and never missed a day of work. One should not generalize about people, but it is not unfair to say that in my experience, over the time I spent in Costa Rica, most of the men were irresponsible and dishonest, while the women were responsible and honest. Period.

During my 12 years in business in Costa Rica, I had over 20 lawyers. The Legislative Assembly, made up almost entirely of attorneys, passed a law shortly after I got there that required every business to have an attorney on retainer. All my attorneys, without exception, defrauded me in one way or another, including one I regarded as a close personal friend.

We always had cash flow problems. People were slow to pay, and the government was even worse. When I won a good contract through public bidding, I had to wait as much as six months after completion to get my final payment. This provided an unwelcome but rewarding test of my faith. In one 18 month period, every Friday morning my excellent secretary, Mayela, would say, "*Don* Fred, we don't have enough money in the bank to make our payroll this afternoon." To which I invariably replied, "Don't worry, Mayela, we'll be all right." During those 18 months, we never missed a payroll. During the day, someone who owed us money would finally pay up, or a new contract would come with the 50% deposit we required, and we could make our payroll.

How I Beat the IRS

Toward the end of my second year in Costa Rica, an American businessman dressed in the usual Washington, D.C., suit and power tie came to my office. He was from the Internal Revenue Service and explained he came down every year to audit the accounts of some of the US-owned businesses. My little company had come up, and he wanted to see the books. I complied.

About a week later, he handed back my books and said they were messy, but all seemed to be in order. However, he had a few questions. He noted my income was entirely from M. y C. and I was a 25% partner. The other 75% of the company belonged to Tereza.

"Why does she have 75% and you only 25%," he asked, "especially since you are the president and manager of the company?"

"Well, she is an attorney and more qualified in business than I am, so we set it up that way."

He continued. "I see your wife didn't file an income tax return. Why was that?"

"Well, I guess she didn't want to," I said. He flushed noticeably and said, "But that's not right. Everyone has to file a return."

I paused like I was thinking about it a bit. "Well, you see, she's not a US citizen; she's Brazilian, so she decided not to file a return to the US IRS. She doesn't have to."

He gulped and said, "You know, you've got a good thing going here. Putting the lion's share of the company's profit into her account, then you don't really have enough income to make any difference. I have one more question: you took an additional 15% off your adjusted gross income for living in a 'hardship' area here in Costa Rica. Don't you live in San Pedro? I know that area. It's a very nice suburb."

At this point, I pulled out the 40-page flier for US citizens living overseas that the IRS had sent me and turned to the page listing the areas in Costa Rica that were "hardship areas." And, sure enough, there was San Pedro. I underlined it and handed it to the gentleman. He sat back in his chair quietly and then said, "Okay. Let me make a suggestion. If you change your company from a partnership to a corporation, nobody from the IRS can come and demand to see your books. Also, if anyone comes down and wants to audit you in the next five years, tell them to jump in the lake. Once you are audited and cleared, we cannot touch you again for at least five years." And he got up and left. The very next day, I went to my attorney and began the process of changing our company to a corporation.

Mesoamerica—Perhaps the Most Creative Thing I Ever Did

In the summer of 1981 we'd been in Costa Rica for five years. Our little company had established itself as a leader in roofing and waterproofing. Jessica was four, and Erick was a year and a half. My marriage to Tereza was stumbling along.

I received a letter from my friend, David Weimer, a professor of English literature at Rutgers University in New Jersey. David had spent time in Brazil as a Fulbright scholar. He wrote to let me know that Amnesty International USA was looking for a new executive director. He wanted to recommend me for the position as he was on the Board of the New York branch of A.I. I readily agreed.

I was excited about getting back into the fray of working for justice. I got a letter of recommendation from Dom Hélder Câmara, and I pursued the job. However, as is often the case, they no doubt already had the candidate chosen and were just going through the motions of a search to satisfy public expectations. I was surprised to learn I made the shortlist of three but not surprised to learn they'd decided on someone else.

My years of association with Dom Hélder had been vital to me. He was a significant figure in the world struggle for justice. At the time, I didn't see myself as important in that struggle, but the ecumenical work symbolized peace and harmony. The few things I could do for Dom Hélder gave me great satisfaction. My work at the Community Center provided hope and opportunity for people. Having that taken away with my expulsion from Brazil was a real blow. Now that I was out of survival mode, I more acutely felt the loss of engagement in something worthwhile.

A short while later, Parke Renshaw contacted me. Parke was the director of the Language School in Campinas, where we learned Portuguese. He had retired and was living in Atlanta. He told me an organization that studied and supported international projects was looking for an executive director. They invited me to Atlanta for an interview. The interview went splendidly, and I was sure I would get the job. But at the end of the interview, they explained there wasn't really a job open. They didn't have any funding.

I continued my travels and speaking engagements. Everywhere I went, I made my presentation about the Nicaraguan Revolution and Central America in general. During the question period following my talk, people asked, "Where do you get your information? It doesn't jibe with what we read in the papers or hear on TV" I explained that my information came from firsthand contacts with people on the ground. I didn't hesitate to say that the Reagan administration was lying.

On my return to Costa Rica, I met with two friends, Plutarco Bonilla, a professor of Biblical studies at the Universidad Biblica and a world-renowned Bible translator, and Bill Cook, a missionary in Costa Rica with the Latin American Mission. Bill had written a book about the Christian base communities in Latin America, especially Brazil. I told Plutarco and Bill about the questions I received in the States and the desire for more adequate information about Central America. I suggested we start publishing a newsletter on the region. They agreed and said, "You do it."

We formed a non-profit corporation called the Institute for Central American Studies (El Centro para Estudios Centroamericanos) (ICAS), and I started publishing a monthly newsletter. I recruited Lyle Prescott, an expatriate living in Costa Rica, married to a Tico, and working for the English-language weekly published in San José. Lyle was a good writer and shared our concerns. I also recruited Linda Ferris, another expatriate, married to an Episcopalian priest who was in exile from Guatemala, to be the secretary and help with translations. Using funds from M. y C., I rented office space on the second floor of an older building behind the Magaly Theatre in downtown San José. We put in a telephone, basic office furniture, and a portable electric typewriter.

I wrote to the Board of Global Ministries of the United Methodist Church asking for a grant of $1,500 to help us get started. My request was declined, with no explanation offered. I sent letters to the publishers of Spanish-language magazines and newsletters in the region, asking them to exchange their publications for ours. We also got newspapers from Nicaragua *(La Prensa, El Nuevo Diario,* and *Barricada* (the Sandinista publication) and from Costa Rica *(La Nación).* We got papers from Honduras and El Salvador, as well as a subscription to the *Miami Herald,* which in those days was a reliable source of information on significant events in the region, and *The New York Times,* which was still considered "the newspaper of record" by most in the US.

We did not have the resources to be doing on the ground journalism in the region, though when I went to Nicaragua for *ABC News,* I did not hesitate to interview all the people I could. As significant players from the area came to Costa Rica, we also tried to get interviews. Lyle and I clipped all the sources available daily and putting the clips into files on each country under the headings of Religion, Politics, Economy, US Relations, and Human Rights. Then, we sorted through all the material we'd clipped and wrote summaries based on firsthand information and material reported from at least three sources. Lyle converted our typewritten reports into a printed newsletter that expanded to 12 pages.

We called the newsletter *Mesoamerica,* an anthropological term referring to the area from Mexico's southern border to the Isthmus of Panama. I got a copy of the College and University Directory from the US Embassy library and recruited a half-dozen women at the Union Church to address and stuff envelopes. We sent a copy of the first edition in January of 1982 with a subscription form to more than 3,000 addresses. To colleges of fewer than 1,000 students, we addressed an envelope to the head of the History Department. For schools with up to 3,000 students, we sent the material to the heads of the History Department and the Political Science Department. For schools larger than 3,000, we sent a third copy to the head of Latin American Studies. On page one of the first edition, I wrote:

> *Long aware of the lack of consistently reliable information in English about Central America, a group of persons residing in Costa Rica decided to form the Institute for Central American Studies (ICAS). The founders of the Institute are Latin Americans or persons with long experience in Latin America. The Board of Directors comprises four Costa Ricans, one Argentine, one Chilean, and one North American. All are persons with long-standing and deep commitment to the cause of justice and peace in Latin America . . . . The information published will be gathered from various sources, including firsthand contacts in the Central American countries. Strenuous efforts will be made to guarantee the factual accuracy of the material presented.*

The response to the first issue was amazingly gratifying. The February issue brought in more subscriptions. I traveled to Washington, D.C., in May to attend the Latin American Studies Association (LASA) bi-annual convention. I took a trunk of 1,500 copies of *Mesoamerica* and a slightly larger number of subscription forms. While I was waiting for my flight, I was approached by two men from security who asked why I was taking all that printed material to the United States. I always carried a copy of the Costa Rican Constitution, which I pulled out and read about the freedom of speech guaranteed to anyone in Costa Rica. I asked why they were enquiring about material leaving the country. They demanded I give them a few copies, but I refused, suggesting they could go to the airport newsstand across the hall and buy a copy for one dollar.

At the convention, I placed a copy of the newsletter and subscription form on every chair in the main auditorium. By mid-June, we had nearly 1,500 paid subscriptions. We sent a copy of *Mesoamerica* to every member of Congress. On several occasions over the next few years, we were cited on the floor of Congress and got into the Congressional Record.

One afternoon, I got a phone call from Nora Boots, the executive for Latin America for the Board of Global Ministries. She had turned down my request for a $1,500 seed money grant for *Mesoamerica.* She was in Costa Rica and asked if I could have breakfast with her. I accepted, and when we met, she began by saying she was quite impressed with the newsletter. "It is really quite professional," she said.

"Thank you," I said, not knowing where this was going.

"Where do you get the funding for such a fine publication?" she asked.

I could tell from the way she phrased that question and from the expression on her face that she was implying I was being funded by some nefarious group. So I got up and left, saying, "Fuck you,

Nora," on my way out. I wasn't going to defend myself and the newsletter to her. She didn't deserve an explanation.

In November 1982, we held our first *Mesoamerica* Study Seminar, a 10-day experience in Costa Rica and Nicaragua. We brought participants to Costa Rica for four days of intensive study of the Central American Region, and to tour places like the Irazú Volcano, where on a clear day one can see the Atlantic and Pacific oceans. We had speakers from each country in Central America, including both a Sandinista and a *contra* speaker from Nicaragua, as well as Brooklyn Rivera, a Miskito Indian leader in exile in Costa Rica.

Next, everyone flew to Managua for a six-day experience, including a briefing by the US Embassy and interviews with people involved in the Land Reform, the Popular Church, and some opposed to the Sandinista project. We visited *La Prensa* to interview Violetta Chamorro, widow of Pedro Joaquin Chamorro, the founder of the paper who had been murdered in 1978 by Somoza and his allies. Under Violetta, *La Prensa* was leading the opposition to the Sandinistas. Violetta became the opposition candidate to Daniel Ortega in 1990 and was elected to the presidency. We also visited *El Nuevo Diario,* which had been formed by dissident La Prensa employees who supported the Revolution. Another visit was made to *Barricada,* the Sandinista paper. We had interviews with Father Miguel D'Escoto, a Maryknoll priest and the Sandinista Foreign Minister; Nora Astorga, guerrilla fighter and Vice-Minister of the Exterior; Comandante *Omar Cabezas,* Vice Minister of Defense and the author of a best-selling autobiography of a Sandinista guerrilla fighter, *Fire From the Mountain;* Father Ernesto Cardinal, Minister of Culture; Alfonso Robelo, former member of the Junta de Reconstrucción, and opposition leader, among others. This was the first of 40 *Mesoamerica* study seminars we were to carry out over the next eight years. More than 600 people participated in these seminars, coming mainly from colleges, universities and religious groups in solidarity with the people of Central America.

One day, my phone rang at the *Mesoamerica* office. When I answered, the person at the other end asked to speak to Fred Morris. "Speaking," I said.

The caller introduced himself as Noam Chomsky and suggested perhaps I had heard of him.

"Yes, Dr. Chomsky," I replied. "I've heard of you."

He explained that his daughter worked in Managua for the international version of the Sandinista newspaper *Barricada.* He planned to visit her over the holidays and had a three-hour layover in San Jose on January 1.

"I have been reading your newsletter and would like to meet you and learn more about it," he said.

Hardly able to contain my excitement, I replied that I thought I could work him into my schedule.

On New Year's Day 1983, I drove to the Juan Santamaria International Airport and spent three hours drinking Bloody Marys with Noam Chomsky. I told him about my misadventures in Brazil and my friendship with Dom Hélder Câmara. He was impressed with my history and liked *Mesoamerica* greatly. This began a long-term friendship.[5]

Mesoamerica became part of the growing US opposition to Reagan's maniacal opposition to the Sandinistas and any other popular-based movement in Central America. In addition to providing factual information, we gave participants of the study seminars a firsthand experience of the Sandinista Revolution. *Mesoamerica* published the first reports of the Iran-Contra scandal a month before any US media.

As a result of these efforts, I became a marked man in San José. We noticed an American standing at the street corner near our office, taking pictures of people who went in and out. He carried a purse attached to his wrist, a *mariconera* in Costa Rican Spanish. We could clearly see the outline of his pistol. Every time I returned from Nicaragua, I was taken aside by airport security and asked questions about why I was going to a "communist" country so often, what I was doing there, etc. It got to the point where I simply walked up to the man at security and said, "Okay. Where do we go?"

Our telephones were tapped, and we could hear the clicking of their cheap equipment every time we picked up the phone. Our offices were broken into at least twice. Nothing was taken, but our files were ransacked. Some Communist literature was placed in our files, and if we had not discovered it and thrown it in the trash, we might have had to explain to some police types why we had it.

Tereza . . .

My relationship with Tereza continued to be rocky. One day, she informed me her mother had decided she should return to Brazil to take her mid-term exams at the Law School. I suggested there were eleven universities in the D.C. area and she could enroll in any of them. But Francisquinha decided that Tereza should finish her final year in Law and get her degree, even though we had no hope of returning to Brazil.

Tereza flew down to Recife, and her sister Maria Helena died the very day she arrived. Maria Helena was 21 years old and doing exceptionally well at the university. She had gone to Caruarú on a weekend trip and, on arrival, complained of a headache. Within a few hours, she was in the local hospital, diagnosed with meningitis. She died before morning. The whole family was devastated. Tereza completed her mid-term exams and returned to Virginia but carried the burden of grief. There wasn't much I could do to relieve her of the pain.

In June, she returned to Brazil for exams. She was gone for about six weeks. I was under continued financial stress, and we were not getting along very well. She went again in December to take her final exams and graduate. She came back around Christmas with her brother Henrique. In high school, Tereza spent a year in the States on an exchange program. She'd learned English quite well and had a wonderful year, so she and her mother decided that Henrique should have a similar experience. But Henrique had never been interested in learning English. At 17, he was a sullen teenager, not the least interested in being in the United States. I registered Henrique in the local high school, but he simply sat in his classes looking out the window.

I asked Tereza to go with me to a counselor, but she was uninterested. Finally, after nearly 11 years of conflict, I invited her to walk with me down to the Sabanilla Plaza, about three blocks from our house. We sat on a bench in a lovely little park, and I said we must get help. She said our only problem was that I didn't come home for lunch every day. If I did that, all would be well. But I knew another mealtime would mean more arguments. The kids were clearly being torn asunder. Then she said she didn't have time for all this and had to prepare for a meeting with the Association of Brazilian Women. She went to her meeting, and I packed a suitcase and moved into my office at *Mesoamerica*.

CHAPTER 8

Rosa Argentina Molina Marín

On October 13, 1977, a group of Sandinista youth in San Carlos, Nicaragua, launched an armed attack on the military headquarters of the Somoza's National Guard. The FSLN, Sandinista Front for National Liberation, planned to attack five military outposts in cities nationwide. But one of their members had betrayed them and informed Somoza's National Guard of the attacks. The group in San Carlos didn't know about this and went ahead even as the other four attacks were called off. They ended up killing most of the Somoza troops in San Carlos. But since the other attacks didn't take place, Somoza was able to mobilize a rapid response, and the Sandinistas were forced to flee across to Costa Rica, which gave asylum to the refugees from San Carlos.

As the stringer for *ABC News* in Costa Rica, I reported on these events and interviewed some of the youth from San Carlos. I found myself becoming invaluable to the network. At that time, I was the only person working for any networks covering Central America who spoke Spanish. So when the *ABC* reporters came to San José, I was responsible for making contacts for them with local TV and arranging for interviews with influential persons in the government. That took me frequently to the Presidential House (Casa Presidencial) to translate for the *ABC* reporter in interviews with government officials, including President Rodrigo Carazo.

On one of these trips, I encountered one of the most beautiful women I had ever seen, a Black Costa Rican from Puerto Limon, who was the private correspondence secretary of *don* Rodrigo. My situation with Tereza was not improving, but I didn't feel free to do more than speak to this woman, Rosa Argentina Molina Marín. Argentina set up interviews with the president, but our relationship was limited to that. The Sandinista Revolution heated up over the next few years. *ABC*'s visits became more frequent, and I spoke with Argentina frequently.

After I finally made the break from Tereza, I thought about women I had met over the years that interested me. Argentina was at the top of that list. I had recently seen her on the streets of San José by chance. She was no longer in the presidential office as the elections in 1982 brought Luis Alberto Monge into power as president of a different party. When I saw her, I asked where she was working. She said she had been transferred to the Proveduria, the department that handles government purchases.

I didn't see her again for nearly a year, but I got the number of the Proveduria and asked to speak to Argentina Molina. When she came on the line, I identified myself as the *ABC* reporter she'd met in *don* Rodrigo's office. She recalled me. I asked if she'd be willing to meet me for a conversation over coffee. Her response was, "But aren't you married?"

"Yes," I said, "but we're separated and will be getting a divorce."

"I've heard that one at least a thousand times," she said. But I persisted, and she agreed to meet me for coffee. After I explained my sad story, she told me hers. She'd been dating a Costa Rican she'd met at university for eight years. They were preparing to get married. But one Saturday, when he told her he was going camping with some friends, she got a call from a mutual friend suggesting she go to a particular address in the Moravia neighborhood of San

José. She went to the address, and when she rang the doorbell, her fiancé opened the door in his boxers. An American woman, also partially dressed, was standing behind him. So there we were, two basket cases stumbling out of failed relationships. We talked for three hours, and I invited her to have dinner with me. She accepted. We've been together ever since.

One of the things that intrigued Argentina was my support for the Sandinista Revolution in Nicaragua. She never expected that from a *gringo*. Some of her first cousins had been in the attack on the military outpost in San Carlos in 1977 that started the Insurrection that became the Sandinista Revolution. I told her about my work with *ABC News* and my trips to Nicaragua. I also told her about *Mesoamerica* and the support I was trying to give the Revolution. She told me of her background, spending the first 14 years of her life moving back and forth between Nicaragua and Costa Rica. Her mother, *dona* Olga, had 21 live births in her marriage to her father, Agustin. Sixteen of them had died before they were two years old. Her father was usually not at home, spending time with other women, as was the custom for too many Nicaraguan men. They had to move every three or four months when they lived in San Carlos. Her mom could not make enough money doing laundry in the San Juan River, or cooking and selling food on the streets of San Carlos to keep up with the rent. In third and fourth grades, she would often faint mid-morning, having not eaten anything the day before.

When Argentina was 14, the family fled to Costa Rica. Her father was a member of the National Guard, driving Somoza's son's boat on Lake Nicaragua. He made the mistake of saying he wouldn't vote for Somoza in the next election. The son gave orders to have Agustin Molina and his entire family murdered, so Argentina's father took the boat and fled down the San Juan River, about two hours ahead of the National Guard in hot pursuit, until they reached Barra de Colorado, Costa Rica. She finished high school in Costa Rica, delayed because she had to help her mother support the five surviving children. She then moved to San José to attend university.

After graduating from secretarial school, she became the president's private correspondence secretary, where I found her. Our lives blended marvelously. I was 50 when we got married. I already had four children and thought I was too old to start a new family. But Argentina asked if we couldn't have at least one together. I recall very vividly one night, about three a.m., waking up, looking at her and feeling a tremendous desire to have a child with her, something I'd never felt before. So I agreed to have one.

On December 10, 1985, our son, Frederick, was born weighing 10 pounds 8 oz. A beautiful baby and delightful. But then Argentina began saying she really would like to have a girl. In April of 1987, our daughter, Raquel Ambar Morris, was born. And on September 27, 1988, our second daughter and my seventh child, Gabriela Argentina Morris, was born.

Argentina joined one of our *Mesoamerica* trips to Nicaragua. When we returned, she was arrested at the airport. They hassled her before one of the security people suggested to the inquisitor that they had made a mistake, as this young woman was employed by the Casa Presidencial. They gave a left-handed apology and let her go. We will celebrate 40 years of unbelievably happy marriage, heading for our 50th and Golden Anniversary when I celebrate my 100th birthday.

CHAPTER 9

Brasil Bloque

I'D BEEN IN COSTA RICA for about seven years when one day, a strange person appeared in my office. He was roughly 6'1", lanky, and sported a "Pancho Villa" mustache, a Western hat, and cowboy boots. He introduced himself as Agustin de Neymet, the owner of a company based in Mexico City that manufactured a line of concrete admixtures and epoxy products. He'd seen my announcement in the Costa Rican Yellow Pages indicating that I sold a line of Spanish-made admixtures and wanted to make a proposal to me.

Agustin's father was a chemical engineer and founded their company over 25 years ago. He invented a variety of chemicals that would change the characteristics of concrete. One of the more important of those admixtures was a retardant, which slowed down the concrete's setting up or hardening. This was especially important in hot climates because concrete is exothermic, meaning it generates heat as it hardens. If that happens too rapidly, the concrete cracks, reducing its quality and strength.

Some six months before, the Mexican economy entered a severe crisis, harshly affecting the construction business. Agustin could not let his workers go because most had been with the company for over 10 years. Under Mexican labor law, if one fires or terminates an employee without just cause, they must pay a month's salary and benefits for each year they had been with the company. Neymet didn't have the cash to pay off the workers, but he couldn't keep them on the payroll. So, he was looking to sell the technology to obtain the cash to ride out the crises.

He'd contacted several companies in San José with his offer without success. Costa Rican engineers and business people were conservative and didn't trust a Mexican. So we began to discuss then negotiate. I ended up using a new company I had formed a couple of years before called Brasil Bloque, S.A. Within three weeks of being capitalized by a loan of $200,000 from the Inter-American Bank, Costa Rica entered a crisis of its own. The *colon* went from 8 to 42 for a dollar, and the Bank decided not to make the loan. I paid Agustin de Neymet a few thousand dollars and gave him some shares in Brasil Bloque. He was required to provide us with the technical advice to start producing the products.

I brought Bob Holiday in as a partner as he was a civil engineer. All of a sudden, I had a new venture underway. The concrete admixtures were better than any other products on the market. Within a year, we won a public contract with the National Electric Company (ICE) for one million liters of our principal retardant, Durotard. However, the conservative attitudes of the engineering class in Costa Rica worked against us. We could show them in their own labs that our products outperformed others, and they preferred to stick with Sika products, as they were well-known and made in Italy. Our product was as much as 35% cheaper, so convincing them to buy it was difficult.

At one point, I flew to Florida and visited the largest Redi-Mix company in that state. They liked the product but said they needed 25,000 gallons a month for their 35+ plants. We couldn't produce that much product, so I returned home without selling anything. In short, I was caught in the trap of living by doing roofing while publishing *Mesoamerica,* which remained my real vocation.

From Costa Rica to Malta and Broadway

Argentina and I discussed possibly moving to the US for some time. I wanted our children to be bi-cultural and bi-lingual. If we remodeled the house to add a bedroom, we could easily rent it for a good income. Then, after 10–12 years in the States, I would be eligible for retirement, and we could return to Costa Rica and our lovely home.

I contacted my dear friend, Jim Reed, a D.S. in the Northern Illinois Annual Conference, and told him we wanted an appointment. We then arranged to visit the States, first in Washington to see Jennifer and then Chicago, stopping for a night in Pittsburgh for a visit with Dick Sherwood and his wife. Dick was my high school and college tennis partner and was the east coast vice president of J.C. Penney. In Chicago, we stayed with Jim Reed and his wife. We had good interviews, and things were set up for our return in June to take a church somewhere in Northern Illinois.

From January until May, I had been thinking about what kind of appointment I would get. My dad always said the Methodist Church punished missionaries when they returned home by putting them at entry-level churches. I had many friends in the conference, and my father had been a D.S. and pastor of the largest church in the conference, so I thought they might put me in a middle-sized congregation. However, in May, I got a phone call from Bruce, the D.S. in the DeKalb District, saying they wanted me to serve at Malta, an entry-level church.

We finished packing and struggled to get our exit visas from Costa Rica. Bob Holliday, my former business associate, had filed a suit against me, claiming that I owed him money—which I didn't, as he had actually scammed me out of several thousand dollars while working for me at M. y C.—but as long as his suit was in place, I couldn't leave. I finally had to give him $16,000 to lift the suit. Bob later worked for USAID in El Salvador in the middle of

Reagan's genocidal war against the people of that country. He spent the rest of his career as an engineer for USAID, which has now been exposed as a global front for the CIA.

We went to Nicaragua to say goodbye to family and friends. We spent a few days in Managua, and I visited Comandante Omar Cabezas and Comandante Moises Hassan. Moises, who had been mayor of Managua for several years, asked me why we had decided to leave. "Moises," I said, "I just can't stand dealing with Ticos anymore." He burst out laughing. He told me how once, during the insurrection against Somoza, Carlos Fonseca Amador, the intellectual leader of modern Sandinismo, made an interesting comment. They were sitting around a campfire one night up in the mountains. Fonseca said, "One should never generalize about a people and say 'the Chinese are like this, or the Germans are like that.' Except in the case of Costa Rica, because they are all sons-of-bitches."

Our move to the States was somewhat complicated because Argentina was seven months pregnant with Gabriela. Knowing we would have three babies under three years of age, we decided to see if Lizbeth would be willing to come to the States. She'd been part of my family since she was eleven, when she began babysitting for Jessica and Erick. Somewhere along the line, Lizbeth moved in with us. After my separation from Tereza, she stayed with Tereza and the kids until Tereza went back to Brazil. Shortly after that, I invited her to come back and help with Freddie and Raquel.

Lizbeth was devastated by our decision to move to the States, as she had come to love not just Freddie and Raquel but Argentina. So when I offered her the chance to go to the States with us, she jumped at it. English was her first language, as her family were all from Puerto Limon on the Caribbean coast, and many of the people there speak Jamaican English. We agreed to pay her and get her into the community college at Kishwaukee.

On June 19, 1988, all six of us arrived in Chicago. My longtime friend, Bill Campbell, met us at the airport and loaned us his

Chevy station wagon so we could drive out to Malta. That same evening, we met with the Staff/Parish Relations Committee and the DS, Bruce, to see if they would accept us as their new parsonage family. Bruce had told them nothing about us except that I'd been in Latin America as a missionary. He deliberately did not mention that Argentina was African-Central American.

Roger Hueber, representing the Northwest church, said only, "It seems to me that you are significantly overqualified for this parish." Florence Butler introduced herself. She had been at the Annual Conference in 1986 when I spoke and was ecstatic that I would be her pastor. Tom Plotte, the Chair of the Trustees, had yet to prepare the parsonage for us, though he'd known for three months that a new family would be arriving. The A.C. had been out for several months, and the temperature had been over 100 for a few weeks.

Our goods took about a month to arrive from Costa Rica, so we were camping out in the parsonage. We bought a car and went furniture shopping. Before we moved in, O.J. Cunningham, one of the leading laypersons of the Malta church, came by for a visit. O.J. had worked for G.E. in DeKalb and was now retired. He had started a food-sharing program in the DeKalb District. Farmers from all over the area donated vast quantities of food for one of the inner-city churches in Chicago. He raised funds to rent several trucks to haul the food into the city. He also implemented a program whereby kids from the inner-city parish came out to the country to spend time on a farm.

He did, however, warn me that LaVerne Johnson, one of the major players in the church and in DeKalb County, was upset by the fact that the new pastor's wife was not white. LaVerne was a wealthy retired farmer and the leading bigot of the region. The first Sunday I took the pulpit when LaVerne saw Argentina walk in with Freddie and Raquel, he very conspicuously got up and walked out, slamming the door on his way out. He never returned but made frequent house calls on members of the church, openly calling for action to "get the N——s out of the parsonage." He operated like a kind of Godfather in the area. People in the church found that he was generous in loaning money to them on favorable terms to help put their children through college. That meant they had a debt to LaVerne.

On that same first Sunday, Argentina stood with me at the church door after the service to meet the congregation's people. Most of them were cordial and charmed by Argentina's beauty and graciousness. But one woman, Beth Duffield, president of the United Methodist Women's group, refused to take Argentina's extended hand and walked right by. This performance was repeated the following two Sundays. After that, Argentina did not stand with me at the door anymore.

Most of the people in the community were salt of the earth farmers and kind to us. However, the church was suffering financial difficulties. Several felt that LaVerne's absence was the reason, as it was assumed he was the source of significant financial support. I also discovered that the six pastors who preceded me had all left due to a nervous breakdown or death, or simply left the ministry. Malta was clearly one of the infamous clergy-killing congregations. Having survived torture at the hands of the Brazilian army, I was determined they would not kill me.

Marcia Huber, Roger's wife at the Northwest Church, came to see me shortly after our arrival. She shared that her niece, Amy, who had grown up in Malta, had recently been diagnosed with melanoma cancer. She was not expected to live much longer. The following Sunday, I announced I would form a Prayer/Healing group to pray for Amy. Nearly 40 people showed up for the first meeting. I began by explaining that illness was never the Will of God, no matter what some churches had been saying for a few centuries.

I pointed out that Jesus' ministry of healing was unconditional. He never conditioned his healing on the behavior of the sick person, nor did he blame them for being ill. I then said we can assume God *always* wants to bring healing into our lives. But God needs our help and cooperation. As followers of Jesus, we can be instruments God uses to bring healing into any situation. This wasn't magic nor a matter of negotiating with God. Learning how to allow God to work with and through us was a matter of learning. I said that spiritual healing is, as Agnes had taught me, "an adventure of the human soul with God that may or may not bring physical healing, but always brings an increase of wholeness." I began explaining the ways of praying that I learned from Agnes Sanford.

The group met every Tuesday for the next six weeks, praying first and foremost for Amy but then for other people as we received requests. We had a core group of about 10–12 who continued to meet every Tuesday for three years—and continued even after we moved on. Amy seemed to improve, according to reports we received from her mother. But our group arrived on the scene too late, and after some 10 months, Amy died. However, she was spared the horrendous pain that usually accompanies the final states of melanoma cancer, for which everyone was grateful. And she showed a vibrant and joyful spirit right to the end.

In November 1988, I got a letter from our Bishop, Sheldon Duecker. It was a form letter sent to all the clergy inquiring how we felt about our ministerial appointment. I composed a fairly long letter stating that the parsonage was great and the people were responding well to my ministry for the most part, but I needed clarification as to why I was appointed to this place. I had 25 years of urban ministry experience and spoke three languages. I got no answer.

At Christmas, we received hate mail in the form of Christmas cards signed by "the Vipers," who expressed hopes that we would all die in an accident and put an end to our presence in their parsonage. The following November, I received the same mimeographed letter from Bishop Duecker, to which I responded with the same letter from the year before. Again, no answer.

When I was reappointed to Malta for the third year, I decided to take some direct action against this deliberate undermining of our ministry. I used my prerogative of being the pastor in charge to look at the financial records of the giving of the church members. I'd always avoided doing this but needed to see what was happening. I discovered eleven families had stopped giving altogether shortly after our arrival. Then, I found the Gospel lesson in the Lectionary for the following Sunday: the story in the Book of Acts about Ananias and Saphira, two early followers of Jesus. They were members of the Jerusalem Church, who sold their property like the other early Christians but did not turn over the proceeds to the Apostles. I called a few of the faithful members of the congregation, telling them we were facing a shortfall because some families had stopped giving. I asked if they would stand up in church the next day and publicly increase their pledge by $5 or $10 a week. They all agreed.

In my sermon, I pointed out that Ananias and Saphira had both dropped dead when confronted by St. Peter over their withholding. I announced there were eleven families in our congregation, most of whom were present that Sunday, who had stopped giving after our arrival. I didn't threaten them with death but simply said that they would have six weeks to pay up, or I would publish their names in the church newsletter with the amounts they'd been giving before and the zero amounts given during the past two years. I then invited others in the congregation to stand up and pledge to make up the shortfall so that the church would not be held hostage by these families. Six families immediately stood up and increased their pledges for a total amount more than the others were withholding.

By August, nine of the families had brought up to date their giving, so I only had to publish the names of two families. That included LaVerne. Everyone was shocked to learn he'd only been giving $1,200 a year. They'd been led to believe he was the major donor of the congregation and the pillar of the church. Several families gave two or three times more. The following November, Bishop Duecker and I again exchanged the same letters. But this time I called him at his home at ten o'clock in the evening. "Sheldon," I said, "I haven't heard from you about my appointment."

"Well, Fred," he responded, "we have several *important* appointments to deal with this year and aren't going to be able to deal with yours."

"If that's the case," I said, "I will need to ask you to aid me in transferring to another Annual Conference that will want to use my 'gifts and graces' in an appropriate place." I added that I understood he was having difficulties making an appointment to Broadway UMC in Chicago. "I would be happy to go there," I said. He responded, "You know they have unusual ministries there?"

"You mean because they minister to gays and lesbians?"

"Oh, you know that?"

"Sheldon, *everyone* knows that." He had tried to appoint six pastors to Broadway. Five had turned it down, and the congregation turned one down. Four days later, I was appointed to Broadway. When we arrived, I found 92 members listed on the books but could only locate 72. In my four years there, it grew to a membership of 256, being the fastest-growing congregation in the Annual Conference in terms of growth percentage.

I put in place some programs that enabled us to capture some of our many visitors as members of the church. I recruited church folks to visit on Sunday afternoons, taking a loaf of homemade date-nut bread and some literature about Broadway United Methodist Church. They were instructed *not* to go into the visitors' home but to stand at the door, express our joy at their worshiping with us, and invite them to return. If interested, they were asked to participate in the get-acquainted classes I had every month. We received 56 new members in the first year.

Broadway UMC became the home to three A.A. groups, one ALANON group, and several other community organizations.

Broadway led the Annual Conference in Missions giving in our second year there. We had an excellent music program led by a medical doctor, Rochelle Parker, who played the pipe organ and directed the choir. Many visitors came for the first time because they heard our choir as they walked past the church.

At the beginning of 1993, I looked at the scales one morning and saw I weighed 220 pounds. I was obese. I went to my doctor and asked for a physical. My blood pressure was in the 160s. He put me on a 1,100-calorie-per-day diet and urged me to start walking at least three miles a day. Argentina and I got up early every morning and walked to Lake Michigan, just a block away, and walked down to Lincoln Park and then back home—3.5 miles every morning, except Sundays. In two months, I lost 38 pounds. I felt great and bought a new wardrobe. All was well until a couple of months later, I woke up at two a.m. with excruciating pain in my abdomen. By the time I got to the E.R., the pain had diminished. They gave me some Mylanta, said I must have eaten something that didn't agree with me, and sent me home. The next day I saw my doctor, who said the same thing.

Nearly two months later, I was all dressed up and getting ready to drive up to Loyola University, where Noam Chomsky was getting an honorary degree. Without warning, I fell to the floor and began vomiting. I was nearly paralyzed by the pain. An ambulance took me to Illinois Masonic Hospital. Argentina had flown to Costa Rica with Freddie to visit her family, leaving the girls with me. Lizbeth had "graduated" to another household. While waiting in the E.R., I called her and asked her to take care of the girls when they got home from school, and to contact Argentina in Costa Rica.

After what seemed like an interminable wait, a doctor came as I was sitting on a gurney in agonizing pain and said the blood work indicated I probably had pancreatitis, a disease I knew absolutely nothing about. He asked me how much I drank. When I said I didn't, he said, "Yeah, I've heard that before." About 90% of the cases of pancreatitis are caused by alcohol abuse. They gave me a shot of Demerol to help with the pain and put me into a hospital bed, where I stayed for the next 28 days. Eventually, a specialist in gastro problems came and confirmed I had pancreatitis, and there was nothing they could do except give me liquids intravenously and look to see if I had died yet. The pain was unremitting. I read later that pancreatitis is considered to produce the closest thing to childbirth pains a man could experience. They gave me Demerol every two hours, but it wore off in less than an hour and left me begging for another shot like a heroin junkie.

My personal physician came to the hospital but didn't dare to go to my room. I was to find out later he should have done an ultrasound on my gall bladder when I was in the Emergency Room earlier. That would have revealed gallstones, as when people have a significant weight loss in a short period, they have a 50% chance of developing gallstones. One of the stones popped out and blocked my common bile duct and backed up all the bile onto my pancreas, which began to digest itself—pancreatitis.

By chance, a member of Broadway UMC, who worked in the hospital as a psychologist, happened to walk by and see me sitting in pain. He didn't know I was hospitalized and asked what was going on. I contacted our children's pediatrician through him, who had just changed his practice to General Medicine. He came to see me, and I said I would hire him to take charge of my case if he put me on a pain pump. He agreed, so I fired my doctor.

After eight days in the hospital in severe and debilitating pain, I was put on a pain pump, which is simply a device that allowed me to push a button and I would receive a dose of morphine. I could push the button as much as I wanted, but the device would only give me so much morphine per hour. Within five hours, the pain was gone, and I could sleep. The pain was feeding on itself, keeping my body tense and cramped, which provoked more pain. Once that cycle was broken by the morphine pump, the pain went away and didn't come back.

I wasn't fed until the very last day. I had an intravenous drip that put some kind of swamp water into my veins for nourishment. The hospital charged my insurance company $1,000 a day for that bag of stuff they made in their own pharmacy. They also charged $4 for one Tylenol. And they charged $15,000 rent for the pump. I discovered later that I could have bought one of those pumps for about $10,000. My final bill was $158,000 for the 28 days.

Argentina flew home as soon as she could and came to hold my hand as often as possible. After about 18 days, I called Florence Butler in Malta. She had been one of the members of our prayer/healing group at that church. I asked her to come pray for me. Florence confessed she was afraid to drive into the city. So she drove to DeKalb and took the train and then a taxi. She entered my room, and after a short conversation, she laid hands on me and prayed. That's when I began to get well. I was visited by several of my clergy friends, but none of them prayed with or for me. They would chat for a while and then, on their way out, would say, "I'll be praying for you." But I knew they wouldn't. Or if they did, it would be an "if it be thy will" kind of prayer, which is useless at best.

The nursing care at Illinois Masonic was terrible. I was not bathed once, not even a sponge bath. I don't blame the nurses. They were overworked and didn't have time for luxuries like baths. I would hear the night nurse, a sweet Filipino woman, crying in desperation at three-thirty a.m. She had 15 patients and simply could not keep up with their needs.

After 20 days, they had me start walking up and down the hallways to regain strength. On day 26, a light meal came for me. I looked at it carefully and threw it in the wastebasket. The chief dietitian came charging up, demanding to know why I'd thrown out the food. When I told her it was filled with fat and oil, she apologized and admitted I was right and should not have been given that meal. She actually thanked me for not eating it.

When I was released, I walked the six blocks to our home on Broadway. I was in my pulpit the following Sunday, thanking the congregation for their prayers. Florence Butler was in the congregation, and I told everyone her prayers had begun my healing. I had to return to the hospital six weeks later to have my gallbladder removed. It was gangrenous and had to be removed the old-fashioned way. I had 14 inches of staples to show for it. Three days later, I walked home again and was in my pulpit the following Sunday.

About a year later, I noticed what looked like a canker sore on my tongue. Providentially, I had an appointment with my dentist that very day. I asked him what to do for it, thinking he would give me some stuff for canker sores. He looked at it carefully and said he wanted me to see an oncological dentist. The next week, I saw the specialist who did a biopsy. A couple days later, he called to say it was malignant and needed to be removed ASAP.

I went to his office the following Tuesday. He numbed my tongue and took out a slice in the middle, about ¼ inch thick and ½ inch into my tongue, getting what he called "clear margins." The biopsy looked good. I had to go back every three months for the next year, then every six months, and finally once a year. Then, I was declared healed. I had smoked a pipe for about five years, though I had quit five years before all this happened, and it most likely was the tobacco that caused the cancer. The doctor also said I was fortunate I had seen my dentist that day. If I had waited even as little as a month or two, it could have spread uncontrollably and been fatal.

Somewhere along this timeline, I discovered that the original church building had burned down in 1979. The church had been able to build a new sanctuary on top of the foundations of the original church. Still, they didn't have enough money to put in an elevator, so the City of Chicago would not allow the use of the basement. It had become a dumping ground. I contacted the

National Board of Missions of the United Methodist Church and discovered they would loan us $90,000 to build out the basement. I found a company that would put in a lift that satisfied the City for only $15,000. So we rehired the architect who had designed the sanctuary, and with an increase of only $200/month on the mortgage payment, we added an additional 5,000 square feet of space for the church, doubling the size of the building. Our architect designed a kitchen and bathrooms with showers so we could receive youth groups and other visitors. We even had a TV corner, where on Sunday afternoons, people could gather to watch the Chicago Bears or, later in the year, Michal Jordan and the Bulls.

By the end of the second year, we had standing room only in the sanctuary. I called the architect to see if we could knock out a wall and expand the seating, but he said all the walls were weight-bearing and could not be removed. He added that when he was designing the sanctuary, he suggested they allow for expansion, but the leadership at the time didn't seem to want the church to grow. So we had to go to two services, which can be problematic as it creates two congregations that are inevitably hard to blend.

Our choir did not have a choir room, so we made the choir president the Chair of the new Building Committee, wanting to have the "new" basement provide space for one. Our architect designed a huge choir room with soundproofing so that the choir could practice while other groups were using the basement. I served as the general contractor, which saved the church at least $12,000.

All was going along splendidly until July, when Rochelle Parker, our choir director, came to me and said the choir didn't want to go to the basement. Her husband, a former Navy pilot, was paraplegic, having been injured in an accident while crop-dusting after he left the Navy. He was to be the principal beneficiary of the new lift to the basement. As a favor to me, I asked her to encourage the choir to go to their new choir room in September, when the basement was to be finished. If, by the end of the year, they found it to be unsatisfactory, I would go to the Administrative Council on their behalf and ask for a change of venue. After a long conversation, she agreed.

But at the close of the August meeting of the Administrative Council, when the chairperson asked for any new business, Rochelle informed the Council that the choir refused to go to the basement. Keith Eccarius, the choir president and the building committee chair, knew nothing of this. A long and heated discussion ensued. I said that though we had instigated and carried out the build-out primarily for the choir to have their room, I did not care where they met. They could meet in my garage if they wanted to. But the decision was up to the Council, not the pastor. With that, I excused myself and went home.

After a lengthy discussion, the Council decided that the choir could continue in the bright and airy room on the upper level it had been sharing with the Sunday School children. The children would be transferred to the choir room in the basement—with no windows at all. This created tremendous tension within the choir and among the congregation as a whole. I tried to stay out of it, but of course, that was impossible. I somehow became the villain.

Rochelle began playing 20–25-minute preludes to the service, starting at 10:25 and ending between 10:45 and 10:50. This meant our service ended at 11:45 rather than at 11:30. This seemed to be necessary to many of our members, as the yuppies in Lakeview had full social calendars, including Sunday afternoon activities, ranging from a Cubs or Bears game to a visit to the Lincoln Park Zoo, or shopping at a nearby mall. Those 20 additional minutes to our worship time threw off their schedules. And, naturally, the preacher got the blame for the extended service, though the actual time of the service had not changed at all, except for the mini-organ concert at the beginning.

The Staff/Parish Relations Committee (personnel) frequently met with Rochelle to insist that her prelude was to be just that: a prelude of 5–7 minutes, as she had been doing for years. To no avail. Her mini-concerts continued. Tensions mounted until, in May, the Staff/Parish Relations Committee, of which I was not a member, fired Rochelle, having warned her multiple times about that as an inevitable outcome if she didn't change her ways. This was a total shock to the congregation. The reaction was violent, in part, because David Gunnel, one of the choir members, broke into my office and stole the church mailing list. Along with some cohorts, he began sending out hate mail aimed at me. He got Eleanor Bose, one of the oldest church members, to sign the letters attacking me as the "unreasonable pastor" who fired the beloved choir director without cause.

Things got to the point that Argentina stopped attending the services and wrote a letter to Bishop Duecker announcing her resignation from the United Methodist Church. She said she could not continue to be part of a so-called Christian community that was so hate-filled and malicious toward its pastor. Our D.S. did nothing to help in the situation. After I announced my early retirement, she only communicated with me to ask who I thought might be a good replacement. I suggested my dear friend, the Rev. Greg Dell, then pastor at Euclid Avenue UMC in Oak Park, as he had a very positive position on LGBTQ issues. He was, in fact, appointed to Broadway to follow us.

In June 1995, I would have completed 40 years in the United Methodist Church's ministry, qualifying me for retirement. I would be 62 and qualify for early Social Security. I began exploring possibilities for a place to land. I had gone to Brazil in February to help the Church of the Brethren deal with a problem they were having with a church in Rio Verde. While there, I spent a week in Rio testing the waters as a possible place to retire. I was still suffering from my love affair with Brazil and was dying to return. Argentina had enjoyed our month there as a tourist and was willing to go.

In June of 1995, we went to DeKalb, Illinois, for the Northern Illinois Annual Conference. As is their custom, they had a special recognition service for the retiring pastors one afternoon. Each pastor was given ten minutes to say whatever they wanted about their years in the Methodist ministry. When it was my turn, I said God had been very good to me through the ups and downs of the past 40 years. I said I was eternally grateful to all who prayed for me and made phone calls to members of Congress when I was in prison. But, I added, as an institution, the United Methodist Church has crapped on me at pretty much every opportunity.

When I returned from Brazil after 17 days in their torture chambers, I was met at JFK airport in New York by two executives of the Board of Global Ministries. They promptly told me I had resigned. They didn't fire me—they *resigned* me. Without any explanation or physical examination, they simply ushered me out the door without honoring their obligations for separation benefits. I spent the next 22 months unemployed and finally went to Costa Rica, where I spent 12 years making a living running my own company. Then, when I returned to the conference, I was sent to an entry-level church despite having 25 years of pastoral experience and speaking three languages. My dad had told me when I accepted the call to be a missionary in Brazil that I had just ruined my career.

So, I concluded, I'm grateful to God. Oh, by the way, the Church of the Brethren has asked me to be their supervising elder for their work in Brazil, which, I believe, is the same as being a Bishop. Bishop Dueker handed me my retirement certificate but didn't shake my hand.

Return to Brazil

The Rev. Acyr Goulart had been a seminary student in São Paulo and followed me at the church in Itaipava. By 1995, he was vice-rector of Bennett Metodista Universidade, the Methodist University in Rio. He said he would like for me to teach at the university and guaranteed me a job there, which would complete what we needed to live in Rio. While in Rio, I did a market study, checking the cost of living, and discovered it was about 90% of what it costs to live in Chicago. Doing all the numbers, it looked like we could return to Brazil. In mid-June 1995, we started on another chapter in our adventure through life.

Just before leaving Broadway, one of our closest friends in the church, who had been supportive of me when I was in the hospital and through the Rochelle saga, came to me and asked, "Fred, how do you know this is what God wants you to do—going to Brazil?"

I responded, "That's an excellent question. And I have to say I don't *know* with certainty this is God's will for us. But we have looked at it carefully, and it seems to be going in the right direction. But I know that if I'm wrong, and this is not God's plan for us, God will help us find the right direction. That's how it has worked out for me before, and as I read 'The Story' in the Scriptures, I see that God has done that for others through the ages." I then went a step further and reminded her of the experience of John Wesley, who went to Georgia, sure that God wanted him to convert the Indians, but after three years of total failure, returned home to find his encounter with God's Spirit that led him to travel up and down all of England for the next 50 years preaching the unconditional love of God for all.

We packed up and flew to Rio via Miami. After about 90 minutes flying south over the Caribbean, we turned around. In another 90 minutes, we were landing again in Miami. The airline did not inform us of anything; it just said we had to wait at our gate before re-embarking. We waited until two a.m. At that point, the passengers were in near-revolt. The airline said our flight would not continue. They put us into an airport hotel and scheduled us to leave at ten p.m. the following evening. Finally, they explained that a generator on one of the engines had shown a defect.

Acyr had assured me he'd be waiting at the airport, but we didn't see him. So, I loaded my family and our 10 suitcases into two Volkswagen Beetle taxis, and we headed to Bennett Methodist University in Flamengo. I inquired for Acyr and was told he was in his new home on the Barra da Tijuca beach, a new extension of the luxury beach areas of Rio, past Copacabana, Leblon, and Ipanema. His secretary said his new apartment had just been handed over to him, and he was busy moving. He didn't have a phone installed yet, so there was no way to communicate with him. He hadn't made any arrangements for a place for us to stay. No one knew we were arriving.

We were offered a place to stay in the dormitory of the Colegio, in a large room with 20 bunk beds and a bathroom. Acyr had also assured me that he and my dear friend, Rev. Wilson Guerierro[6], would have scouted three or four apartments for us near Bennett. But the next day, no Acyr, no way to communicate with him, and no flats in sight. So, I looked for a Realtor. After about two hours, I found one willing to assist us, though he said there wasn't much available. There had been an economic downturn since I last visited, and the apartment owners were simply not putting their apartments on the market. Real estate laws in Brazil made it difficult to evict a renter, so the owners preferred to have the apartment empty.

After two days of searching, we found nothing of interest and we finally got in touch with Acyr. With no apologies, he said he had a cousin who had a lovely apartment for rent in Petropolis, the former summer capital of Emperor Dom Pedro. It was only an hour away from the university. He said he could loan us a car to go see it.

We didn't hear from Acyr again, and no car showed up. So, semi-desperate, we rented a car and drove to Petropolis. However, we couldn't find the cousin's address, and no one answered the phone number Acyr had given us. So, we went over the mountains to Teresópolis, where I lived from 1966 to 1967. I enjoyed showing it to Argentina and our children. I located Sr. Josía, who had been the lay leader at the Methodist Church when I was pastor there.

In those days, he was poor, living in a shack with a dirt floor with his wife and three children. He would arrive on Sunday with all five of them on his bicycle. But now he was a prosperous attorney, having served as the city attorney for several years, and was the proud owner of a lovely home and a new car. He received us with open arms and offered to help us find a place to live in Teresópolis.

I knew commuting would be a stretch, but I assumed I would teach only two days a week. Josía contacted a friend who had a place for sale outside the city. He drove us out there, and we met the owner. It was a charming summer place set on a large piece of land. We negotiated the price and decided to move in.

As I had agreed with the Church of the Brethren to be their supervising elder in Brazil, I needed to drive out to Rio Verde, Goiás, so we needed to buy a car. Josía had a friend who was selling a recent model Fiat. It met our needs, and we bought it on the spot. The next day, we headed out to Rio Verde. When we arrived, the lay leader of the local Church of the Brethren, Divino Onaldo, was expecting us. He welcomed us into his home with his wife and two children. He was a local businessman, working in public relations with some radio stations. The former pastor, who had founded the church, had tried to sell the property and take off with the funds. I managed to get an attorney to block that, so the local congregation kept the property. It was a close call, but we won.

Next, we drove to Goiás Velho, the original capital of the State of Goiás, today a colonial and UNESCO relic, where my dear friend, Father Marcelo, had founded a Benedictine monastery with a community of a dozen brothers. Marcelo had been there for more than 25 years, and the community reflected his dedication to following in the footsteps of Jesus of Nazareth and Frei Bento, the founder of the Benedictine order. They had a marvelous chapel decorated with local art, including wood carvings by one of the Brothers. The refectory was like a medieval monastery; homemade bread was a staple of all their meals. Traditional beans, rice, and occasional meat, with salads made from vegetables that the Brothers had grown themselves, completed the menus.

We enjoyed three days at the monastery. Argentina and the children enjoyed it immensely. Some children from the neighborhood played with us. Then we headed back to Teresópolis. But at this time, I had an exceedingly painful recurrence of pancreatitis. It was the trip from hell for me, as I doubled up over the steering wheel with intense pain in my abdomen.

We had planned to stop at the colonial city of Ouro Preto in the State of Minas Gerais on our way home. However, my health was such that we only stayed overnight and a couple of hours the next day before heading home to get some medical care. I spent a couple of days in the hospital in Teresópolis. When we got back to our new home, Argentina observed it would be nearly impossible for us to live there in the long run, as it was 11 kilometers (six and a half miles) from the city of Teresópolis on a dirt/gravel road that would be nearly impassable during the rainy season. So, we had to undo the purchase agreement and look for another place. We finally found a lovely home we could not afford but felt we had no choice, so we signed a rental contract for one year, hoping to find something else during that time.

I then went to the private school that had been recommended to us for our children: CEM. It was owned and operated by an understanding and helpful Portuguese-Brazilian woman. Our three children did not speak Portuguese, and the school year in Brazil ran from February to December, so they would drop in the middle of the year. It was agreed they would be accepted as "auditors" from September to December then register as regular students in February. All three were fluent in Brazilian Portuguese within the three months of auditing. They insisted that Argentina and I never speak English with them in public, as they didn't want anyone to know they were not Brazilian.

I started teaching at Bennett in September. Acyr had assigned me three courses to teach: Ethics, Anthropology, and Contemporary Ideologies. I felt unqualified to teach any of those subjects. I took a course in Ethics at the seminary in 1958. I had never taken a course in Anthropology, though I had read Margaret Mead, Ashley Montague, Oscar Lewis, Malinowski, and others. As to Contemporary Ideologies, I had no idea what that even meant. My "dear friend" Acyr, had assigned me to teach three nights a week, from seven to ten p.m., which meant I either had to drive up the mountain to Teresópolis or take the subway across Rio at ten p.m. and then catch a bus up to Teresópolis, in either case arriving home after midnight.

I spent my mornings reading everything possible to prepare for the evening classes. As I had never taught these subjects, I felt I was staying one chapter ahead of my students. Then, I discovered that Bennett Methodist University was simply a diploma mill. For my Ethics course, I had 90 students jammed into a room about 15 feet wide by 65 feet long. There was no P.A. system, so I was forced to give most of my lectures to disinterested students by yelling. About 70% of the students smoked all the time, so I usually could not even see the people in the back through the haze. Ethics was a required course for Law and Architecture students who had no interest in the subject. The Architecture students simply didn't show up for the seven p.m. class but went across the street to a bar and enjoyed drinking beer for an hour. I didn't take that personally. They didn't even know what I looked like, so it wasn't me. But they were outraged when I flunked them for not attending the class, not doing any of the work or taking the mid-term and final exams. They circulated a petition to have me removed from the university faculty.

For the Anthropology class, I chose *O Povo Brasileiro* (The Brazilian People) by the world-famous Brazilian anthropologist Darcy Ribeiro as the textbook. It was a truly magnificent work that traced the history and development of the people of Brazil. The book cost $20. This produced another petition for my removal. Students were accustomed to having their professor take one textbook to the Xerox center of the university and have it copied, chapter by chapter. The students would buy each chapter from the Center instead of purchasing the book. I explained that those copied chapters would cost twice the amount of the book and that copying and selling copies of a copyrighted book was unethical and even illegal. To no avail. They would be damned before they would actually buy a book.

I discovered that the rector of the university, a man I had in my Systematic Theology class back in 1966 whose Portuguese I had to correct and who hardly passed the course because of his limited intellectual capacity, was being paid $10,000 a month, plus a new car each year, plus several expenses paid like lunches at expensive restaurants. During my first year at Bennett, the university paid the medical costs for his pregnant lover/secretary without his wife's knowledge. I also found out he'd employed some 200 people, primarily members of his extended family, to work at the university in various capacities, ranging from the kitchen to the laundry to the cleaning staff and some teachers. Acyr was vice rector, paid $8,500 per month, plus car. He showed up at the university two or three times a week for a few hours, and that was it.

Meanwhile, I was paid $12.00 per class hour. I was given 12 class hours per week, earning $144 each week. I got no pay for class preparation, preparing and correcting exams, not to mention all the travel. And I was paid more than most professors because I had *two* Master's degrees. The others were paid only $10 per class hour. The students were charged $12 per credit, which meant $36 for a three-credit course. This meant that the 90 students in my unethical Ethics class paid the university $3,240 to attend my lectures three nights a week for 12 weeks, while I, the professor, was getting paid $432 for that semester of teaching. It did not come as a surprise that the university was declared totally bankrupt in 2015 for not having paid to the government the Social Security taxes they'd withheld from all their employees for more than 15 years.

At the same time, our children were doing very well in school and had a circle of friends that kept them busy and happy. Regarding our family, all was well, and we were enjoying ourselves—however, there were other problems. Argentina was constantly constrained by the racism she felt at nearly every point.

CHAPTER 10

Praise the Lord!

I will extol the Lord at all times; his praise will always be on my lips.

I will glory in the Lord; let the afflicted hear and rejoice.

Glorify the Lord with me; let us exalt his name together.

I sought the Lord, and he answered me; he delivered me from all my fears.

Those who look to him are radiant; their faces are never covered with shame.

This poor man called, and the Lord heard him; he saved him out of all his troubles.

The angel of the Lord encamps around those who fear him, and he delivers them.

Taste and see that the Lord is good; blessed is the one who takes refuge in him.

Fear the Lord, you his holy people, for those who fear him lack nothing.

The lions may grow weak and hungry, but those who seek the Lord lack no good thing.

Come, my children, listen to me; I will teach you the fear of the Lord.

Whoever of you loves life and desires to see many good days, keep your tongue from evil and your lips from telling lies.

Turn from evil and do good; seek peace and pursue it.

The eyes of the Lord are on the righteous, and his ears are attentive to their cry;

But the face of the Lord is against those who do evil, to blot out their name from the earth.

The righteous cry out, and the Lord hears them; he delivers them from all their troubles.

The Lord is close to the brokenhearted and saves those who are crushed in spirit.

The righteous person may have many troubles, but the Lord delivers him from them all; he protects all his bones, not one of them will be broken.

Evil will slay the wicked; the foes of the righteous will be condemned.

The Lord will rescue his servants; no one who takes refuge in him will be condemned.

—Psalm 34 New International Version (NIV)

AGNES SANFORD HAD an excellent illustration of why our prayers often seem to go unanswered. What about the woman, Agnes said, who drops into your home on a hot summer's day for an unexpected visit. After sitting down, she asks if you could provide her some lemonade to help her cool off. Of course, you say, and go to the kitchen. Soon, you return with a tall glass of icy lemonade. As you offer it to her, instead of taking it and enjoying it, your friend says, "Won't you please bring me some lemonade?" Again, you say, "Here. Enjoy this lemonade." To which she replies, "Please, please, please, I'm dying of thirst. Please just get me some lemonade."

Our prayers are often like that: we spend all of our time begging God for something but don't know how to receive it and say *Thank You*. We never open our hands and hearts to receive what God is offering us.

Merlin Carothers, a Methodist pastor, wrote a series of books about Praising the Lord. The first, *From Prison to Praise,* described his journey of becoming a pastor. He proclaimed that praising God is the way to allow God to give us the blessings of the Abundant Life that Jesus talked about. I am not able to thank God and offer praise when I hear of a child with leukemia or how a drunken driver killed a whole family. I don't believe that everything happens for a reason.

But in my own life, when I can respond with a feeling of underlying joy, good things can come even in and through bad things. That's what St. Paul meant in Romans 8: *And we know that in all things God works for the good of those who love Him, who have been called according to His purpose.* Paul doesn't mean that everything that happens is God's plan. Instead, God can work in and through us as we follow God's purpose to bring good out of every situation and event.

I would not dream of saying it was God's will that the Brazilian military kidnapped and tortured and then expelled me from Brazil. I cannot say it was God's will that the CIA and the Methodist Church shit-listed me so that I couldn't get work in the US. That was a tremendously painful experience. And I don't think that God "willed" my marriage to Tereza to fail. But I do insist, as a declaration of faith, that my underlying faith posture through all of this was one of affirming God's presence in my life and a desire to be of service to God's purpose of love, peace, and justice in this world, God was able to bring to me, in and through and despite all of the above—and more—the most beautiful blessing imaginable—a rewarding and fulfilling marriage to a wonderful woman—after two failures. *Praise the Lord!* I say. But there is more.

My decision to return to Brazil was a colossal mistake. I'd told Argentina wonderful things about Brazil, how there wasn't any racism, how more than 60% of the population was of some sort of mixed race, how there are over 40 different words in Brazilian Portuguese to describe racial color—which meant that it was nearly impossible for them to discriminate against people based on color. It wasn't just Black and White. It was *café com leite; Pelé; mulato, pardo, negrito, moreno, moreno da terra,* etc. We went to Brazil excited about "going home" and Argentina and our kids finding a place in the sun.

Even before we left the Rio airport on our arrival, Argentina found people looking at her strangely, a beautiful *morena,* or *mulata,* in the company of a *gringo,* with three small children of mixed race. She felt an unspoken antagonism. I'd been looking at Brazil the only way I'd learned to: as a white, educated male. It looked pretty good to me. But it wasn't the same for my Black wife.

When I was in Costa Rica (1976–1988), I purchased the technology for manufacturing a complete line of additives for concrete from a Mexican who sold the formulas because he was having terrible economic problems due to Mexico's financial difficulties (1982). The products were excellent, and we actually got into the business of making them in Costa Rica.

To complement my teaching income at Bennett, I decided to manufacture and sell the line of concrete additives for which I'd purchased the technology in Costa Rica. I formed a company called Technocreto, Ltd. and set up a small plant in Teresópolis. However, the products did not work as well with Brazilian cement as in Costa Rica. After floundering around, I encountered a chemical engineer who taught at the University of Rio de Janeiro in *Nova Friburgo.* He also manufactured concrete additives and had sold about a million dollars' worth of them to the company that built the enormous hydroelectric dam at *Itaipú,* on the border with Paraguay. After that, he sold the plant and had to sign an agreement that he would never again manufacture additives. But he knew more about the chemistry of additives than anyone in Brazil and, I suspect, anywhere else. He was fascinated with concrete and loved to make it work better.

I drove the 60 miles across the mountains to *Friburgo* to talk with this chemical engineer. He was interested in my products, and after some negotiation, he agreed to study the formulas and see what he could do to improve them. Within a couple of weeks, he came up with a fantastic solution: we added an ingredient to our retardant, the principal additive we made to slow the process of setting and avoid cracking in hot climates. I took a sample to the engineer in Rio, who reported that it was absolutely marvelous. He said that by switching to our product, *Durotard,* he could increase the net profit per cubic meter of concrete from his plant by $2. Since he was churning out 20,000 cubic meters each month, that was a $40,000 increase in net profit per month.

Expecting to get a massive order from him, I was stunned when he told me he wouldn't buy any. "I'm a salaried employee," he said, "and I get a good salary. When I came to this job two years ago, they were already using the additive I've got now. If I make a change and anything goes wrong in the next couple of years, I will lose my job. And I won't even get to smell the additional profit the company will make using your product. I'm going to play it safe." No amount of persuasion convinced him to change his mind. I found the same response from a half-dozen other engineers in other plants. Everyone loved the product. But they were all afraid to make any changes.

By this time, we'd been in Brazil for about 15 months. We enjoyed our home in Teresópolis. The kids were happy in their school and had lots of friends. However, my teaching experience was frustrating, and our financial situation was deteriorating month by month. By August of 1996, I was feeling desperate. We were sinking into poverty. I couldn't see how we could keep the children in their school the following year. Putting them in the public school in Brazil would guarantee a lousy education and a permanent blight on their future.

I had another attack of pancreatitis, which put me in the hospital for several days. I went to Dr. Rómulo, who did an ultrasound and discovered I had developed a pseudo-cyst on my pancreas. It held about a pint of liquid and was putting pressure on my intestines and stomach. I needed surgery to drain it. Argentina and I had been praying for my health. One evening, in a symbolic gesture, she placed a sharp kitchen knife on the bedside table next to me, along with a bottle of alcohol and some cotton balls. She lit a votive candle, and we prayed together that the Spirit of God would come into my body and do whatever was needed to restore my health. We concluded with a prayer of thanksgiving, simply offering our heartfelt gratitude to God that our prayer was being heard.

The following day, I awoke feeling much better. I had an appointment with my doctor that afternoon to schedule the surgery. Instead, I said I wanted another ultrasound, as I felt much better. He said there was no point in that, but I insisted. Finally, with a measure of disgust, he ordered me to get another ultrasound.

He shook his head when he looked at the results. The pseudo-cyst was gone. I told him about our prayers. "If I were not a Christian, I would not believe this," he said. However, as a good scientist, he still had doubts and ordered a CT scan to confirm all was well. The CT Scan showed only a tiny shadow, about an inch in diameter, indicating that there might have been a problem at one point, but it was gone. Dr. Rómulo was literally stunned. He asked for my permission to take my case to a meeting of gastro physicians in Belo Horizonte. He'd never seen a case of a documented pseudo-cyst that "went away."

Meanwhile, our financial problems continued. The cost of living was going up, and the exchange rate for the dollar, in which our pensions were paid, was going down. It became clear I needed more income or we'd have to take our children out of their private school. I went to Acyr at Bennett and asked if I could get more teaching hours. No. I approached Bishop Paulo Lockman to see if he could appoint me to a Methodist church. He didn't reply to my request nor accept my solicitation for a person-to-person interview. Nothing.

I became increasingly depressed and desperate. Then, I recalled what I'd been preaching for many years: Praise God in all circumstances. That is how we open ourselves up and allow God to work through difficult situations. I proposed to Argentina that we start our day by praising God. We decided to read together Psalm 34 as a kind of mantra, a way of praising God in our difficult situation. Things got worse. But we continued praising God for being with us, caring about us, and caring for us. Psalm 34. Every day.

About two weeks later, I noticed on the last page of my current issue of *Christian Century* magazine a small one-inch box saying that the Florida Council of Churches was looking for a new executive director. Persons interested were requested to send a resume to the Rev. Dr. Barry Snowden in Altamonte Springs, Florida. I got together the requested papers and sent them off. I was not too hopeful, but felt it was worth a shot. I didn't have any other real options. I didn't tell Argentina because I didn't want to raise false hopes.

I made an international phone call to former Methodist Bishop Jim Armstrong, who I knew was then serving as pastor of a Congregational Church in the Orlando area. I asked Jim if I could use him as a reference. After I explained what I was requesting, he laughed at the other end of the phone call and said, "I guess you don't know that I am the president of the Florida Council of Churches."

Jim said he was glad to let me use his name as a reference, but I knew he wouldn't push my name in an inappropriate way. So I waited. Much to my surprise, even while reading Psalm 34 and praising God in our morning devotions daily, I got a package with a letter, a VHS cassette, and a set of questions to answer on camera. The letter said I had made the shortlist and they were doing this virtual interview with three other people. So, at that point, I told Argentina what I had done. We set up our video camera, and she recorded my interview for the Florida Council of Churches. We sent off the video and continued praising God daily with Psalm 34.

Three weeks later, when I got home from my daily labors, Argentina met me enthusiastically, saying Jim Armstrong had called and wanted me to call him as soon as possible. She was convinced I had gotten the job. I tried to calm her (and myself) and made the call. When Jim came on the line, the news was not good. He said that the Committee had decided to go with another candidate, Dr. Barry Snowden, a Lutheran pastor (ELCA), who happened to be the vice-president of the Council. Snowden was a Florida native and pastor of a church in Winter Springs, Florida, wouldn't incur money transferring him from another country. He was well-known, well-liked and seemed to be the perfect candidate.

We continued to Praise the Lord in all things and began every day with Psalm 34 and our prayers of thanksgiving. I kept looking for ways to increase my income. By then, we were into the first week of December, and the new school year loomed.

The week before Christmas, when I got home from my deeply frustrating day at work with Tecnocreto, Argentina met me with word that Jim had called again and wanted me to call him ASAP. He said that Barry Snowden's Bishop could not allow him to be executive director of the Council. He had just started a new congregation, and the Bishop felt the new congregation would fall apart if Barry left at that time. So, the Council wanted to know if I would be willing to accept the post as an interim director for 18 months. Without hesitation, I said, "Yes!" Jim said I had to fly to Orlando the first week in January for an interview with the Committee. If all went well, I would start work as the interim exec on March 1.

I felt confident that being back in the States as interim executive director of the Florida Council of Churches for 18 months would allow me to find a more permanent position. This was a life preserver for me and our family. Praise the Lord!

On the first Tuesday of January 1997, I flew to Orlando, where Jim Armstrong met me at the airport. He had arranged for me to have breakfast the next day with Barry Snowden to get to know him and some of his hopes and dreams for the Council. The Committee would meet the following morning at ten a.m. at the First Congregational Church of Winter Springs, where Jim was the senior pastor. Barry and I hit it off well during our breakfast. We were clearly on the same page regarding ecumenism. At ten a.m. I went across the street to the church for my meeting with the Committee.

To my surprise, one of the members of the Committee was Dr. Peter Duisberg, whom I had known years before in Costa Rica. Peter was a soil scientist in Costa Rica on a contract with USAID, providing technical support for a Costa Rican organization and advising on various development projects. He and his wife, Annabelle, had been active members of the Union Church in San José, where I had been Associate Pastor. They were members of the Prayer/Healing group that had met in our home for five years.

Jim was the Chair of the Committee and began by introducing the 12 members, representing various denominational members of the Council. They asked all the right questions. About 30 minutes into the interview, Peter interrupted and said, "The question isn't if Fred Morris is good enough for the Florida Council of Churches, but whether the Council is good enough for Fred Morris." I was thoroughly embarrassed by this declaration, but it was pretty well received, as they had clearly been impressed by my answers to their questions.

Barry stuck his head into the room and asked Jim to step out briefly. Jim excused himself and left. The Committee continued asking me questions. At one point, they asked me if I had any questions. The only thing I insisted was I would not accept the post if it meant I couldn't be considered for the permanent position as executive director if circumstances changed. They agreed. Jim returned and resumed the Chair. He then said Barry's Bishop had told him that morning he could not be considered for the post even in 18 months. There was no way to keep that a secret, and he would immediately become a lame-duck pastor, which would, the Bishop feared, break up the fledgling congregation. So, Barry had to withdraw his name permanently.

This was a stunning development for the Committee, but they responded by asking if I'd be willing to accept the position of executive director and how long I would be willing to serve. They didn't know I was 64. I said that I'd be willing to serve for ten years. They agreed, and I accepted the position.

Praise the Lord! Again, I say. *Rejoice!*

Jim and I returned to his home, where I had to wait until evening to call Argentina with the news. Then, we began looking for a place to live. Jim contacted a Realtor in his congregation, and we went house hunting the following day. Next, Jim took me to the offices of the Council in Orlando and introduced me to the staff. We had a Secretary/Treasurer and an associate director, Basil Nichols, a former Catholic priest who had left the priesthood to marry. Basil headed up an employment agency for immigrants that the Council ran, financed by funding from the National Council of Churches. There were five women on the staff of that agency. They were all Latinas and were delighted that I spoke Spanish.

At five p.m., which was eight p.m. in Brazil, I called Argentina with the news. As anticipated, she was ecstatic, really couldn't believe it. I told her I'd look for a house for us the next day. The Realtor did what he called a windshield search, driving by eight houses that met my criteria: at least three bedrooms and two baths and under $100k. Of the eight, I eliminated five from the windshield, then after lunch, we went back to the three I liked. By four p.m., I made an offer on a house in a residential community on Blades Court in Winter Springs. It was accepted the next morning, and I filled out a ton of papers. That evening, Jim and his wife took me to see the film *Evita.* Saturday morning, I boarded a plane to Brazil and prepared for the new chapter in our life together.

CHAPTER 11

Florida Council of Churches

To our dismay, we discovered that Argentina's green card had expired. When we moved to Brazil, the law stated that those with green cards could be outside the US for no more than 24 months, or their residency status would be canceled. We had been planning for her to return to the US for a month in June and then return to Brazil. But now we were planning to return to the US indefinitely, we were informed that the law had changed, and after only 12 months away, Argentina's residency had been canceled. We had to apply for a new visa for her.

At that point, we encountered what people worldwide know: the US Consulate is not the least bit friendly toward foreigners who want to travel to the US, either as tourists or as people seeking permanent residency. We were given a pile of papers to fill out and then informed that she would have to take a special HIV blood test. That would take at least a week. The fact that we had tickets purchased for travel in five days didn't interest them.

Argentina went to Dr. Rómulo's office on Thursday to explain the situation. He took her to the lab himself, ordered the test, and said he wanted the results that afternoon. She showed up at the Consulate in Rio with the required paperwork and the negative HIV test results. But they weren't through. When she returned to pick up her visa on Monday, they said all their computers were down. On Tuesday, I went to the airport in Rio with our three children and eight suitcases and boarded our eleven p.m. flight to Miami without Argentina. She stayed with some friends in Rio, hoping her visa would be ready the next day.

I rented a vehicle for us and our eight suitcases. Freddie was 12, Raquel, 11 and Gabriela 10. I drove to an Orlando motel, where I unloaded the kids and bags. Then, I went to our realtor's office to sign the final papers on our house and get the keys. The following day, we drove back to the Orlando Airport, stopping at IHOP for breakfast, and then waited anxiously to see if Argentina had made it. Finally, her plane from Miami arrived—and she was on it!

The immigration officials in Miami had treated her like they do so many "immigrants" and tourists. She had been taken into a windowless room and interrogated with questions that implied that she was either coming illegally or was a terrorist. After about 90 minutes, they let her go, and she made her connecting flight to Orlando at the very last minute.

We had checked out of our motel and had all our bags in the car, so we drove to our new house, which I had purchased without Argentina even having had a chance to see pictures. I was more than nervous, fearing she might not like it. But she loved it, as did the children. The next day, I went to the local school, which was new and marvelous, and registered the children. They started classes the following Monday.

On March 1, I went to the Ecumenical Center in Orlando, where the Florida Council of Churches had its offices, the Florida Presbytery, and the Christian Church to begin my new job. The woman who was the Secretary/Treasurer told me on arrival that she had more than $20,000 of outstanding bills to be paid, and we did not have funds to pay them. One of the questions I neglected to ask during my interview was about the Council's finances. It was destitute. The 26 denominations that comprised the Council needed to contribute more to keep us going, and we needed an endowment.

I immediately ran to Jim Armstrong and asked, "What am I supposed to do to pay these bills and meet our payroll?" Jim and I contacted the denominations with pleas for support. The Florida Annual Conference of the United Methodist Church, with seven hundred local churches, being the largest Annual Conference in the US, was in the habit of giving something like $5,000 a year to the Council, a far cry from what happened in Wisconsin, where the Methodists gave $90,000 a year. We managed to get a couple of fairly large donations to cover the outstanding bills, and I went to work.

I discovered my salary would be $60,000 yearly, more than I had made in any Methodist churches I had served. In my joy at being offered the job, I forgot to ask about such a detail as the salary. I had been in the office only a couple of days when I got a phone call from a woman named Roberta (Bert) Perry. She was the head of the Farm Workers' Ministry in Florida. Without delay, she said she wanted me to join her during Holy Week for a demonstration with the International Teamsters Union in front of the MinuteMaid orange juice processing plant at Auburndale, Florida, just down the Interstate from Orlando. I invited her to come to the office to explain the situation to me.

Bert was there the next day, and we began a friendship that deepened over the next eight years. She told me that Coca-Cola had owned the plant in Auburndale since its opening but had recently sold it to a Brazilian company, Cutrale. It seems that Coke wanted to pass off their labor problems to others by selling off the plants and handling only the marketing of the finished products. This was a strategy I was very familiar with, as Chiquita Banana and Standard Fruit had done a similar thing in Costa Rica. As the labor unions in Costa Rica had successfully pressured companies to pay decent wages and benefits, they stopped the production of bananas and sold their plantations and packaging operations to local farmers.

Coca-Cola had decided to do the same with its orange juice operations. It turned out that the Cutrale operation was really a Coke-sponsored entity. Some years before, Coca-Cola had financed a rather sleazy Brazilian to help him buy some orange plantations in São Paulo state. He leveraged himself into being one of the major producers in Brazil, but along the way, he left a trail of exploited workers, mainly children, who could climb up into the branches to pick oranges without damaging the trees. He managed to escape serious punishment through influence and bribes and continued to expand his operations.

In 1997, Coca-Cola sold the MinuteMaid operations in Auburndale to Cutrale. The first thing Cutrale did was fire the workers who had been there long enough to have some seniority and were trying to organize a union. The workers had contacted Bert Perry, the representative of the Farm Workers' Ministry in Florida. She, in turn, had contacted the United Farmworkers, the union that César Chavez had led so successfully in California. Now, the Teamsters had come on board. They had scheduled a candlelight vigil at the plant in Auburndale for the evening of Holy Thursday, which was a couple of weeks away. Bert wanted me to speak on behalf of the workers and share my knowledge of Cutrale's checkered career in Brazil.

I didn't even know where Auburndale was, but I agreed to be there. So, on Thursday afternoon, along with Argentina and the children, I drove to Auburndale and found the MinuteMaid plant. Bert was there and received us warmly. She introduced us to Carin Zelenko, Director of the Office of Strategic Initiatives of the International Brotherhood of Teamsters. Carin had flown down from Washington, D.C., to show the Teamsters' flag. Around seven p.m., the Vigil got underway, with more than 50 workers walking up and down in front of the plant with their candles. After about 25 minutes, they gathered together. Bert introduced me as the executive director of the Florida Council of Churches, adding that I had just returned from Brazil, where I had lived for several years.

I spoke briefly, affirming that all 26 denominations in the Florida Council of Churches had strong positions on workers' rights to organize into unions to defend their interests. I also affirmed that the National Labor Relations Board of the federal government existed to protect the right to organize. I added that Cutrale, the new plant owner, was considered a violator of human rights in Brazil. I wore my clerical collar, and the workers were surprised to see someone from the church supporting them. On top of that, they were happy to see my beautiful wife and children there, marching with them.

About a month later, I got a phone call from Carin Zelenko in Washington asking if I could fly to Atlanta for a demonstration outside the main offices of Coca-Cola. I agreed and arrived in Atlanta on a chilly spring day. I joined the group of Teamsters in a picket line. We carried placards calling on Coca-Cola to recognize the workers' rights in Auburndale and organize a union. Also in the group of pickets was the Rev. Joseph Lowery, a fellow United Methodist pastor and head of the Southern Christian Leadership Conference, organized by the Rev. Martin Luther King, Jr. in the 1960s, to get churches to support the civil rights movement.

We marched for about an hour and then made some speeches. Someone from Coke came out and told us they didn't own the Auburndale plant anymore and had nothing to do with these matters. We responded by saying they had a moral obligation as the only buyer from the plant to insist that their producer obey the law.

Carin called me about a month later and said that Cutrale had finally allowed the Teamsters to organize the workers in Auburndale. She said our solidarity with the workers we represented was very important. Coke was clearly fearful of the 26 denominations in the Council, and she felt our support had been crucial in getting them to pressure Cutrale.[7]

Quincy Farms

Another item on my plate was Quincy Farms, a plant in Quincy, Florida, about 40 minutes west of Tallahassee. The company produced vast quantities of mushrooms in the dark inside warehouses, utilizing Haitian and mostly Mexican Latinx labor. A few months earlier, some workers marched around the plant on their lunch hour calling for an election to authorize the formation of a union. This wildcat strike did not stop production and lasted only for the lunch hour. The result was firing the workers who participated, which was illegal as US law does not allow workers to be fired for seeking to organize.

The Florida Catholic Conference, led by Mike McCarren, and the Florida Council of Churches issued statements supporting the workers. Jim Armstrong urged me to go to Tallahassee to talk with Mike McCarren and see what we might do about this together. The National Farmworkers Union also became interested. In a few months, a protest march was planned in Quincy.

I drove up to Tallahassee with Argentina and our children, and on the appointed day, we drove to Quincy. There was a meeting at the local African Methodist Episcopal Church where I was invited to read the Scripture lesson. The Rev. Dr. Joseph Lowery was the preacher. I was one of three or four white people in the sanctuary. Then we marched through the streets of Quincy, joined by the Latinxs. Quincy Farms had maintained a policy of divide and conquer with the African Americans and the Latinxs, having them work in different departments and on different shifts. But they joined together for the march.

Our demonstration elicited no response from the owners or managers, so we returned to Orlando. Shortly after that, I heard from Arturo Cruz, César Chavez's successor, urging me to write a letter to the President of Pizza Hut in Dallas, Texas, asking them to stop buying mushrooms from Quincy Farms until they allowed an election. I sent the following letter:

Michael S. Rawlings, President,
Pizza Hut USA
14841 Dallas Parkway
Dallas, TX 75240

Dear Mr. Rawlings,

I am writing to you on behalf of the Florida Council of Churches. For many years, all of our constituent churches, along with the Roman Catholic Church, have had a clear and consistent position in favor of the right of workers to organize to defend their legitimate interests in the marketplace. You know that the results of such organization in our US history have made us the wealthiest in the world today. There are a number of issues being raised by the workers, but the issue that concerns us at the Florida Council of Churches is their right to organize.

Unfortunately, however, not all agree with this principle. For more than two years, there have been conflicts between the workers and management at Quincy Farms in Quincy, Florida.

On March 14, 1996, a number of workers engaged in a protest demonstration, insisting that they be allowed to organize a union to represent their interests. The result of that demonstration was the arrest of 24 workers and the subsequent firing of more than 40. Despite repeated efforts by groups like the Florida Council of Churches and the Florida Catholic Conference, the management of Quincy Farms has refused to discuss the situation. In the spring of this year, the workers sued Quincy Farms, demanding back pay and benefits since their firing for trying to organize. It appears they will win this suit, and Quincy Farms management is finally beginning to talk with them. However, there is still no willingness to allow them to form a union to represent them.

At a time when the gap between rich and poor is widening in this country, making it more and more like what we have traditionally called "third world countries," the Florida Council of Churches feels that this principle of the right to organize is absolutely crucial to permit workers a chance to enjoy the benefits of the wealth that this country enjoys and that they help create.

Knowing that Pizza Hut is a significant customer of Quincy Farms mushrooms, we want to ask that you use your obvious commercial and moral influence with Quincy Farms management to encourage them to allow the workers to organize a union of their choice. We want to ask you to cease using Quincy Farms mushrooms until they have agreed to respect this important right of the workers.

This was written on the letterhead of the Florida Council of Churches, which had the names of the 26 denominations that made up the Council. I received no answer. But three weeks later, Pizza Hut canceled its contract with Quincy Farms. The manager of Quincy Farms retired for "family reasons," and the president of the Philadelphia-based parent corporation, Sylvan Industries, flew to Florida and sat down with representatives of the National Farmworkers Union. An election was held in which the workers overwhelmingly voted in favor of the union, and a union contract was signed, being the very first of its kind in Florida between farmworkers and a corporation.

Shortly after this, I got a letter from Arturo Cruz stating he felt the letter from the Florida Council of Churches was the determining factor in getting Pizza Hut to cancel their contract and force the owners of Quincy Farms to sit down and negotiate.

Coalition for Immokalee Workers

While all this was going on, Bert Perry insisted I go down to Immokalee in the south of Florida, where farm workers were being abused in incredible ways, including actual cases of slavery. So,

I drove about 200 miles to the northern edge of the Everglades, where I met with Lucas Benitez, one of the founding leaders of the newly formed Coalition for Immokalee Workers. This group sought a modicum of justice from the tomato growers of that area, who produced most of the tomatoes used in the US fast food industry. They were asking for an increase of $0.01 per pound with the condition that the penny would increase the wages of those picking the tomatoes.

I took Lucas' request to the Council's Committee on Social Action, urging them to approve his request that we urge a boycott of Publix Supermarkets, McDonald's, Wendy's, Taco Bell, Burger King, and all the other food makers that used tomatoes. Publix stonewalled.[8] They would not even discuss the issue. However, over the next few years, all other companies except Wendy's accepted the CIW's proposals.

One of the most joyful moments of my eight years with the Florida Council of Churches was in 2003 when the Free Trade Association of the Americas (FTAA) held its final meeting in Miami to push through a trade agreement that would exploit the entire hemisphere to the benefit of the United States. More than 20,000 people showed up in Miami to protest. I was standing on a street corner with a group of protesters from the Council when a farm wagon, pulled by a tractor loaded with CIW farm workers, drove by slowly. Suddenly, Lucas Benitez jumped off the wagon and ran across the street to embrace me, thanking the Council for its support. He later said that the Florida Council of Churches was the very first religious organization to provide any encouragement and support for their efforts toward justice and dignity.

My son, Erick, who was a student at Florida International University in Miami, getting his Master's degree in Political Science, joined the protesters and was arrested by the Miami police. He was kept in jail for 24 hours and released the next day when his attorney, John de Leon, who defended the rights of immigrants, went to the jail. His case was dismissed when his trial date came because the arresting officer never showed up. Amnesty International won a major lawsuit against the City of Miami for its violation of the human rights of several hundred protesters.

I was asked to be the spokesperson for many of the protesters. When interviewed by Miami TV stations, I warned that the aggressive attitude of the Miami Police would lead to illegal actions that would cost the city a lot of money. I saw a man standing nearby with a name tag that read Tom Hayden. I'd been in Chicago during the trial of the famous Chicago Seven, who'd been accused of several outlandish charges related to the Democratic Convention of 1968, and I recalled that Tom Hayden was one of the defendants. He later married Jane Fonda.

I approached him after the news conference and asked if he was *the* Tom Hayden, and he confessed he was. I told him I'd participated in protest marches in Chicago during the trial. He invited Argentina and me to join him for cocktails at his hotel. He was teaching a course at Harvard and brought a group of students to Miami to observe and participate in the protests. I shared my experience of being kidnapped and tortured by the Brazilian army, and my friendship with Dom Hélder Câmara. This made us instant friends.

Mt. Olive Pickles

In March 1999, the Farm Labor Organizing Committee (FLOC) called for a boycott of Mt. Olive Pickles. Mt. Olive was the largest producer and supplier of pickles on the East Coast. FLOC was founded in 1967 by Baldemar Velasquez, himself a farmworker. By 1999, FLOC was a force to be reckoned with. The boycott began to take shape. Mt. Olive Pickles used the same argument that the fast food companies used against CIW: "We don't hire any farm workers. We simply buy cucumbers from the farmers. Thus, we have nothing to do with the working conditions on the farms."

But CIW defeated that argument when it got Duke University to throw Taco Bell off its campus when it refused to aid the tomato workers. FLOC took the same arguments to Mt. Olive. I took the matter to the FCC Commission on Social Justice. They agreed unanimously to urge the member churches and all their congregations to boycott Mt. Olive pickles until the company negotiated a contract with the workers. About a month later, I was awakened at six-thirty a.m. by a call from Bill Bryan, President of Mt. Olive Pickles. He and his family were active United Methodists in North Carolina, and he'd discovered I was a United Methodist pastor. He was deeply concerned to learn that the FCC had joined an unjust boycott against Mt. Olive Pickles and wanted to know what he might do to stop that action.

I explained that the decision to take part in the boycott had been taken by our Commission on Social Justice, and I could not simply reverse that decision on my own. Mr. Bryan asked when he could meet with the Commission. I said he would be most welcome to join the next meeting in Tampa for an hour to plead his case. He said he would be there. Two weeks later, Mr. Bryan flew in on the company jet with four of his staff to present his case to the Commission. He explained how the boycott was unfair because Mt. Olive had no farm workers.

The Commission members were familiar with this argument and quickly shot it down, pointing out that Mt. Olive was the purchaser of all of the cucumbers produced in North Carolina. Thus, they had a total influence on the producers and a moral responsibility for the health and well-being of the workers. The Commissioners also reported they knew of the precarious housing offered to the migrant workers and the lack of healthcare and other basic benefits.

Bill Bryan was clearly unprepared for the level of detail the Commission members knew. He reiterated his argument that Mt. Olive had no farm workers in its employ, adding that he'd visited some of the farms and the housing was like the cabins at the Methodist Summer Church Camps his kids went to. That produced a round of laughter from the Commission. After going around several times, the Commission voted unanimously to maintain the boycott and thanked Bill Bryan for his visit.

Baldemar Velasquez, the founder and director of FLOC, later told me that Mr. Bryan was devastated by his inability to snowball the FCC. Shortly after his trip to Florida, he signed a contract with FLOC to guarantee decent pay and dignity for the farm workers.

Interfaith Coalition for Worker Justice

In 1998, we participated in the formation of the South Florida Interfaith for Worker Justice. In 1991, Kim Bobo, a Methodist community organizer, founded the Chicago Interfaith Committee on Worker Issues. I had gotten to know and respect her when I was pastor of Broadway United Methodist Church. Her organization had evolved into the Interfaith Committee on Worker Justice and began reaching out to help form committees throughout the United States.

Modeled on the organization Kim had founded, the Florida Council of Churches aided in the formation of two interfaith coalitions for worker justice, one in Miami and one in Central Florida, Recognizing that the federal minimum wage had long lost its original purpose of providing for the health and welfare of working families, coalitions sought to get counties to pass what were called "Living Wage Ordinances." This hourly wage, usually calculated by members of a local college or university Economics department, would provide for a family of four, including health insurance. That usually resulted in an hourly wage of $2 above the federal minimum wage.

We managed to be victorious in Miami-Dade County, and all the workers at the expansion of the Miami International Airport, a $1.5 billion project, would benefit from this ordinance, along with the road-building and maintenance workers throughout the Miami area contracted by the county. We also formed the Interfaith Coalition for Worker Justice in Central Florida but did not get the Orange County Supervisors (Greater Orlando, including Disney World and Universal and all the huge resorts and hotels) to sign on. I met with the mayor on more than one occasion to explain that the increased income produced by a living wage ordinance would significantly boost the local economy but to no avail.

South Florida Seminary

Father Patrick O'Neill, a most unusual, independently wealthy Catholic priest in Miami, had decided, I believe with the prompting and encouragement of Jim Armstrong, to form an interfaith seminary in Miami. It was located on the Campus of First Presbyterian Church on Brickell Avenue, a large, famous, and dying church with a huge endowment. It had 35–40 students when I first learned of it. Father Pat was the Chancellor of the Archdiocese of Miami. Through him, I met Archbishop Favalora, a charming and sympathetic church leader, but a bit reluctant to go too far in his relations with Protestants. I met with him several times, and he spoke of the Catholics joining the Florida Council of Churches. He was intrigued, but it never happened. In one moment of startling frankness, he asked, "What's in it for us?"

One year, I got Bishop Dorsey, Bishop of Central Florida, to be the keynote speaker at the Annual Assembly of the Council. We never got beyond that. The Bishop of Jacksonville was a violent homophobe, as was the Bishop of Tampa. The Bishop of West Palm Beach was most cordial, and I thought we might actually break through there. Yet, he suddenly resigned under accusations of improper relations with a seminary student and disappeared from the map.

In my third or fourth year in Orlando, I was invited to participate in a weekly radio show on Catholic Radio with Father Bob

Markunas. It became the most popular show on the Catholic radio station. Listeners were intrigued to hear a Methodist pastor and a Catholic priest discussing social justice issues similarly. We did this for several years until one day, my priest friend disappeared with no explanation.

In 2000, Father Pat asked me to be the dean of the to-be-formed Orlando Campus of the South Florida Seminary. I had taught Systematic Theology for a couple of years at our Methodist seminary in Rio. I was excited about this ecumenical enterprise, so I accepted. The new school grew slowly but was blessed with an excellent faculty. Some former theology professors from the Episcopal Church and other denominations who had retired in the Orlando area were happy to "suit up" again and teach a course. By the second year, we had more than a dozen students on the Orlando Campus, usually meeting on Saturdays on the campus of a large Disciples of Christ (Christian) Church, and the student body was growing. Almost all of the students were part-time with secular jobs. But there was a lot of enthusiasm and dedication on their part, and it was exciting to work with them.

9/11

One beautiful day in September of 2001, I drove to Jim Armstrong's home to meet with some of his seminary students. I was listening to the radio when the news came over that a plane had struck one of the Trade Towers in New York. When I got to Jim's house, he and the students gathered around his TV, looking at footage of the tragedy in New York City. While we all watched, the second plane struck. About 30 minutes later, one of the towers fell, collapsing into its own footprint. Everything changed for us that morning and for the world.

One of the first and most important things that happened was the anger and hatred spewed forth against non-Christians. Osama bin Laden was immediately identified as the mastermind behind the attack, even though it was simultaneously announced—not as loudly—that he was in a hospital in the Middle East suffering from serious kidney disease, and no proof was ever presented of his involvement in the attack. So much hatred was immediately addressed toward Muslim communities in the US. Sikhs, Hindus, Jews, and others were lumped together as the "foreigners" who were responsible for this attack. Hate was spewed forth from all sides.

Recognizing this as a dangerous trend, I immediately invited leaders of all faith groups in the Orlando area to meet at the Ecumenical Center to discuss how we might counteract this hatred. The first meeting was attended by more than 15 faith leaders, a mixture of Protestants, Jews, Muslims, Hindus, and Sikhs, accompanied by Scott Maxwell, a columnist of the *Orlando Sentinel,* whose column, *Naming Names,* was popular for its clear thinking and straight talk.

We quickly agreed on the idea of a joint worship service, inviting as many faith groups as possible to participate in a service of prayer for harmony and understanding. We chose a Rabbi and a Muslim woman to co-emcee the event. One of the principal resort owners of Orlando, a Jewish man named Harris Rosen, offered one of his huge resort hotels as a venue for free, and we started working toward a January event. We soon had Protestant, Catholic, Jewish, Muslim, Hindu, Sikh, Native American, and New Age groups all participating. We asked each group to lead prayers in their own way in their principal language. I was asked to do a final presentation with a mini-sermon on the theme.

The event, held on a Sunday afternoon in January, was a significant success with more than 800 attendees. The fact that a Jewish Rabbi shared the leading spotlight with a Muslim woman was not lost on anyone. Bishop Dorsey of the Catholic Diocese of Orlando led the Catholic part. The Sikhs, nearly unknown to most attendees, shared a profound message of unity. An African Methodist

Episcopal Church choir presented some excellent music in their tradition. The Native Americans made a powerful presentation, calling for the unity of the children of the Great Spirit. The New Age folks mystified us all.

I summed up the event by observing that modern astronomy has made it clear that there are at least 100 billion stars like our sun in our Milky Way, one of more than 100 billion galaxies in what we call the "Known Universe." I then observed that as all of our religions claim to believe in a Creator God, in one manner or another, it was patently absurd for any of us to claim that the Creator God was Presbyterian, Methodist, Lutheran, Episcopal, Catholic, Sikh, Jewish, Muslim, Hindu—or any particular brand, etc. The God we all claimed to worship was much more than we could even begin to understand. It would behoove us all to recognize that, for the most part, we simply don't know what we are talking about but are merely repeating what we have been told about God and the Creation by our parents and our culture of origin. My final word was let's lighten up and learn to live together and love each other.

I was disappointed to note that among the 800+ persons present, only the AME and the United Methodists from St. Paul's United Methodist Church in Windermere were present. Virtually all other Florida Council of Churches denominations were conspicuous by their absence.

Cherishing the Creation

When we were still in Teresópolis and Argentina was videotaping my interview for the personnel committee at the Florida Council of Churches, one of their questions was, "What do you see as a high priority for the Council? And how would you address it?" My answer was that we needed to earnestly promote the Unity of the Churches today and get beyond our traditional parochialism and individualism. I said that the environmental crisis could be the vehicle for doing this, along with a solid theological emphasis on Jesus' words in John 17: 2. I worked as hard as I could to develop a program to attract the attention and commitment of the churches, to a common action toward combating global warming.

We came up with a program called Cherishing the Creation. We put together a series of workshops in various parts of Florida, calling together persons interested in the problems facing the planet in this time of environmental crisis and offering some educational tools to take back to their denominations and local congregations to enlist the members in a statewide effort to attack the problem. I found a few extraordinarily well-informed and dedicated persons in various denominations. We put together a program that we presented to the Annual Assembly of the Council. The recruited persons put on an excellent program with well-developed literature and program outlines for District and local presentations.

A central emphasis was the role that the churches should play in educating our members as to their responsibility to lead in the changing of how we do pretty much everything to reduce our carbon footprint and seek to lower the output of CO2, carbon dioxide, recognized by virtually all scientists to be the principal culprit in global warming. This included a campaign to get local congregations to do an energy audit of their physical plant to see how they might reduce their energy consumption and thus the production of CO2, as in Florida, the majority of electricity was produced by a dozen coal-fired power plants. Then, we encouraged individual church members to do a similar audit on their homes, changing light bulbs to more efficient and less energy-consuming ones. And so on.

I was proud of what the laypersons on our team put together. However, to our dismay, we discovered that our Cherishing the Creation campaign produced a huge collective yawn on the part of the member churches. Only those church members who were already on board and members of the Sierra Club showed any interest—and were already doing what we were recommending. By the year 2000, our campaign died a slow death.

GW Bush's War on Iraq

On February 15, 2003, I gave two speeches at anti-war rallies in Orlando. I said if we went to war in Iraq, we would generate more terrorism in the world than we could imagine. We would destroy Iraq, which was the most developed country in the area at that time, with an excellent university system, health care, water, and electricity. I also noted that our military did not know how to fight urban guerrillas and would be bogged down in endless and brutal combat, which would kill massive numbers of civilians, as well as our soldiers. I also observed that the reasons for going to war were based entirely on lies. More than 15 million people around the world gathered that day to protest against the war on Iraq. All in vain. And, unfortunately, my dire predictions proved to be true.

A local weekly in Orlando that happened to hear the first of my anti-war speeches published a report about it entitled *Raising Hell for Jesus.* However, none of this made much difference. In 2002, the National Council of Churches held its annual meeting in Tampa. At one point, Bob Edgar, the general secretary of the council, announced that the Rev. Oscar Bolioli, a Uruguayan Methodist, would be retiring from his post as director for Latin American Relations of the Council.

I approached Bob and told him that I should be hired as Bolioli's successor, giving him my credentials as one who was fluent in Spanish and Portuguese and had a significant history in Latin America. He responded by saying, "Great. If you can raise your salary, you're hired." I'm sure he thought I could not do that, but two months later, I raised the funds to pay my salary. He kept his word, and I became the new director of Latin-American Relations for the National Council of Churches.

In that capacity, I flew to Brazil, where my dear friend, Father Marcelo Barros, one of the two leading liberation theologians of that country, had arranged for me to meet with President Lula to present a letter to him from the Rev. Bob Edgar. The letter asked Lula to use his offices to mobilize support from the non-aligned countries to oppose the pending attack on Iraq by President GW Bush. Similar letters had been delivered to the heads of state in England, France, Germany, Italy, and other European countries.

On March 17, 2003, at five p.m. I sat down with President Lula in his equivalent of an Oval Office and presented him with the letter of appeal. He knew who I was, thanks to his chief of staff and Father Marcelo—meaning he knew I had been kidnapped, tortured, and expelled from Brazil by the military dictatorship, which had imprisoned him more than once as a labor leader in São Paulo. We had a marvelous meeting for more than an hour.

When I left Lula's office, I was met outside by about 25 Brazilian journalists, intrigued by an American clergy coming to talk with Lula about the impending war. They also knew of my history as a political prisoner of the military dictatorship. It was clear that my encounter with Lula would be front-page news in Brazilian papers the next morning. However, at nine p.m. Brazilian time, George W. Bush announced that the US would be attacking Iraq within the next two days. So *that* was obviously on the front page the next morning.

In July 2003, I got a call from *MoveOn,* a Washington, D.C.-based group, asking if the Florida Council of Churches would be willing to co-sponsor a full-page ad in the *Orlando Sentinel* calling for a congressional investigation of the lies the Bush administration told in the run-up to the attacks on Iraq. *MoveOn* would pay $50,000 for the ad, wanting only our participation as a Florida-based organization. As Executive Director, I had no authority to decide, so I forwarded their request and a mock-up of the ad to the executive committee. The ad was a full-page photo of George Bush, with the headline *Misleader.* On the right-hand side, five of G.W.'s lies were listed. Across the bottom was a call for the congressional investigation. The executive committee unanimously approved the council's participation in co-sponsoring the ad.

By nine a.m. on the day it ran, Argentina, who was working as my secretary, had already fielded two death threats aimed at me by United Methodists in Orlando. They said they wouldn't stand for such attacks on our Methodist president and would be firebombing our home. I immediately called the police, and we were given protection for two weeks, with squad cars driving by our house at irregular intervals.

The United Methodist Bishop began getting calls from wealthy Methodists, demanding that the Florida Annual Conference withdraw from membership in the Council. The Bishop of the Evangelical Lutheran Church in America, one of the larger Protestant denominations in Florida, had driven to Orlando that day from his home in Tampa to celebrate his daughter's wedding and was blindsided after the wedding by some wealthy Lutherans who were also outraged to think that the Florida Council of Churches would "attack our President." They demanded that the ELCA withdraw from membership in the Council.

As the executive director, I naturally received full credit for the Council's participation in this "nefarious attack" on our Methodist president. The United Methodist Bishop, who had been a good friend, went underground. The financial support from the Methodists of Florida nearly disappeared, and the Lutherans also reduced their support.

We had already downsized considerably, closing our offices at the Ecumenical Center and moving them to my home in Winter Springs. My salary had been cut in half. When I began working for the NCC, Bob Edgar had gladly taken me on staff when the Rev. Oscar Bolioli, a Methodist pastor refugee from Uruguay, retired after many years as the director of Latin American Relations for the NCC.

When I was announced as the new director of Latin American Relations for the NCC, I went to the Directors of Church World Service, where I was met with a great deal of suspicion, bordering on hostility. I explained I would not be controlling any funds or trying to manage our partners in Latin America. That totally changed their attitude.

One of my first trips to Latin America was to attend an event in São Paulo with the Rev. Dr Tony Kieropolis, Bob Edgar's Associate General Secretary. Tony did not speak Spanish or Portuguese, so I was his guide and translator. Many of the church leaders at the event had known me during my time as a Methodist missionary in Brazil, and others knew of me as a survivor of the military, giving me considerable status. Tony read a speech in Spanish, which was well received, and we got along quite well on the trip, though he clearly felt upstaged by me because of my reception by the Brazilians.

My second trip was to attend the Assembly of CLAI, the Latin American Council of Churches, in Buenos Aires. There, I discovered that both Oscar Bololi and Nora Boots, the executive secretary of the United Methodist Board of Global Ministries, were totally disrespected by the Latin American churches. Both had used their positions and funds to dominate the partner churches throughout Latin America. When I made it clear I saw my role as one of deepening relationships and not telling them what to do, they embraced me warmly and clearly longed for the kind of relationship the NCC had had during the days of the military dictatorships.

I discovered that virtually no one at the NCC remembered the role the NCC had played during the 70s and 80s in Latin America. Bob had fired over 100 staff members upon assuming his position as General Secretary. The Rev. Eileen Lindner knew some of that history, but Bob was busy sidelining her as he consolidated his power in the NCC. But the Latin American church leaders remembered the NCC's role during those dark years and deeply appreciated that history. I was able to establish a budding friendship with Israel

Batista, the executive director of CLAI, as well as the Episcopal Bishop of Panama, Bishop Murray, who was elected President of CLAI at that meeting and who would prove to be a good friend later on when Argentina and I moved to Panama.

My New Hobby: Real Estate in Orlando

During the summer of 1997, we spent a week at a time-share resort in the Florida Keys. We were enthralled by the splendor of the Keys. Since it was vacation time, we relaxed the controls we had on our children regarding bedtime, and they watched some TV late into the evening. One morning, our daughter, Raquel, who was just 11, told me she'd watched a program where a man named Carlton Sheets explained he could make anyone wealthy in real estate by following his "No Money Down" program. Suspecting this to be one more late-night scam, I didn't take it very seriously, but Raquel insisted. She said, "Daddy, you could do this." So I finally agreed to watch the program the next night.

Carlton Sheets was personable and made some excellent arguments. As our finances were pretty precarious, I decided to invest in his offer and get his tapes on how to buy real estate with "No Money Down." It proved to be the best investment of my life. I spent $189 to purchase a set of some 40 cassette tapes, in which Carlton explained his program for buying real estate without putting down any money. I listened to the recordings as I drove about 40 minutes to and from the Ecumenical Center in Orlando. I actually listened to each tape at least twice before doing anything.

Carlton's program was quite simple: any bank in 1997 would gladly loan 80% of the appraised price of a house. The secret was to ask the seller to hold a second mortgage for the 20% balance. Most sellers were afraid to do that, so about eight out of ten were uninterested. But I also discovered that in Florida, as a purchaser,

I had the right to be present when the real estate agent presented my offer to the seller, and I could correct any misinformation.

In 1997, hardly anyone would pay the asking price of a home. They would offer 90% and haggle with the seller, paying 93 to 95%. Following Carlton's advice, I would tell the seller I would pay the asking price if they held the second mortgage of 20%. Then, I would ask that we amortize the 20% over 15 years, with the promise of a balloon payment of the balance due no later than five years from the closing date. The other secret Carlton offered was to only buy houses you could rent for a bread-and-butter price, which was about $500 a month at that time. That was good enough if $500 would cover the PITI (principal, interest, taxes, and insurance). No profit is expected in the first year. But at the end of the first year, increase the rent by $25 a month. No one moves out because of that kind of rent increase, and suddenly, you are making $300 a year. The second year, another $25, and now $600 a year.

With much fear and trembling, I found a house for sale for $50,000 in Sanford. I was confident I could rent it for $500 a month. I made the offer and bought the house. Then another, and another. Argentina and I would spend our Saturdays looking at houses until we found one to buy. Within a year, we owned and rented 10 houses. I found a partner with an outstanding balance sheet, and with his credit rating, we purchased a 22-unit apartment complex in Winter Haven and a strip mall in Sanford—all with no money down.

Argentina and I became adept at evaluating houses and finding renters. But it became hard to manage, so I made a deal with a Realtor in Sanford to manage all the homes for a 3% commission on the rent. We did this for most of the nine years we remained in Orlando. Then, we began selling them when planning to retire and move to Panama. We sold the last one, our own home, exactly one month before the crash in 2006.

The Bitter Ending

We enjoyed our years in Orlando. As a totally unexpected surprise, we got a pass to Disney World. I had been in my new job just a few weeks when I got a phone call from Diana, a woman in Disney's PR department. Every year, Disney World gave $500,000 to non-profits in the Greater Orlando area. Each year, they formed a jury of community leaders to evaluate the 400–500 applicants. Diana wanted to know if I was willing to serve. It would involve meeting with the other jury members three or four times, reviewing and grading the applications. I agreed.

It was a much larger job than I thought. Wading through nearly 500 applications occupied many hours of my evenings for the next three months. There was a huge breakfast event at Disney World where the winners were announced. Seeing so many worthy organizations in the area doing good work for the community was inspiring. Afterward, I got a letter signed by Michael Eisner, the head honcho of Disney World, inviting Argentina and me to be their guests at a dinner meeting at the not-yet-opened Animal Kingdom. Then, about three weeks later, I got another letter from Michael Eisner. It contained a year-long pass for five people to go to Disney World for an entire year.

This was a mixed blessing. Until then, we had gone to Disney World once, as we could not afford it. So, I had been able to honestly tell our children we could not go more than once a year. But now, virtually every week, one of our children would say, "Daddy, can you take me and three of my friends to Disney this Saturday?" So, Argentina and I had to drive to Disney almost every weekend for the following year. At the end of that year, I got another letter and another pass. This went on for five years. Obviously, the kids were in Hog Heaven, being able to invite two or three of their friends to go to Disney World. But we really got tired of going pretty much each weekend.

Meanwhile, the work of the Council was gratifying to me. Being able to make a difference in the lives of Florida farmworkers was satisfying. The ecumenical aspects did not move along nearly as well, however. It seemed the ethos of the Southern Baptist Church, the largest Protestant group in Florida, had seeped into the other denominations. For instance, the Episcopal Church was nearly totally homophobic in Florida. The United Methodists, who had not yet dealt with this matter nationally, had developed reconciling congregations. Several hundred churches across the country took a public stand affirming LGBTQ persons. They declared that everyone was welcome, regardless of race, ethnic background, or sexual orientation. But among the 700 congregations in Florida, only two had declared themselves to be reconciling congregations. The attitudes toward women were also largely misogynistic. There were not many female clergy in the state.

The financial support for the Council continued to decline. The United Methodist and the Lutheran Bishop's suggested that a "less controversial" executive director might help. Both reduced their financial support for the Council. I supplemented my income by taking on the deanship of the seminary, which paid a token salary, then the position at the NCC. But both of those eventually faded away. I called a special Council's executive committee meeting to deal with this. At that meeting of the executive committee, the then-president of the Council, the Rev. Clark Campbell-Evans, a United Methodist clergy who had been quite supportive of me all along, openly declared that he had not opened the mock-up of the ad that ran in the *Orlando Sentinel* with his approval, and said that if he had seen it, he would not have approved.

The Episcopal Bishop of Miami, Bishop Frade, a good friend and who had followed the Rev. Campbell-Evans as president when his term was over, resigned from his post as president of the Council because he was being attacked in his diocese by homophobes threatening to leave the denomination because of the favorable position the Episcopalians had taken nationally regarding the LBGTQ issue. In his place was the vice president, the Rev. Russell Meyer, a Lutheran pastor based in Tampa, whom I had nominated for the position. As president, Rev. Meyer formed a special committee to deal with the financial crisis. They held a meeting to which I was not invited and then invited me to a luncheon to share their conclusion: I should retire and be replaced by a pastor with other income. Two members of the committee told me in the men's room at the restaurant where we were meeting that Russell had said I wanted to retire, and for this reason, they had voted with him on the matter. This was news to me, but it was too late by then. So, Argentina and I made plans to move to Panama.

Russell announced he would become the new executive director as soon as this die was cast. He was informed by other members of the council that he could not be both President and E.D., so he resigned as president and took over as E.D. My dear friend Bishop Chuck Leigh[9] was elected president, a position he held for the next few years. Russell mainly traveled to the National Council of Churches annual assembly and other national ecumenical opportunities. Still, the Council practically ceased to exist, except for the letters Bishop Chuck sent out supporting justice issues. It had been a good run and a rewarding time, though I was shocked by the betrayal by a man I had considered a friend and ally, and disappointed at the responses of the denominations.

CHAPTER 12

How We Got to Panama

AT THE BEGINNING OF 2005, I formed a non-profit called Faith Partners of the Americas, Inc. to develop relationships of solidarity between churches of North America and the peoples of Latin America and the Caribbean. I hoped to build on the history of relationships in the 70s and 80s and even into the 90s between the National Council of Churches and the churches of Latin America. Since June of 2003, I had been serving as Director for Latin American and Caribbean Relations of the NCC. Even though the NCC no longer had deep pockets, there was enthusiasm over the fact that the NCC was once more extending a hand in solidarity.

Unfortunately, I discovered the NCC had little interest in Latin America. Since early 2003, they'd been overwhelmingly involved in opposing the war in Iraq. But when Bob Edgar became the general secretary, his first responsibility was to deal with the financial crisis he inherited. He began by eliminating 100 staff positions.[10] When that was done, there was no institutional memory of the NCC's role in Latin America and the Caribbean in earlier times.

In October 2004, Dr. Tony Kireopoulos, the Associate General Secretary for International Affairs and Peace Issues, whom I reported to, came to Orlando with his family. He called me to his hotel at the Disney complex. He said it had been decided that starting in January, I would no longer hold the Director for Latin American and Caribbean Relations title. Instead, I would be a "Latin American Consultant," and my compensation would be per diem. The information on how to document payment requests was never provided. When I presented my first invoice at the end of January, it was rejected. Tony said I had not been requested to do any of the work I was billing them for, even though it was all a matter of following up on projects that had begun in 2004.

So, on March 9, 2005, I sent a letter of resignation to Tony, stating that the lack of support and general disinterest in Latin America made it impossible for me to continue. In May of 2004, after great insistence, I was allowed to attend an Encounter of Faith Families sponsored by CLAI in Santiago, Chile, together with Eileen Lindner of the NCC. CLAI had urgently pleaded for a delegation of several heads of communions of the NCC, as there would be some 50 such persons there from throughout the hemisphere. Still, nothing was done to make that happen, so Eileen and I were the representatives of the Council.

On my way home from Santiago, I stopped in Quito, Ecuador, for a couple of days to visit with the Rev. Israel Batista, General Secretary of CLAI. Israel showed me around and shared his dreams for projects the NCC could collaborate on. One was to provide support for Indigenous Evangelical communities in that country. He introduced me to the Rev. Marco Murillo, the president of FEINE, a federation of 2,500 Indigenous Evangelical churches. We agreed to continue pursuing the project. However, on returning to the States and talking with Tony about the possibility of our serving as a broker for some solidarity actions with FEINE, I was informed that would not be possible. No explanation was given.

When I resigned from the NCC and formed Faith Partners of the Americas, I renewed my contacts with Israel and Marco with an eye toward Faith Partners being the broker. I put on paper the idea of taking 12–15 medical personnel from the US to Ecuador to provide initial support for the indigenous communities and to begin exploring further avenues of cooperation. I laid out an 8–10 day experience, including six days of service in the indigenous communities.

Israel and I agreed to spend 2–3 days with him and Marco, looking at the project's specifics. In the meantime, I shared this idea with some of the leaders of the Northland Community Church in Longwood, Florida, a non-denominational mega-church whose senior pastor, the Rev. Joel Hunter, was a former United Methodist and a close friend. Joel and Northland showed interest and agreed to pay my expenses for this trip, along with another Northland member, Dr. Larry, a physician who had experience in similar projects in Mexico and Guatemala.

When I purchased my ticket to Ecuador, my travel agent said if I stayed overnight in Panama, I could save $250, so I planned my trip to spend March 29–31 in Ecuador, fly to Panama on April 1 and spend April 2 in Panama. While researching Panama, I discovered several websites describing it as the perfect place to retire. The government of Panama gives retirees benefits; it has a lower cost of living, great weather, and no earthquakes, hurricanes, or tornadoes.

On arriving in Panama, I stayed at the Caesar Park Hotel, a four-star hotel, for only $92 for the night. The next morning, I set out with my video camera, driving around the city. Panama City is modern with attractive architecture. The city is clean, with signs announcing a $1,000 fine for littering. In the afternoon, I drove past a shopping mall, the Multi-Plex, and discovered it was an American-style mall with lower prices than the US. I shared with Argentina what I had learned about Panama as a place for retiring. One of the things that interested her most was its proximity to Costa Rica.

Just up the hill from David, the second-largest city in Panama, Boquete was a favorite retirement place. With the mountains on one side and the ocean in the distance on the other, Boquete has always had comfortable weather. At 3,000 feet above sea level, it is rated as one of the best places in the world for Americans to retire.

Argentina and I decided to make another visit to Panama in August. When we arrived, we met Karina and Mario Vilar, the owners of the movetopanama.com website, through whom we'd made arrangements for our trip and lodging. We headed into Panama City in their SUV. The apartment they provided for $30 a day was a suite in Mario's parents' home on Via Argentina in downtown Panama City. The following day, we had breakfast at a sidewalk café and enjoyed just looking and savoring the sights and sounds. We were back at the apartment at nine a.m., where Mario's sister, Mariela, and her husband, Max, were waiting for us. They had programmed two seminars for the morning: one on real estate and the other on insurance. Argentina could get health insurance better than we had in Orlando for about half the price. Auto and property insurance were also cheap.

In the afternoon, Mariela gave us a city tour, showing us a dozen neighborhoods. We arranged to meet Diana Bishop in Coronado, a resort community on the Pacific coast. She ran the panama-realtor.com website and took us to see a four-bedroom furnished house that was charming and rustic and in the gated community at the Coronado Golf and Beach Resort. The asking price was only $105,000. She took us to see another house in the resort that had just come on the market. It was a block from the hotel's tennis courts and a much more substantial house with three bedrooms, three baths, and two maid's rooms. It had a lovely backyard and a marvelous porch. The asking price was $165,000.

Next, we traveled to Boquete, a charming town with a population of about 20,000. The average year-round temperature was 72. But Argentina began sneezing shortly after arriving. We found a place we had heard about called Valle Escondido, a condo-type community built around a 9-hole golf course. Most units were two bedrooms with Spanish-type architecture and an entire village with stores, shops, and restaurants. However, it was pricey, small, and had a weird floor plan. From there, we drove to a development called the Molinos. The houses were on individual lots, and some had a beautiful view of the Volcano Baru up behind and the Pacific Ocean in the distance.

However, Boquete struck me as a place to go and wait to die. There were only about six restaurants in the town and it was a 40 minute drive to see a movie. No thanks. Then *don* Mario, the owner of the nicer house in Coronado, told us he also had an apartment in Panama City that he purchased for one of his daughters. It was a two-bedroom apartment with about 1,350 square feet in the Marbella district. He was asking $90,000. When he took us to see it, we thought it was lovely on the second floor, just a block away from the ocean (Avenida Balboa). Very spacious and completely furnished.

We decided to buy both the house in Coronado and the apartment, which we would rent for income. We took Mario, Karina, Mariela, and Max out to dinner. They chose a place on the causeway, a long spit of land near the canal developed for tourism and night spots. The next night, I took Argentina to dinner at the Caesar Park Hotel, where I had stayed in April. We had an elegant fish dinner, complete with a splendid wine. The whole bill, including the tip, was only $23!

We flew one hour to Costa Rica to visit Argentina's family the next day. We rented a car at the airport and drove to Heredia to visit the family Argentina lived with when she was in college. They were delighted to see her. We then went to Tres Rios, where we spent an hour with Plutarco Bonilla (a world-renowned Bible scholar) and his wife, Esperanza. Plutarco had been one of the co-founders of *Mesoamerica.* Then we continued to Limón, staying at Argentina's family's home until Tuesday. We drove back to San José, I flew back to the States, and Argentina remained for another two weeks.

We really felt good about the whole project. Argentina was excited that we would be close to Costa Rica. I was excited about living near the beach. We thought the house would be a wonderful place for us to spend the rest of our lives. Back in Florida, we proceeded to get ready to move to Panama. I filled out a ton of paperwork to get our residency status. We checked out shipping our car and made arrangements with a moving company. In August 2006, we flew down to Panama to begin the next chapter in our lives. We inherited a maid, Marcela, from *don* Mario and Sadith and a gardener, José, and began to settle into our new home.

Shortly after, Argentina and I were in Panama City to get her physical exam for her health insurance. We were standing on a corner of Via España looking for a taxi. One stopped, and the occupying passenger opened the tinted window and asked us where we were going. "Hospital Nacional," we said.

In English, the passenger replied, "That's where I'm going. Get in."

That's how we met Nick Ruggerio, a recent arrival in Panama. He lived in Altos del Maria, a largely expatriate community in the mountains about 35–40 minutes from Coronado. He was going to the hospital to pick up his wife, Sue, who had broken her foot. Later that afternoon, we spotted Nick and Sue at the hospital café and ate lunch together. We instantly bonded, and they simply adored Argentina. I mentioned we were thinking of starting a church in Coronado. They immediately jumped on that, saying they'd been looking for a church. That's how we got the first two "members" of our first branch of the Church Without BS.

The Church without Bullshit

I went to see the manager of the resort hotel. There was a 5-star restaurant on the hotel's second floor in Coronado, and I explained that we wanted to start an ecumenical church. I asked if we could use some space in the hotel for a few hours on Sunday mornings. To my joyful surprise, she said on Sundays the restaurant didn't open until two p.m. and we could use it as long as we put the tables and chairs back in place.

Nick and Sue were very excited about the new English language church, and they spread the word among the expats in Los Altos del Maria. We printed up some flyers and posted them around Coronado. One week later, we held the first service of the Church Without Bullshit. About 20 people showed up, and I introduced myself and said I would be happy to serve as pastor of this new English-language congregation without salary. I explained the meaning of the name, saying I would not be telling them what they could wear or do or not do. I would just be telling them, each week, in as many different ways as I could, about the infinite and unconditional love our Creator God has for all God's children.

They were intrigued and expressed excitement at what kind of church this would be. We gradually grew to a group of 30–35. We took up an offering dedicated to book scholarships to Panamanian university students. Most of the participants were pleased with my emphasis on the unconditional love of God rather than the kind of threats they had been used to in the churches they'd attended in North America.

However, after about 18 months, Nick told me some older participants had second thoughts. "I really like Fred and his preaching," some said, "but what if he's wrong?" They obviously worried about their impending passing and just wanted their tickets punched for Heaven.

As our friendship developed, Nick and I decided to venture into building inexpensive houses for the expat market. We found a contractor and negotiated with him to build for us on lots that we purchased. Though we were less successful than we hoped, largely due to our lack of marketing capacity and ability, we did build and sell three lovely homes for a profit. Our contractor proved to be a crook, but he only hurt us a bit before we called it quits.

CHAPTER 13

How We Got to Nicaragua

THIS IS A LETTER I wrote in 2007 to my oldest daughter, Jennifer, to tell her about our decision to leave Panama and move to Nicaragua.

Dear Jeny,

I hope this finds you OK and enjoying your life again. You are in my prayers every day. We are in Nicaragua and have been here since July 1. Argentina had been dreaming about living in Nicaragua for a long time, as she has this wonderful extended family here. Our first thought was to buy a "second home" for extended visits, as we both love Panama. But that week, we saw several very nice properties that cost less than half of similar properties in Panama, so we began to think seriously about the possibility of moving here. We also discovered that though Nicaragua is a very poor country, thanks to Ronald Reagan and George Bush, Sr. and their genocidal wars of the 80s, a rather extensive "first world" island has grown up in Managua, mainly on the road to Masaya, which today is a very modern four-lane divided highway that goes all the way to Granada. It is, of course, a First World island surrounded by a sea of Third World poverty, but on that island, one can live with all the comforts of Orlando or Panama, including cable TV, internet, and shopping malls.

So we decided to look carefully for a place to buy to live in. Since I am 21 years older than Argentina, the odds are that she will spend several years alone. Here in Nicaragua, she will be surrounded by people who love her and can provide support and care. Also, I still have a significant amount of debt that has accumulated over our years in Florida when my salary did not quite keep up with the demands of our family. Selling our properties in Panama will enable us to pay off our debts and still buy a place for us in Nicaragua.

Much to our surprise, Raquel decided to come with us the day before we left Panama. We have rented a lovely cottage on kilometer 14 of the Carretera a Masaya for the month while we begin looking for a new home. We drove to the other side of Managua and went out on the Old Road to León, about 16 kilometers away, to see a house we saw online. It was a lovely place, similar to a Swiss chalet in its architectural flavor, with steep roofs and gables. It has an entire manzana of land, just under two acres. We were charmed, and the price was right.

The next day, we went out with Marlon Gonzales, a young Realtor who showed us five or six homes. He showed us a home in Nindirí in April, just across the highway from Masaya. It is a picturesque place that has won the title of "best municipality in Nicaragua." As you come into Nindirí, a lovely tree-lined boulevard is in the middle of the paving-stone street. Being a traditional village, there is a town square with a colonial Catholic Church on one side and some commerce on the other.

Raquel has fallen in love with Nicaragua and has decided that she wants to study veterinary medicine. We visited the Universidad de Ciencias Comerciales in Managua, Nicaragua's most reputed school for that career. The campus is lovely, and the people at the Veterinary School were clearly competent and on top of their subject.

In addition, I am excited about the possibility of re-activating Faith Partners of the Americas to work on a couple of projects in Nicaragua. There is a clamoring need here for environmental education. I have been working on the idea of working with local churches, utilizing my contacts with CEPAD (a Church World Service-type organization) and CLAI, the Latin American Council of Churches, to get some environmental education at the grassroots level. A second project will involve education against domestic violence, which is nearly endemic here. So, as a surprise to all, I may not be retired yet after all.

Last Saturday, we went to the Plaza of Faith and the Plaza of the Revolution to share in the 29th Anniversary of the Sandinista victory against Somoza and his patrons. There were more people than gathered for the Pope! President Hugo Chavez of Venezuela spoke, as did ex-Bishop Lugo, the new president of Paraguay, and President Zelaya of Honduras. Cuba's Vice President was there, as well as the Vice President of Guatemala. El Salvador and Costa Rica were very conspicuous by their absence. Panama at least sent a warm letter of congratulation. Chavez made an impassioned plea for a resurgence of Liberation Theology. It was an exciting afternoon and evening, and we had a great time.

Well, must close this for now. Please fill me in on what is going on with you. I miss hearing from you.

Much love,
Dad

As we hoped, we sold our properties in Panama and prepared to move to Nicaragua. Our cat, Muffin, was nowhere to be found on the day of our move. After looking for her for over an hour, we finally decided we couldn't wait any longer and asked José, the man who had been taking care of our grounds for the past three years if he would be willing to care for her when she showed up. He knew her well and said his wife and daughter would love her. We had two dogs, Duchess, our German Shepherd, and Cookie, Argentina's Yorkie. Off we went. I drove our Nissan Frontier, and Raquel drove Argentina's Hyundai Santa Fe. We had brought those two cars to Panama from Orlando, and now we were taking them to Nicaragua.

About an hour into Nicaragua, we were stopped by the police, as we had no license plate on the front of the Nissan. I explained that Panama only used one plate in the back, but that explanation wasn't satisfactory. The gendarme wanted a fine of five hundred *cordobas,* the Nicaraguan currency, or he said he would have to impound the vehicle. I negotiated the fine down to three hundred, and we drove on. I was to be stopped an average of once a week for the next 12 months by local police for not having a front plate. This began a wonderful six years in *Patria Libre,* Free Nicaragua.

We found Nindirí to be a delightful place to live. Our realtor, Marlon, recommended a young woman, Maria Elena Calero, as our maid. She came to work every morning on her bicycle at seven a.m. and worked until five p.m. She was with us for the entire six years we lived in Nicaragua.

Please Forgive

While we were in the process of packing our household goods for our move to Nicaragua, I got an email from *Brasília.* Sueli Aparecida Bellato, who identified herself as the Vice President of the Amnesty Commission of the Ministry of Justice of the Government of Brazil, said that the Commission would be meeting to deal with several persons who'd been victims of torture at the hands of the military regime during the dictatorship. My case would be dealt with then, and she invited me to be present. The Ministry of Justice would pay my plane fare to and from Brasília.

My son, Erick, who lived in Recife, had contracted an attorney more than a year before to represent me before the Commission and apply for my status as an "amnestied" person, a misnomer the government was applying to all the people being recognized as having been victims of the dictatorship. On September 24, Argentina and I flew from Panama City to Rio and Brasília, where our friend, Sergio Pereira, received us.

On the evening of the 25th, we went to an elegant restaurant in Brasília for a pre-Commission celebration. To our surprise, we met up with my dear friend, fellow prisoner and victim, Alanir Cardoso, and his wife, Maria. He was accompanied by one of the members of the Commission, who was also a member of the Central Committee of the Communist Party of Brazil (PC do B). Since being freed from political prison, Alanir had been the regional head of the PC do B for the Northeast of Brazil. At the same dinner table, my daughter, Jessica, her brother, Erick, and their mother, my former wife, Tereza, appeared. Another amazing but delightful surprise.

The next day, about 200 people were present: many Catholic Bishops, the head of the Brazilian Council of Churches, several ministers and/or vice-ministers of the Brazilian government, a Bishop of the Brazilian Methodist Church representing the College of Bishops, and many friends and other persons concerned with human rights.

Two of the ministers made welcoming speeches, some quite eloquent and heroic in their affirmation of human rights and their denunciations of the abuses that were committed by the military dictatorship from 1964 to 1985. One of the ministers had been a victim of that regime himself. The most remarkable part of this to me was that the Brazilian Methodist Bishop, speaking in the name of the College of Bishops of the Brazilian Methodist Church, formally asked me for forgiveness for the fact that my own church, the Brazilian Methodist Church, did not support me in any way in 1974.

There were 13 of us there to be recognized that day. All were Brazilians, except me. My case was the first to be dealt with. It began with the president of the Commission, Dr. Paulo Abrão Pires Junior, standing before me and saying, "Reverend Morris, on behalf of the Government of Brazil, I want to ask your forgiveness for what was done to you 34 years ago by agents of our government."[11]

Dr. Paulo then asked me to make any remarks I might wish to make, suggesting I had 10 minutes. I began by commenting that after 34 years, they could not expect a Methodist preacher to speak for only 10 minutes. I then outlined my nearly 11 years in Brazil as a Methodist missionary and described what had been done to me by the Brazilian army's torturers. I concluded by reading the declaration made by the National Conference of Brazilian Bishops on my behalf while I was still in prison. They published this note in the *Estado de São Paulo,* the most prestigious newspaper in the country:

> *On September 30, in front of his home, Pastor Fred Morris was taken prisoner, and only on the fourth day was his imprisonment acknowledged and was he allowed to have contact with the General Consul of the United States. Many notices and accusations have been published about Pastor Fred, and what is to be hoped is that, in a regular process, it will be possible to clarify everything regarding him, with ample possibility for defense. The testimony of his brothers and sisters of the Methodist Church, pastors of Evangelical churches, and Catholic priests and lay persons make clear, based on long association in ecumenical activities, the conviction that an objective examination of the facts and a judgment made with an ample possibility for defense will bring to the public an image very different from that being emphasized in the press." Just last week, the members of the Brotherhood Team* (Equipe Fraterna), *an ecumenical action group that advises the CNBB in the Second Region of*

the Northeast, held a public prayer meeting. On Monday, at eight p.m., this group will meet at the Church of the Monastery of São Bento in Olinda for a prayer vigil.

My testimony produced a very emotional response from the people gathered there. My beloved wife, Argentina, and my ex-wife, Tereza, were sitting together, embracing one another and weeping. Many were shedding tears of shame, theirs because I brought back memories of their own suffering at the hands of the military dictatorship or that of a loved one who may have even been killed under torture. After my testimony, there was a break for lunch. I was greeted and embraced by dozens of those attending. Mauricio Andrade, the primate Bishop of the Episcopal Church in Brazil, was especially effusive. We both recalled Bishop Ted Sherrill, an American who lived and served in Brazil for more than 40 years and had become a close friend of mine.

The Methodist Bishop who had read the letter from the College of Bishops tried to convince me that they were really sorry, but I wasn't convinced. One of their numbers had denounced my friend Anivaldo Padilha to the Brazilian Secret Police (DOPS) as a communist back in 1970, with no evidence. Anivaldo was kidnapped and held in the infamous *Operation Banderantes,* the principal torture center in São Paulo, for nine months of near-constant torture.

I felt totally alienated from the Brazilian Methodist Church for several reasons:

1. My name had been erased from the records of the First Region;
2. My former colleague in Recife, the Rev. Adolpho Evarista de Souza, one of the most mediocre pastors I've ever known and who'd withdrawn from the *Equipe Fraterna* when he saw Catholic priests in it, had managed to get himself elected to the Methodist episcopacy; and

3. The General Conference of the Brazilian Methodist Church had, at its last meeting, voted to withdraw from any organization that had Roman Catholics and "other non-Christians" in it!

That meant withdrawing from the Brazilian Council of Churches (CONIC), which the Methodist Church had founded and whose director was a Methodist pastor, and from CESE, the Brazilian equivalent of Church World Service, an ecumenical agency that tried to meet human needs in a cooperative manner, and whose director was a Methodist.

I was more than willing to forgive the actual Government of Brazil for what its predecessors had done some 34 years before because they were showing that the spirit and style of the government had really changed. They were making significant gestures of repentance, but I saw that the Methodist Church of Brazil had only gone downhill during that period. Their hypocrisy in making what they called an "apology" was nearly total.

CHAPTER 14

How Rancho Don Quijote Came to Be

When we moved to Nindirí in November 2008, we all thought this would be our last move. We loved the house, and it was close enough to Managua for Raquel to enjoy frequent contact with the many friends she had developed over the prior 3–4 months. When she started her classes at the *Universidad de Ciencias Comerciales,* she made more friends and began to get a feel for upper-middle-class Nicaraguan society. Argentina was delighted to be back "home" in her native Nicaragua. We were only a 30-minute drive from Sabana Grande, where many of her cousins and aunt lived. I settled into a routine of starting to work on this book, reading, and just generally enjoying being retired.

In January, we had a wonderful visit with two couples we love: Gil and Inez Dawes and Sid and Ellie Greenfield. I had met Sid when I returned from Brazil in 1974. My dear friend Brady Tyson introduced us. Sid and Ellie were both anthropologists. Sid had been Margaret Mead's disciple and specialized in Brazil, so we had much in common. The two couples hadn't known each other before arriving at our home. Still, we had a delightful couple of weeks traveling around the country and visiting the *Masaya* Volcano, Lake *Managua* in *Granada, Laguna del Apoyo* in *Catarina,* and *San Juan del Sur* beach.

Raquel started discussing the possibility of a *finca* (rural place) for weekends. Most of her new friends in Managua had a *finca* somewhere. She and Argentina were captivated by the idea of having a place for some animals and for planting. At first, it seemed pretty unnecessary to me, but we had just received the compensation funds from the Brazilian government and had a bit of cash in the bank for the first time ever, so we began "looking around" for a small plot of land where we could build a little cabin and plant trees, bushes, flowers, etc. Argentina had always wanted someplace to raise chickens and plant flowers. Our lovely home in Nindirí had only one defect: absolutely no yard.

In January, we made another trip to San Juan del Sur. We enjoyed the beach and found a delightful restaurant, *El Timón,* right on the beach, with great seafood and a lovely view. That evening, we decided to go for supper at *Pelican Eyes,* the posh resort hotel restaurant. As we were driving up the hill, we saw a *"gringo"* couple walking up the hill, so we stopped and asked if they would like a ride. They did. However, when we got to the top, the restaurant was closed. Our new friends, David and Charlene Friend, from Canada, said that Pelican Eyes has another restaurant down below that would be open. It was a delightful place, with the tables on a terrace around an infinity pool and a spectacular ocean view.

The Friends had a lovely place on the hillside overlooking San Juan and the ocean. We invited them to visit Nindirí and stay with us the following week. They asked if we could watch their house while they were in Canada, as they didn't plan to retire in Nicaragua for a few more years. We agreed and suddenly had a beach house.

We continued to be interested in the possibility of buying a *finca.* I contacted *Momotombo* Realtors and asked about *fincas* available in the Masaya area. A charming young woman, Liliam, came to see us and, shortly after that, made a date to show us some properties near Nindirí. We looked at 6–8 properties and finally saw one that looked like a good possibility for us. It was eight *manzanas* (about

13 acres). It was already heavily planted with about 700 citrus trees and 200 *tamarinda* trees. The property also had two wells already in place. We met with the owner and negotiated the price and terms.

We contacted Marlon, the realtor who'd found us the house in Nindiri. We had established a very cordial relationship with him, and he frequently came to our home for lunch or in the evening to *volar pico* (talk, talk, talk) with Argentina. He was gay and had suffered a lot in *macho* Nicaragua. When he discovered we couldn't care less about his orientation, he quickly made us his best friends. We asked Marlon to come with us to look at the property. He didn't seem to be terribly enthusiastic and suggested we drive around the area a bit to see if there might not be some other properties available.

When we got to *San Ramón de Tisma,* Marlon saw a sign indicating a *finca* for sale, about 10 *manzanas* (17 acres). We drove down to look at it. At first look, it wasn't very attractive, as it had been used as pasture for about 25 cows, which had beaten down the soil. It was also quite overgrown with some pretty ugly weed-like plants. However, it had a couple of hills on it. From the top of them was a startlingly beautiful view of the *Charco de Tisma,* a huge wetland connecting Lake Managua *(Xolotlan)* with Lake Nicaragua *(Cocibocla).* From the *finca,* it looked like a lovely lake about two miles away, with the mountains of *Chontales* on the other side.

Argentina and I were immediately attracted to this by the lovely view. Marlon called the number on the sign, and within 15 minutes, two brothers, the owner's sons, arrived. I began negotiating, and by the following Monday, we had agreed on a price of $24,000. Three days later, we bought the place. We weren't really sure what we wanted to do with it, but we drove out to it regularly and began dreaming.

Liliam, who had lost the sale of the other property, told us that her father had a business in *La Paz Centro* near *León,* building *ranchos,* a popular indigenous structure made of eucalyptus tree trunks with a palm-thatched roof. We found a company that agreed to come out and give us a bid on the construction of a large *rancho* (25 x 33 feet) and a small cabin of the same kind of structure but with exposed brick walls. We negotiated a price, and within three weeks, they had built the cabin and the *Rancho Grande.*

Then *don* Concepción, one of the partners from *La Paz Centro,* came out, and together, we decided to add another Rancho and cabin for our caretaker, *don* Julio. We were becoming increasingly enamored of our *finca* and its beauty. Once we got rid of the cows, the place began to bloom. We then asked Harvey, a young brick-layer/contractor, who had done some work for us in building out the patio at our house in Nindirí, to finish up the cabin, do the plumbing work, and put in the floor in the Rancho Grande with *piedra laja negra* (black flagstone).

We began spending more and more time out on our little farm. We had *don* Julio start hacking away at the weeds and began having events there with the family. Meals were all cooked on an open fire. Every time we went out there, we loved it even more. We also discovered that there is a constant pleasant breeze blowing up off of the Charco. We found ourselves dreaming about building a permanent residence on our farm. We began thinking of giving our farm a name. After a few weeks of mulling it over, I came up with *Rancho Don Quixote* in honor of the *Impossible Dream* of justice and peace, which has been pretty central in my life and the theme of Cervantes' Spanish classic.

In June 2010, we finally decided to build our home on the farm. Argentina had always wanted a "Granada-style" house built around a central garden. The living room area is at the entrance, which opens up to the garden. The bedrooms and kitchen are built around the garden. By this time, I had convinced Argentina that we should borrow funds from the bank to start the work, not wait to sell the Nindirí house to begin. Our bank, BanCentro, *LaFise,* agreed to finance the work.

Starting in June 2010, we began a reforestation project for *Rancho Don Quijote,* planting more than 500 trees by the end of June. 400 are flowering trees; the remaining are coconut and fruit trees (lemon, orange, mango, papaya, and avocado). We planned on planting another 1,000 trees in June 2011, as we discovered that 500 trees are not as much as it sounds on 17 acres. Along the way, we purchased two *criollo* horses, Rosinante and Lucero, and let them loose on our 17 acres. Rosinante gained 85 pounds in the first month, while Lucero gained 55. In addition, we had eight dogs, two goats, five parrots, two cats, and a small flock of about 30 chickens.

We spent the next three years on *Rancho Don Quijote*. It was literally paradise on earth. The real joy was the planting we did. We made innumerable trips to *Catarina,* a village just up the road from Masaya, famous for its nurseries, selling dozens of plants, flowers, and flowering bushes. We filled the back of our Nissan pickup a dozen times with plants and flowers and made a marvelous garden in the internal garden of our house and the surrounding yard. Seeing this old cow pasture turn into a horticultural paradise was a delight.

I had a couple of beautiful hammocks made in Masaya; one had *Don Quijote* embroidered on the sides, and the other had "Dulcinea." One for me and the other for Argentina. They were permanently strung in our huge living room, decorated with eight beautiful rocking chairs, four of white wicker and the other four of lovely hardwood. Maria cleaned and cooked, so Argentina and I had the idyllic existence of a couple of expat retirees.

There was a small Methodist presence in Nicaragua. Still, the closest little Methodist church was a semi-Pentecostal group, and that was not our cup of tea, so we were, in effect, unchurched during our six years in Nicaragua. I was asked to baptize a couple of children of members of the family and did a couple of weddings, but that was it. We got to travel around Nicaragua quite a bit, enjoying its beauty. Matagalpa, in the mountains, was lovely. Leon, at one time the capital of the country, has one of the oldest and largest churches in Central America, as well as a noted university, and was the home of Reuben Dario, the most famous literary Nicaraguan, recognized throughout the Spanish-speaking world as a worthy heir to the English Shakespeare, for his eloquent writings and poetry.

We would have a barbeque at *Don Quijote* with some regularity for the family and sometimes have 30–40 people. Occasionally, they would bring hammocks, string them up in our living room, and spend the weekend with us, enjoying our pool and two horses. Lorenzo, our caretaker, would take the smaller kids on rides on Rocinante, while the older ones who knew how to ride would enjoy taking both of the horses up and around our 17 acres. The pool was a great attraction for all, and we had made it child-friendly, no more than 45 inches deep.

Rancho Don Quijote became a landmark in the area. People would use it as a point of reference for giving directions to their homes: "from the entrance to *Rancho Don Quijote,* 150 meters west, 25 meters south, etc."

CHAPTER 15

Homesickness Leads Us to California

At the end of our second year on *Rancho Don Quijote*, our fifth year in Nicaragua, Argentina began to feel serious homesickness for our three adult children. Raquel spent about half her time in Nicaragua and half in San Diego, where she was enrolled in the state university. Gabriela was living and working in Florida, and Freddie was in Los Angeles, having arrived there a year or two before, seeking to follow his dream in the music world.

I sent emails to six Bishops, four Methodist and two Episcopalian, offering myself to do ministry either with Spanish-speaking or Portuguese-speaking communities, including Bishop Minerva Carcaño in Los Angeles. I met Bishop Minerva in 1973 when she was 19 years old, a sophomore at SMU, attending a conference of returning and outgoing Methodist missionaries held at Scarrett College in Memphis. I had not seen her for the 40 years between that conference and when I sent my email. She replied saying there was a small town in Central California, in wine country, that had a UMC congregation she thought I might be able to serve. A place called Shandon, halfway between Los Angeles and San Francisco. The population is about 1,350, 75% of whom are Mexican. Most of those folks worked in the grape-producing fields for the wineries that had grown up since the 1990s. I responded immediately that we would be delighted to serve that congregation.

Argentina was beside herself with joy. We began the whirlwind of seeking to sell the Rancho, pack, and move to California. We arranged to fly to Los Angeles in time to attend the Annual Conference on Redlands University's campus, where I sought out the Rev. Dr. Cedrick Bridgeforth, who was to be my DS. He received me graciously and welcomed me to California. Cedrick is a Black UMC pastor and was, at that time, the president of the Black Methodists for Church Renewal, a national group of African-American UMC pastors. He was a very handsome man in his early 40s, clearly destined, in my mind, for the episcopacy in the not-too-distant future.

I called Gerson Mendez, a realtor in Paso Robles, letting him know we would be driving to the area on Sunday afternoon and needed to find a home starting Monday. He said nothing was available in Shandon, but it was only 18 miles east of Paso Robles. Gerson showed us two condos that were for rent, 2/2s. He then showed us a couple of houses that were 3/2s, the same price. The last house he showed us had yet to come onto the market, a 4/2 on Samantha Lane. We decided it was for us. We signed the lease and got the keys that evening.

The next morning, my phone rang. Our daughter Gabriela was calling from Norfolk, Virginia, where she had just moved with Ben, her significant other. She asked if she could come live with us in California. She didn't say why, but I said yes, of course, we would be delighted to have her live with us. She arrived four days later. A week later, much to our delight, Raquel asked if she could move in with us as well. She had been spending part of her summer with an internship at the Denver Zoo, but that was over.

Pastor Terry, who was leaving Shandon, invited us to have dinner with him at Jack Ranch restaurant, about ten minutes east of

Shandon. It is, we discovered, a famous landmark, as it is where the famous movie star, James Dean, died in an auto crash at the age of 24. Terry gave me the phone numbers of some key members and filled me in on some of the church's history. He had been pastor there for seven years.

The Methodist Church had been there for more than 130 years, but as the demographics of the community changed, the church shrank and shrank until, when we got there, there were only about 25 persons left. They were all Anglos. My appointment was based on the hope that Argentina and I could attract some of the Latino community into the United Methodist family. I contacted the church treasurer and one of the principal leaders, Ellen Schroeder. The church building looked like a Hollywood set. The original building had burned to the ground some years back, but with the insurance funds, it was rebuilt exactly as before.

The following Sunday was my first time at the Shandon United Methodist Church. There were 24 persons in attendance, five of them being our family, as my daughter, Jessica, was visiting us. Lizbeth, our foster daughter from Costa Rica, and her daughter, Zoe, drove down from San Francisco for the occasion. The music was provided by Jerry Perney, a retired music teacher who had taught at Paso Robles High School for 40 years until his retirement. His wife, Gay Perney, was also a former music teacher. Jerry had a wonderful "honky-tonk" style on the piano, which gave an unusual but pleasant flavor to the hymns.

Before the Pastoral Prayer, I asked the congregation members to guide me on what we should pray for. I asked them to start with the larger matters affecting our world, whether related to peace, the environment, or anything else of significance. Then, I asked for requests related to the community of Shandon and its surroundings and, finally, for personal requests.

Things went well in a fairly typical fashion, except that one long-time member of the church, rose to read a Letter to the Editor from the Paso Robles paper, lamenting the influence of gays and lesbians in our community. She asked for prayer that we be able to resist this nefarious impact. I took a deep breath and responded by simply stating that the book of Leviticus gave me permission to sell my daughters into slavery if I so desired. As I had already introduced my three daughters to the congregation, I observed that I thought perhaps the references to selling them into slavery were a bit outdated and that maybe the references to homosexuality might be as well. I suggested that we pray for the love of Jesus Christ to enter the heart of the man who wrote the rather hateful letter and into every heart present in the church that day that we come to understand how much God loves all of God's children. The lady was quite friendly at the coffee hour, as were all the other members of the congregation.

At the announcement time, I did mention I would be beginning a couple of Prayer/Healing groups. I said I would share my experiences with spiritual healing and teach them how we can be instruments for the Holy Spirit of Jesus to touch the lives of people with special needs. I was pleased when eight people actually arrived at the first meeting. I had purchased several copies of Agnes Sanford's little book, *The Healing Light,* and had a copy for each person. I explained I would be using that book as the guide for our group, and we would be reading and discussing one chapter each evening until we finished the book.

One of the people present was April Barnett, the granddaughter of Jerry and Gay Perney. She was married and had two children. Another person who had come was Rhonda, a member of the local Assembly of God. However, when she heard that we were going to be talking about healing from her neighbor, who was a Methodist, she wanted to come, as she had a serious health problem.

After about 40 minutes of my presentation and discussion, I suggested we begin our ministry by forming a prayer list and praying. At that point, Rhonda, a woman in her early 70s, explained why she had come. On the previous Thursday, she had gone to her doctor about a problem with her breathing. He took an X-ray and said that she had a "mass" in one of her lungs. He scheduled her for a biopsy on Wednesday. I invited the group to gather around her chair, and we laid our hands on her and prayed. I encouraged the group to visualize the Spirit of Christ entering into each of us and all of us as a group and then flowing through our hands into Rhonda, purging away anything that didn't belong and renewing and restoring her lungs and body. We stayed with our hands on her for several minutes while I directed the prayer, visualizing the Healing Light of God's Spirit flowing into and through Rhonda's body, healing her, and restoring her health.

On Wednesday morning, I received a call from Rhonda's sister. She said that Rhonda had gone for her biopsy, and the doctor had taken another X-ray to see exactly where he should insert the needle into her lung to extract tissue for the biopsy. But when the X-ray was developed, it showed that the "mass" was gone. Her lungs were normal! A week later, while I was at the church on a Wednesday morning in the hope that perhaps I might be of some use to any of our parishioners who might need some form of pastoral assistance, April Barnett appeared. She immediately told me what happened to her after the Monday evening Prayer/Healing meeting. She told me that her four-year-old daughter, Izzie, had been suffering from asthma. She had been given all kinds of medicines, antibiotics, and steroids by her doctors in the hopes of relieving her from this life-threatening ailment.

April said that when she got home on Monday evening, Izzie awoke from her sleep gasping for breath. She was having another asthma attack, worse than ever before. Her little body was rigid with her struggle for breath. April gave her the inhaler she usually used, but it did no good. The young mother was desperate and getting ready to rush her child to the hospital when she decided to try the kind of prayer we had been talking about in our meetings.

She placed her hands on Izzie's chest and visualized the Spirit of Jesus coming into her hands and flowing through her into the body of her child, relieving her of the spasms of her asthma and allowing her to breathe freely. Following the pattern of prayer we had been learning, she began offering thanks to God for the healing of her child's lungs.[12]

Then, she said, the most marvelous thing happened: as April's hands were on her daughter's chest, the rigidity began to melt away like a block of ice melting in the summer sun. And then Izzie began to breathe freely and normally. Soon, she fell asleep and slept through the night. When she awoke the following morning, she was well.

We continued with the usual activities of a Methodist church. A youth group of high school children met in the church on Tuesday afternoons. Devon Radke, a very active and passionate layperson, led that group. She and her husband had been drug users, along with some other not-to-be-recommended activities, for many years until they had a rather dramatic conversion experience. Devon was attending one of our Prayer/Healing groups, and she told us that her husband had developed a problem with his back. His doctor said that it appeared that he had damaged one or more disks. As a result, he should not try to lift anything more than 25 pounds. A major part of his work was installing air conditioners, so they feared he might have to quit his job and look for something else. This was not a happy prospect, as the job market in the Shandon/Paso Robles area was not very vibrant. So we prayed for him, using Devon as a channel, laying hands on her, and praying for her husband. A week later, she reported that he had been completely healed. After an X-ray of his spine, his doctor said all appeared normal, and he could resume his regular activities.

The church attendance gradually increased to the point where we had nearly 30 persons in church each Sunday. Though that was an almost 50% increase, I was not impressed. We were not bringing in any of the Mexican community in Shandon. The church had a food distribution every other Thursday morning with food provided by the US Department of Agriculture through their offices in Paso Robles. Some 35 or more families came every time to get a significant quantity of fresh food and even some chicken or other protein. Most of the families coming were Latinx, so Argentina and I were present to talk with them while they were picking up their food. They were shocked that the pastor spoke Spanish and his wife was Latina. But that did not translate into any of them coming to our church, even when I announced that we would have a Spanish service. No one showed up.

Just before Christmas, I had an inspiration and visited with the local grade school principal. A Lions Club from Atascadero had donated a huge box of Christmas toys for us to distribute to needy children in Shandon. I asked the principal if she could provide me with the names and addresses of the neediest families in the community. She asked the teachers to name the families with the greatest needs. I then contacted each of those families, asking for the names and ages of all their children. We then put together a Santa's bag for each household with presents for each child and a $50 gift card from the Food-for-Less supermarket. There were an average of 4–5 children in each household.

On Christmas Eve, Argentina and I played Santa Claus and visited each of those homes with the Santa's Bag for the children in the house. It was obvious to us that these would be the only presents the children of those households would be getting in nearly every case. In January, I made follow-up pastoral calls to all those homes to invite them to our church, especially urging the children to attend our Sunday School. Result: one family, Maribel, the wife of a soldier stationed at nearby Camp Edwards, started coming to church and actually ended up joining the church. That was it.

Since September, I had been reading all of the books I could find about starting Hispanic churches in the United States. I wrote my D.S. a letter reflecting on our six months in Shandon and making suggestions about the future. Here is the letter I sent:

January 8, 2014

Dr. Cedrick Bridgeforth
10824 Topanga Canyon Blvd.
Chatsworth, CA 91311-1350

Dear Brother Cedrick:

I hope this finds you well and enjoying a reinvigorated New Year.

We had a wonderful Christmas with three of our children here—the first time in over eight years! And we had four here for Thanksgiving!

We are enjoying our work in Shandon very much. The folks in the UMC there are wonderful and very responsive to our efforts.

However, after six months of labor in these fields, I need to make something of a report and some observations about the future.

The most significant thing during this time has been the formation of two Prayer/Healing groups. One meets on Monday evenings and the other on Tuesday afternoons. We have been studying a little book by Agnes Sanford, The Healing Light, which I have used with such groups since 1958 at the Methodist church I served in Newark, New Jersey, while finishing seminary. It is inspirational and an excellent prayer guide that allows the Holy Spirit to work through us. We have seen many remarkable healings since we started these groups. These have been shared with the congregation, renewing spirituality among the entire group.

Church attendance is gradually creeping upwards. We had 15–20 in worship during the first few weeks, and now we usually have between 30 and 35. As you know, the "old guard" is just that: old. Great people, but most are on fixed incomes, meaning the possibility of increasing the congregation's financial resources is minimal.

I have studied the giving patterns with Ellen Schroeder, our Treasurer. (She is also a treasure!) We will work one-on-one with some of the good folks to encourage them to be more regular in their giving, committing to a certain amount each week, even if they cannot be in the worship service. That alone should bring a modest increase to our income. But even if the $16,000 grant we got last year is renewed for this year, we will still have a shortfall of about $1,000/month, or $12,000 per year.

We have been working hard at forming a Spanish-language congregation. It is slow going. The Latinos are, understandably, somewhat suspicious of the Anglos. Argentina and I have been "working the crowd" on the Food Sharing days (the third Thursday of each month). Most recipients are Latinos and are quite surprised to meet a Spanish-speaking pastor. They are further charmed by my Costa Rican wife. But that has not yet been transformed into a positive response to our invitation to worship at a Spanish-language service.

I have been studying how others have started Latino congregations. The most helpful book I have found is by an Episcopalian priest, Juan Oliver. His book, Ripe Fields: The Promise and Challenge of Latino Ministry, is quite helpful. One of his more important insights is that to be successful, such an effort must have a long-term commitment from the judicatory body, including financial support. As with any new church start, such a commitment must be firm for at least five years, with the necessary finances included.

In Shandon, we have the advantage of having a lovely and attractive building and an Anglo congregation that wants to become inclusive. But we need a financial commitment from the

District and/or the Conference of at least $28,000/year for the next four or five years.

Argentina and I are willing to commit to this work for at least four years. But for that to happen, the District/Conference must also commit.

Thanks for your support. Please let me know what I may do to help this come to pass.

Peace,
Fred Morris

Cedrick's administrative assistant, Dorrel Attaberry, called and asked that I be available for a phone call. Cedrick came on the line and said that the Bishop and her cabinet wanted us to move from Shandon in June to a place called North Hills, in the San Fernando Valley of Los Angeles. North Hills had been the home of the Sepulveda United Methodist Church for many years, and in the 1990s, it was one of the larger UMC churches in Los Angeles, with more than 1,200 members and three pastors. The property was extensive and still hosted the North Valley Caring Services, a service organization formed by the church in the 70s that had evolved into a significant social service agency. A Head Start program also rented the educational wing of the church property. Cedrick said they wanted us to go there and start a new faith community on the former United Methodist Church site.

I was shocked by the request. I said to Cedrick, "You know, of course, that I am 80 years old." To which he replied, "So was Moses." I was greatly flattered that the Bishop and her Cabinet wanted me to start this new ministry. It would be the first time in my 60 years of ministry in the United Methodist Church that I was being asked to go somewhere because of who I am and not just to "plug a hole."

We drove down to North Hills in late February to see the church and to be interviewed by the Rev. Steve Petty, pastor of the nearby Northridge UMC, and Rev. Lew Fry, a retired UMC pastor who was the treasurer of the North District Union, which was the actual owner of the property and who would be paying the bills for the startup, along with Charles Laing, an active Methodist lay person, who was in charge of maintenance of the property.

My three interviewers hastened to say that they would have the house completely rebuilt before we occupied it and that it would be ready by the Annual Conference. We had serious doubts about the possibility of that being done but were excited about what we saw in North Hills. The sanctuary was lovely, complete with a marvelous tracker organ, which we were informed was the finest organ in the San Fernando Valley. The educational wing was occupied by some 122 children in a vibrant head start program—60 in the morning and 62 in the afternoons. North Valley Caring Services was led by its executive director, Ivette Pineda, the daughter of Salvadoran refugees, who had been at NVCS for about nine years and was heading up a vibrant community service program.

Charles Laing informed us of the weekend yard sale in the church's parking lot every Saturday and Sunday. Some years back, the senior lead officer of the LAPD, Officer Charles Chacon, asked Charles if the District Union would allow families in the neighborhood to set up a swap meet in the parking lot on the weekends. Many were trying to earn extra money selling things off the fences in front of their apartment buildings, which was illegal. Officer Chaco didn't like giving them tickets and suggested to Charles that perhaps they could hold a swap meet in the church parking lot. NVCS was willing to administer the program, along with a neighborhood group headed up by *dona* Margarita Diaz, who lived across the street from the parsonage.

With all that activity on the church property, there were good opportunities to form a new faith community. We accepted the appointment and returned home to get ready to move to Los Angeles. Cedrick then told me he would drive up to Shandon to meet with the administrative council to break the news. Argentina and I were disturbed to think they would pull the rug out from under those good folks just as we were beginning to get involved with them and the community. But, I had always followed orders, as it were, in the Methodist system, and I must admit, I was intrigued at the thought of being in Los Angeles.

Cedrick's meeting with the administrative council did not go well. They were utterly shocked by the news of our being transferred to Los Angeles after only one year and were quite upset at what they regarded as a cavalier attitude by the Annual Conference toward them. I had to agree with them; it was clear the Shandon UMC wasn't high on the cabinet's list of priorities. That suspicion was confirmed three years later when the Annual Conference closed the church and took over their bank account and all funds.

On Easter Sunday, the local Assembly of God pastor sponsored a sunrise service at a lovely chapel built by a California millionaire on a hill overlooking Shandon. He invited a Baptist preacher from Paso Robles and me to preach at that service. I was the last to speak and had listened to the haranguing of the first two preachers, who'd spent their time reminding those assembled that if they didn't repent of their ways and accept Jesus as their personal savior, they would spend eternity in Hell.

When it was my turn, I simply shared with them what I regard as the truly good news of Easter, that the love of God is sufficient to overcome even the final enemy, death itself. And, I insisted, as I always did, that love is unconditional, infinite, and meant for all of us. A week later, we had a newcomer in our service, a young woman who introduced herself as Elizabeth Roderick, along with her lovely nine-year-old daughter, Juniper. At the coffee hour, she said she'd been at the sunrise service on Easter Sunday, was intrigued by my message, and wanted to know more.

Not having many visitors or newcomers at our little church, I arrived at Elizabeth's home the next day to get acquainted and answer some of her questions. I gave her a little book about Methodist beliefs and, a couple of weeks later, she asked to be baptized and to join the Shandon United Methodist Church. Maribel, the Latina woman who'd started attending with her four children after our Christmas efforts, also wanted to join. So in May, just a couple of weeks before our final Sunday in Shandon, I received *four* new members, a 20% increase in one fell swoop.

CHAPTER 16

Final Roundup

I HAD BEEN CALLING Charles Laing regularly about the progress of rebuilding the parsonage. He'd had many problems getting the permits to do the work and suggested we delay our move until at least July 15, when he felt sure the house would be ready. On July 15, the movers came to our Paso Robles home, packed our stuff, and hauled it to North Hills. Our daughter, Gabriela, had decided to take over the lease on our house there, together with a couple of roommates. She'd found gainful employment in a childcare center while awaiting approval of her teaching documents by the State of California.

We drove down to North Hills with our two dogs: Tiffany, our Nicaraguan Maltese, and Ziggy, the mutt that Raquel had found on the beach at Coronado, Panama, only 4–5 days old—still not having opened her eyes.

I suddenly had an inspiration about how to start our work in North Hills. The news of those days, on all the TVs and in the papers, was about the children at the frontier, the thousands of unaccompanied minors who'd been showing up at our southern border, fleeing from gang violence in El Salvador, Honduras, and Guatemala. I knew those gangs had their origins in Los Angeles back in the 1990s. The LAPD decided the best way to deal with its unmanageable gang problem was to deport the gang members. Most of them had been brought to the US during the 1980s as their parents fled from the wars Ronald Reagan fought against the people of those countries. Many of the parents had gotten residency and/or citizenship from Reagan through one of the amnesty programs he carried out. Thousands of young gang members were deported to Central America from Los Angeles.

When they arrived in El Salvador, Honduras, and Guatemala, many spoke poor Spanish, as they had grown up in the US. And having dropped out of school, they had few skills other than using guns and extorting money from the citizenry. So, they started doing exactly what they knew: extorting money from the local citizens. Thus, countries that had never had gangs of any significance before suddenly found themselves overwhelmed by violence. These gangs soon made alliances with the narcotraffickers from Colombia and became transhippers of cocaine and marijuana from Colombia to the United States. The final piece of this destructive set of organizations was a set of alliances with the Mexican mafia to facilitate the transport of drugs from Central America to the southern border of the United States.

The unaccompanied minors were children the gangs sought to recruit into their organizations. The standard procedure was for a couple of gang members to approach a child, often as young as 10–12, almost always a boy, and invite him to join their gang. The initiation rite was to take a gun and kill the local baker—to prove their valor—and to get them compromised in such a way that they could never leave the gang. Young girls were frequently raped then told they would be the gang's girlfriend.

Many of these children were terrified and ran home to tell their mothers what had happened. The mothers, in turn, borrowed money from local loan sharks, paying 10% interest per month, and gave a *coyote* $5–6000 to take their child to the US to stay with a brother or sister who'd gone there maybe 20 years earlier. Those were the children arriving on our southern border.

While movers were unloading our things from their truck into our new home, *dona* Margarita Diaz appeared, along with Officer Chacon. Both offered to help as we began our work in North Hills. Margarita said she was the president of a community neighborhood group and would help in any way we needed. I took her at her word and asked if we could gather any folks from the neighborhood the coming Sunday for a prayer service for the children at the frontier.

On Sunday afternoon, open for the first time in five years, the sanctuary was comfortably full, with more than 100 people. I introduced myself as the new pastor and welcomed them to the prayer service. While talking with Margarita, I discovered that most people didn't understand why these children were coming, and many were dumbfounded to think of the mothers who'd let their children make such a trip. In Spanish, I explained why, and I saw the light of comprehension coming into their faces as they suddenly understood why a mother would let her child flee from the gangs, as the alternative was either to become a murderer or, as the gangs threatened, see their own family murdered.

We then had several prayers for the children. I asked Margarita's husband, *don* Carlos Diaz, to lead us in prayer, as she'd told me he was an active Catholic layman. Then I invited others to pray, and I concluded with my prayer for these children, their families back home, and our community here in North Hills so that we might learn ways to welcome and care for these children. During the rest of July and into August, I mostly wandered around the neighborhood, getting acquainted with the place and some of the people.

On the first Sunday in September, I got up early, put on a stole, and walked out to the parking lot as the various families set up their stands to prepare for their Swap Meet. I asked *dona* Margarita, the coordinator of the swap meet, the *yardita,* to invite people to gather around me as I wanted to pray for them and their families. Soon, 30 or 40 people gathered together, and I prayed for each one, and their families, and asked for God's blessing on them during that day's sales. I did that each Sunday for the next two months. Then, in November, I announced at the end of my prayers for them that next Sunday, I would set up an altar in the parking lot and offer the Sacrament of Holy Communion for any who would like to join in.

Dona Rita, one of the vendors, immediately sought me out and asked if she first needed to go to confession before receiving communion. I told her that wasn't necessary. She shared that she hadn't been to mass in nearly 30 years, having been excommunicated by her priest for leaving her abusive husband.

I printed up the sacrament of the Lord's Supper of the United Methodist Church in Spanish and had about 65 copies ready for the following Sunday. I set up the altar on a folding table with a red cloth, two candles, a chalice with Methodist grape juice, and a plate with Mexican bread rolls. Shortly after seven a.m., I had Margarita use her bullhorn to invite the people to gather around the table for the sacrament. Some 40 people paused in setting up for the swap meet and came to the table.

They were clearly surprised to hear the service in Spanish. As we proceeded through the liturgy, they were even more surprised at how similar the Methodist liturgy was to the Catholic Eucharist. Most of the folks were of a Catholic background, though many, like Rita, were not actively part of any Catholic community. I discovered a multitude of reasons for their falling away: many had been excommunicated by a priest, like Rita, because their marriages had fallen apart; others because they used birth control or had had an abortion. Some were angered when the priest wanted to charge as much as $500 to baptize their child, or to bury a family member. Some didn't believe anymore in all the church demanded they profess to believe. Some 15–18 persons actually shared in the Communion that first Sunday. The following week, between 20–25. Then the group grew to 40.

Though California was famous for its sunshine, by mid-January it was cold and blustery at seven a.m. in the parking lot and barely light. After the morning service, during which we were all shaking and shivering, one of the participants said, "Pastor, couldn't we do this inside the church?" To which I replied, "What a great idea!" And the following Sunday at seven a.m., we met inside the sanctuary of the United Methodist Church. I had invited Beto Ruiz, a lay member of the Northridge UMC and a retired music professor at California State University, Northridge, to join us with his guitar to lead us in singing.

Shortly after, I announced one Sunday I wanted to start prayer/healing groups for anyone interested. Within two weeks, we had about 17 people in the Tuesday afternoon group and another 15 on Wednesday evening. As some of those showing up didn't speak Spanish, we did both groups bi-lingually. Again, I used Agnes Sanford's book *The Healing Light* as our textbook.

Early on, a woman in our new faith group, Claudia, told us that her sister Angela had been traveling across Mexico to come to the US when she was kidnapped by a Mexican gang. The gang found Claudia's phone number in Angela's phone and called to demand several thousand dollars as ransom, threatening to kill Angela if the ransom was not paid. We began praying for Angela's release, and while Claudia was seeking the required funds, Angela miraculously escaped from the gang and made her way to California. Soon, she was in our prayer group, too. We also saw several people healed of various ailments, ranging from arthritis to heart problems to cancer. The group's enthusiasm grew as they learned to pray effectively, to be used by God's Spirit as channels for God's healing touch.

In January 2015, Rev. David Farley, a California-Pacific staff member who headed up the Justice and Compassion Ministries, approached me to discuss the problems facing the children at the frontier. With the help of Ivette Pineda at the North Valley Caring Services, we put together a grant request to the United Methodist Committee on Relief (UMCOR), asking for a bit more than $300,000 to aid the formation of four welcome centers in the conference: one in North Hills; another in Claremont; a third in Watts; and the fourth Escondido, near the border with Mexico. The request was to meet the human disaster of the arrival of thousands of unaccompanied minors at our border.

There had been some ugly incidents in some of the border communities, with groups of rednecks gathering to block the transport of some of the children to detention centers in the area, shouting "Go Home" and worse things at these children. David and I wanted to provide places to aid the children and welcome them in through United Methodist churches. Our request was granted, and suddenly, we had some funds to enable us to actually do something.

Argentina saw a couple of men in a shopping mall offering aid to families looking for homes to buy. One was a realtor, William Ordoñez, and the other, Jaime Tapia, head of a company that provided mortgages for home purchases. Argentina mentioned I was the pastor of the UMC Hispanic Mission in North Hills and wanted to start a welcome center for some of the unaccompanied minors coming across our southern border. Both men expressed a strong interest in aiding in that venture.

As soon as David told me we'd receive $15,000 from the UMCOR grant, I invited Jaime and William to be part of a steering committee to assemble a welcome center. Then, I reached out to Gloria Myles and Ivette Pineda as well. Gloria had been part of our congregation in Chicago at Broadway UMC and identified herself to me at the Annual Conference at Redlands when we were appointed to North Hills. I then invited Anchulee Raongthum to join the committee. She had been on the Board of the North Hills East Neighborhood Council.

The steering committee began working on forming the North Hills Welcome Center for Children. We soon put together an event in the neighborhood for July 15, 2015, to launch the Welcome Center. We got several local merchants to donate items for a raffle at a family event at the church. We got two TVs, bicycles, a tablet, and other items. We also had a piñata for the kids. We offered hot dogs and punch for all who came. Result: we had nearly 200 people from our neighborhood at the event.

As we began, I explained our desire to establish a Welcome Center for some of the unaccompanied minors coming across our border, fleeing from gang violence in El Salvador, Guatemala, and Honduras. I went into detail about why they were coming and why they needed our help. The response was very positive. Then, our committee member, Jaime Tapia, took over as master of ceremonies and carried out the raffling off of the various items we had. Every person who came had been given, at the gate, a ticket with a number. The corresponding number was put into a small rotating basket, and we had some of the children present take turns pulling a ticket out of the basket. There was a lot of excitement, followed by screams of joy as people discovered they had won a bicycle or a TV.

The Rev. David Farley was present, and through his efforts, we had three refugee children present, the first "clients" of our new Center. David introduced me to Amanda Escobar, who he explained was originally from Honduras but had lived in El Salvador for several years and worked closely with Archbishop Romero and his group, defending the people of that country from the violence of their army. Amanda had to flee back to Honduras because of her close relationship with Archbishop Romero, but when Hurricane Mitch swept across Honduras, she was forced to flee to the United States, where she came under the rubric of TPS (Temporary Protected Status), along with several thousand others. Amanda was looking for a job, and David recommended her as a person who could make our new Welcome Center work.

He had already designated $15,000 from the UMCOR grant to us, so I sat down with Amanda and asked how much she'd need to work with us to form the Welcome Center. She and her 15-year-old daughter, April, rented a room in a home in Sylmar, about six miles from our church. I worked over her pretty modest numbers, and we devised a proposal allowing her to start almost immediately. The budding North Hills UMC Hispanic Mission had been generating some income from the yard sale, and the North District was giving us $2,000 per month for our needs. I also discovered that many families around the church had a serious parking problem, as the apartments they were renting provided just one parking space per apartment. We began offering overnight parking in the church's parking lot in exchange for a monthly donation of $50. So, I could add to the UMCOR funds some of the church's income to make it possible for us to hire Amanda.

She proved to be a Godsend. As a refugee herself, she had a heartfelt desire to help the children arriving at our border. In addition, she had worked at the Salvadoran Consulate and knew many of the appropriate people and organizations we needed to work with to make this happen. The church building had a large space that became the office for the Welcome Center. The family event had given us some exposure in the area. Jaime Tapia took it upon himself to have 5,000 full-color flyers showing what services we were offering to refugee children.

Soon, foster parents, the aunts and uncles of the children who had been released by the Border Patrol and Immigration and Customs Enforcement (ICE, the largest police force in the country) started showing up at the church. Amanda developed some intake forms to be filled out with the appropriate information about the child and their foster parents. A health center opened shortly at Monroe High School, just a few blocks away, and through that center, we discovered we could get all our children into MediCal, a state-sponsored health insurance program.

It became apparent that the most urgent need for these children was legal assistance. We contacted CARECEN (Central American Resource Center), Esperanza, KIND (Kids in Need of Defense), and Public Counsel to get pro bono legal assistance for nearly all the children who came our way. However, due to the tremendous volume of children coming across the border, it soon became impossible for them to help all of our children. We began to contact a group of "low bono" immigration attorneys who gave us a reduced price. The going rate in Los Angeles to represent a child was between $8,000 and $20,000. But our low bono attorneys would accept one of our children for a fee of $3,700. I negotiated with them to take a retainer of $1,500, then the foster family would assume the responsibility of paying $100 per month for the next 22 months.

Within a year, we had nearly 100 children registered in the Welcome Center. We decided to form a non-profit rather than just doing the work as part of the church. We needed to raise money from various agencies, including foundations, who do not like to give money to religious entities. The second reason was that I wanted the Center to be independent of the goodwill of the ecclesiastical authorities of the UMC. When I was expelled from Brazil, within two months, the pastor who took my place closed the family planning clinic because he "didn't believe in family planning." As a non-profit, the Center would have its own Board of Directors to maintain and control it, independent of the ecclesiastical authorities.

I needed to start the process of getting 501c3 status, which would permit people and entities to take a tax deduction for their donations to the Center. So, our committee became the Board of Directors, and I became the President/Executive Director of the San Fernando Valley Refugee Children Center, Inc. (SFVRCC). It took a year to get that done, but we made it. For the first two years, Amanda and I were the whole show. But then we got an intern from CSUN, Nancy Avelina. As our numbers grew to 200, then 300, we also attracted more interns, some from CSUN and others from UCLA. The National Board of Global Ministries of the United Methodist Church heard about us and showed interest.

Unfortunately, the other three Centers David and I had hoped would do similar work did not prosper. The one in Claremont discovered that only a few families were receiving children in that prosperous community. That Center eventually moved to Riverside, where it did pretty well for a year, but then the pastor was transferred to another church, and the UMC in Riverside was closed. The Center in Watts moved to Huntington Park, where they had fifty-some children, but we could not get any response from the pastor there to know exactly what they were doing. Escondido prospered for a couple of years due to the presence of an outstanding short-term United Methodist missionary who managed to contact a large number of Guatemalans who lived in the area. But when her term was over, that Center simply faded away.

In the meantime, we had two budding congregations at the North Hills UMC Hispanic Mission. One was built around the people participating in the *yardita*. We held a worship service with Holy Communion every Sunday morning at seven a.m. in the parking lot. They came into the sanctuary for a while, but then several complained that some of their goods disappeared while they were in the church, so we went back outside where they could keep an eye on their stands while at worship. At ten-thirty a.m., we had another service in the sanctuary. The *yardita* group stabilized at around 30–35 each Sunday morning, while the other congregation ranged from 30 to 55.

In January 2019, I formed an administrative council of 15 people from the two groups, which became the governing body of the mission. We met monthly to deal with all matters relating to the church, including the *yardita,* the parking lot occupants, and the relationship between the church and the SFVRCC. The North Valley Caring Services (NVCS), our campus partner, was formed in the 1970s. It provided a free breakfast for some 75–80 homeless people. It eventually spun off and became a non-profit, leasing parts of the church property to provide social services. In addition to the breakfasts, it had an excellent English-as-a-second-language program with 30 to 40 women in it. It also had a vibrant afterschool program for neighborhood children.

The Robert and Marion Wilson Foundation provided significant funds to maintain and improve the property, even after the church was closed in 2009. When I arrived, plans were being finalized to remodel the gymnasium and social hall bathrooms. They were dilapidated and inadequate, but when the Wilson Foundation got through, we had four large bathrooms, complete with showers, that allowed people experiencing homelessness to spend 15 minutes getting cleaned up every day of the week from 9:00 to 12:00. That meant that 36 people could have a bath every day of the week.

In 2018, I was approached by the City of Los Angeles about the possibility of our parking lot being used as a safe parking place for families living in their cars. I agreed immediately, only insisting that there would be security all night. As we are in a gang area, I didn't want those families to be victims of gang assaults. It took the City two years to actually get around to doing it, during which I passed the program over to the NVCS, as we couldn't administer it. Soon, 25 families were sleeping in their cars in our parking lot every night. They were required to receive counseling and social assistance to help them to get into permanent housing. That program had a surprising turnover as people graduate to permanent housing and others take their place. Most families had jobs but couldn't get together the first-month/last-month/security deposit required to sign a lease. Many lost their homes when the banks robo-signed foreclosure documents.

In 2018, Ivette Pineda, the executive director of NVCS, told me she would have to look for another job as one of their major funders had pulled out. As SFVRCC had received some good financial support from a fundraising gala at Sportsmen's Lodge, I offered her a half-time position with us, which enabled her to keep NVCS going. However, it also revealed a problem. Amanda had been doing a great job in receiving the children: we had more than 200 then. But I could see that she was developing co-dependent relationships with the children and the foster parents. Most of them saw her as a mother figure, and she seemed to do a lot for them that they could/should be doing for themselves.

In February 2016, David Farley asked me to take one of the unaccompanied minors over to the First Methodist Church in Pasadena to share the center's work with them. I invited a 17-year-old young man, Miguel Muñoz. I translated for him as he told his story to the congregation. He had been in his first year at the university in San Salvador when he had the misfortune to be a witness to a gang murder. The leader of the gang had been a childhood friend of Miguel and recognized him as a witness. A few days later, Miguel was attacked and beaten by the gang and told that if they saw him again, they would kill him. So, his family sent him to Los Angeles, where he had two uncles who'd been here for 20 years or more.

At the end of the service, a man came up to me and said, "I want to help this young man."

"What did you have in mind?" I asked.

"Money," he responded. He handed me his business card and asked me to call him the next day.

The man wanted to be anonymous, so I will call him Tom. He was Jewish, and his parents came to the United States in 1938 as refugees from Nazi Germany. He made his fortune building apartment buildings in Los Angeles, and was "paying it forward." I had no idea what he was doing in a Methodist Church in Pasadena, but he said he wanted to help Miguel finish his education. I told him Miguel was required to repeat 12th grade in high school and learn English. He would be going to a community college in the fall.

Tom wanted to help Miguel finish his education and get him into USC to complete his engineering degree. He asked me how much money Miguel would need. To cut to the chase, Tom sent a check for $25,000 to SFVRCC, with the understanding that half would be a fund for Miguel's education and living expenses so he could study full time, and the other half for SFVRCC.

We had our first fundraising gala in the spring of 2017. None of our Board members had ever participated in such an endeavor, except for Ninette Ayala, who worked at Penny Lane, a social service agency just a block east of our church. Ninette was a grant writer for Penny Lane but had observed fundraising galas, so she was invaluable in helping us stumble through the process. It was marvelously successful. We expected around 125 people coming, each paying $100, but we actually had 174. We had a silent auction with a half dozen autographed books by Noam Chomsky. We raised nearly $100,000 at the event, partly due to a $25,000 donation from a single donor.

Amanda's daughter, April, came on board as a paid intern, working about 15 hours weekly in the office. She was especially helpful to Amanda as her official translator, as April was fluent in English and Spanish. In the spring of 2018, we moved toward our second fundraising gala. This time, we had professional help from Giselle Fernandez, an Emmy-winning TV journalist who had been the Larry King of Latin TV for many years and was the anchor at *Spectrum One*'s morning news program. With her help, we had more than 300 guests and raised a much larger sum than the previous year. Through Giselle, we had the help of several TV figures, mainly some producers and some important Hollywood figures, such as Eva Longoria, who received one of our *Champions for Children* awards.

In 2019, a professor of literature at UCLA got her entire class involved in producing a book about the history of SFVRCC and its work. They interviewed several of our children, translated their stories into English, and then delivered a thousand copies of the book. The Board of Global Ministries of the UMC followed up with a second edition of another thousand copies. It dealt with how the Center came to be and was accompanied by artwork done by the 10 and under children in our therapy meeting.

All the children were dealing with the impact of traumas they'd received before they got to us. I knew that my friends Al Cohen and Faith Sands had a daughter, Heidi Pembroke, a professional trauma therapist, so I contacted her for help. She responded positively but said she was leaving the following week for Geneva, Switzerland, to take part in a program of trauma therapy for refugees from Syria. She recruited an excellent fellow therapist in Pasadena, Dr. Linda Pillsbury, who in turn, recruited a half dozen colleagues, and soon we had a pioneer group trauma therapy program at SFVRCC.

Every other Sunday, from one p.m. to three p.m., some 20 of our children would meet with the therapists. All the therapists were professionals, but none had done group therapy. Since we had so many children with needs, they agreed to share techniques with the children that enabled them to deal with their anxiety attacks and flashbacks to the horrors they'd experienced. This program continued for the next three years, stopping only with the COVID-19 pandemic when we could no longer have face-to-face meetings.

In January 2019, we hired an administrator to work in the office, coordinating the work of SFVRCC and the Church. She was very competent, though she proved somewhat abrasive in her human relations. She had conflicts with Amanda, who did not respond well to having someone coordinate her activities. We tried to work around these conflicts for several months without much success. In July, I had the good fortune to bring on board Mayra Medina-Nuñez as Associate Executive Director. I had known Mayra almost from the beginning of my time in North Hills as she was in charge of a program called CAL-PAC-NIC, a program of the Annual Conference providing workshops periodically at local churches in Southern California for persons needing help with their immigration paperwork.

Without knowing that CAL-PAC-NIC was being shut down for lack of funding by the Annual Conference, I reached out to Mayra to see if she would be interested in working with SFVRCC as my associate on a part-time basis. She said yes and explained that as of July 2019 she would be unemployed, so she was happy to take the position. As she had worked closely with Amanda for several years and had established a close friendship, this was a potential solution to the tensions we had seen growing among our group.

Soon, we hired Mayrimn, an outstanding attorney from Puerto Rico, who was willing to work with us for a relatively small income because her husband had a well-paying job. We were not in a position to provide full-blown immigration services, but she could evaluate cases that came to us and help us know what the next steps should be for our clients—which, at Mayra's suggestion, we began calling participants.

We now had a team of six, including Amanda, Nancy, and April, with Mayra, our attorney, Mayrimn, and myself. At the December meeting of the Board of Directors in 2020, I recommended Mayra be named the Executive Director and that I continue as President of the Board and as a consultant. I felt quite confident that Mayra would take the organization to a higher level when I retired and sailed off into the sunset.

CHAPTER 17

Religion Is mostly BS, but . . .

ALTHOUGH NOT a definitive source, Wikipedia provides a handy definition of religion as "a collection of cultural systems, belief systems, and worldviews that relate humanity to spirituality and, sometimes, to moral values. Many religions have narratives, symbols, traditions, and sacred histories intended to give meaning to life or explain the origin of life or the universe. They tend to derive morality, ethics, religious laws, or a preferred lifestyle from their ideas about the cosmos and human nature."

That is a pretty good anthropological description of religion. But in the everyday lives of most human beings, religion is a concept relating to a particular religion, usually the one dominant in their community of birth. It is more a religious institution than "a collection of cultural systems, belief systems, and worldviews that relate humanity to spirituality and, sometimes, to moral values." In the American experience, it is a church, synagogue, or, more recently, a mosque. So one can easily say, without any further elaboration, "I am a Methodist" or Baptist or Catholic, Jew, or Muslim, or, in increasing numbers, an atheist, meaning that someone has rejected all religious institutions and concepts readily available. One's personal identity is often closely related to one's religious institutional identity. Indeed, much of what passes for morality today is closely connected to institutional religion.

I have been saying, in the pulpit and out, for more than 50 years that religion is primarily a mechanism to enable some people to control other people's lives. Dr. Howard Clark Kee, my New Testament professor at Drew Seminary, once told me, "The history of the Church is mostly the history of the efforts of men to domesticate the Holy Spirit—and their failure to do so." Karl Marx said, long before Dr. Kee or I had an opinion, that "religion is the opiate of the masses." Unfortunately, both my observation and Dr. Kee's are accurate. As well as Marx's.

When I was appointed pastor in Teresópolis, Brazil, in 1965, after my first sermon I was approached by a couple dragging their 14-year-old daughter with them. They told me, "Pastor, please tell our daughter she shouldn't wear such a short skirt." They saw me as the ultimate authority on dress code and, by implication, morality in general. I later discovered that a Baptist church in the same town had a yardstick nailed vertically to the door frame at the entrance to the church, which was marked to show exactly how high a skirt could be off the ground for a woman to be able to enter the church.

When I was transferred to pastor the Methodist church in Pilares, every Monday, the grandmother of Paulo Ayres (a then-seminary student at our Methodist seminary in São Paulo, who later was elected Bishop of the Brazilian Methodist Church) came to my office with a list of young people she knew were smoking cigarettes. I was supposed to discipline them to the extent of excluding them from the church if they didn't repent.

Despite the congregation's expectations, I simply refused to be the moral arbiter of the community. I responded to such requests by suggesting those questions were a matter of individual responsibility and that we, as Christians, must learn to deal with them ourselves and not expect the pastor or some other authority to make decisions for us. Of course, the result was that I was not as popular with the congregations as I would have been had I assumed the authoritarian role that was expected of me—a role that most other pastors gladly accepted.

But these kinds of problems are small potatoes compared with the church's failure to deal with the significant issues facing the people. Instead of confronting important issues like war, poverty, global warming, racism, women's rights, LGBTQ rights, the death penalty, birth control, abortion, the rights of workers, and land ownership, the church and the churches have been silent. Or they have made lofty proclamations at the national level and let it go at that. For instance, we declare our opposition to the death penalty but make minimal effort to educate our congregations on the real issues involved, or to challenge the latent urges for revenge that make nearly three-quarters of people in the US express favor for the death penalty. This is done in the name of Jesus of course, some even citing the Biblical "an eye-for-an-eye" comments to justify the killing of people who've committed murder, conveniently ignoring the horrific way in which our "justice" system eventually manages to kill virtually all of the Black and Brown murderers but rarely executes a White murderer.

We are largely silent about the fact that States that have the death penalty universally have higher murder rates than those that don't. This detail clearly denies the usually offered pretext that the death penalty deters crime.

It is a rare preacher who will take a stand from the pulpit against war because of a well-founded fear that if they challenge the congregation—and the nation—over a war, whether in Vietnam, Grenada, Panama, Nicaragua, Iraq, Afghanistan, Libya, Yemen, Somalia, Syria or Iran, they will be seen as "not supporting our troops." Indeed, the horrendous rate of suicide among current US soldiers clearly indicates that these young men and women are not comfortable with the roles they have been forced into in foreign lands—killing people for reasons they do not understand. At the very least, some of the congregation members will reduce their giving to the church or even leave it, calling into question the financial survival of the pastor and their family. It is a very rare Bishop who will defend a pastor for taking such a stand. "Avoid controversy" is the byword from the hierarchy, as it, too, is under the gun financially.

Being in the Wesleyan tradition of the United Methodist Church, I have always been constrained to be concerned about the social justice issues of our society, whether it be racism, sexism, exploitation of workers, poverty, the death penalty, war, and so on. I have spoken out on those issues. Of course, one result has been I was never appointed to any of the "tall steeple" churches.

Now that I am retired again, but still reflecting on all of the above, and in fact on my whole life, I find myself dealing with even more fundamental issues about the nature of God and the relationship of God with the creation and us, the creatures. I was a good student in seminary, graduating *cum laude* from Drew University (missing *magna cum laude* by 0.02 points on my grade point average). I found the Biblical studies and theology to be challenging and most interesting. But I also found myself involved in two strains of the Christian life that are not always united: spiritual development and prayer and spiritual healing on the one hand, and justice issues on the other.

I got involved in spiritual healing because, reading the New Testament, I saw that the Holy Spirit's actual power was the proof of God's presence in the church. Throughout the New Testament writings, manifestations of the Holy Spirit were presented as expected in the life of the church, whether through healing, by speaking in tongues, or by inspired preaching. This led me to seek to understand why and how such things can happen in the church in our time. But at the same time, the presence of that same Spirit in my own life and my reading of the Biblical prophets, like Amos,

Jeremiah, Isaiah, and Micah, forced me to be concerned about injustice, such as racism, sexism, war, homophobia, and poverty.

I have observed that the churches and synagogues have been used by social and political structures to keep people content with the way things are and allow those in power to continue their ruthless exploitation of any and all. The history of the church, at least from the Fourth Century on, after Emperor Constantine made it the Roman Empire's official religion, is the history of the cross and the sword working together to maintain law and order. This enabled the ruling classes to continue to dominate and exploit the peoples of the earth and the earth itself.

Even the Missionary Movement, of which I was a part for many years of my life, has largely resulted in the domination and exploitation of the people being evangelized. James Michener's incredible book, *Hawaii,* illustrates clearly how the missionaries to those islands ended up owning them—and the people ended up with nothing. Unfortunately, that is not just the story of what happened in the Hawaiian Islands. This reality does not mean that Christian missionaries have consciously and deliberately served the Empire. In most cases, they are dedicated and self-sacrificing people, sincerely seeking to follow the will of God. But that doesn't change the fact that their efforts have been used effectively for other ends.

Basically, the mechanism of domination put in place by the church and the churches is fear. The Gospel has been preached as the only way to salvation, which is portrayed as "going to Heaven," where everything is perfect, and there is "no more pain, sorrow or tears." But the way to that salvation is always conditioned by total obedience to the church. When the Pastor/Priest/Bishop/Pope says jump, you have only to ask "how high" or "how far." If you don't, you will not go to Heaven but instead to Hell, where you will suffer the agonies of fire and brimstone forever.

Even after the Reformation, the preachers and pastors of the reformed churches all too often took on the same role of social control. Check out the preaching of Jonathan Edwards in the pre-revolutionary days of the colonies. Though Hell is not preached often from the pulpits of most churches today, it is still in the background thoughts of the worshippers, as they are encouraged to get ready to "go to Heaven," whatever that might mean. And, of course, the alternative to Heaven is still Hell. And certainly, the promise of Heaven is being held out in virtually all churches as the final reward for being good boys and girls all of our lives—and making contributions to the church.

But today, we no longer know what we are talking about when dealing with Heaven and Hell. The three-storied universe of the Bible doesn't exist. But we still look up to thank whoever might be "up there" when we make a touchdown or hit a home run; we still worry about our friend or relative who wasn't an altogether good person when he/she dies and we have to attend the funeral. Where are they now? Did they go to Heaven? The preacher at the funeral always seems to imply that they must have, even though they never measured up to the standards that have been preached forever. Comfort is given, but pretty much without any content.

So, what happens to the really supreme assholes who wander around this planet for a lifetime, causing pain and damage to untold numbers? I don't just mean the Hitlers and Stalins and Bushes and Donald Trumps, but also the abusive husband, the shrewish wife and mother who makes the life of her husband and children a living Hell until her dying breath. I mean the serial killer, the pedophile, the Wall Street banker who destroys the financial lives of millions with their unbridled greed, the politician who promises to "serve the people" but only lines his own pocket, the political leaders who have ignored the clear warnings about climate change for political and financial gain.

But clearly, Hell is not a geographical place that can be located or even described. The best I have been able to imagine is simply standing before a Holy God and knowing God knows everything you have done that has been harmful to anyone, anytime and anywhere. The embarrassment and shame of such a moment would be infinite and incredibly painful. And inescapable.

In addition to these kinds of speculations, there are still some pretty basic questions about the nature of God. It has always been a complicated subject, even when the earth was regarded as the center of the universe. But today, when modern astronomy has demonstrated that there are more than 100 billion galaxies in the observable universe, each with more than one billion stars like our Sun, with untold numbers of planets out there, questions of *Who is God? Where is God? Is there a God?* are awaiting an acceptable answer. And certainly, the question of whether God is a Baptist, a Methodist, a Lutheran, or an Episcopalian has become totally absurd. From an astronomical perspective, the labels of our religions become meaningless. She might even be Jewish, Hindu, or Buddhist—or, most likely, none of the above.

Is it possible that the God we've been brought up to worship and fear—or ignore—is in charge of all of that? If the Being that we call God is really the Creator of Heaven and Earth, which includes 100+ billion galaxies and all those stars and untold other planets, is it possible that such a God can be in the least concerned about us? Can God really hear my prayers—and respond in some way? Does that really make any sense at all?

In her magnificent book, *A History of God,* Karen Armstrong shows how humans have developed a notion of God over the past 4,000 years or so. She demonstrates how people have, from the beginning of human history, yearned for God or gods. Something innate in humanity causes us to perceive there is something larger and greater than we are. Sometimes, this is seen as nature, but usually, we have given form to concepts of divinity—a Creator-being—or, at the very least, a Rain God, Sun God, or some deity who controls some essential part of our lives.

One of the questions modern skeptics throw up is how can a God possibly pay attention to each person throwing up daily prayers and petitions? George Carlin, one of our modern and much-lamented prophets, asked: "If there is a Divine Plan, what's the point of my praying for God to intervene and change some details? Who am I to ask God to interfere with God's plan?"

I don't pretend to have the answer to questions about the existence or not of God. It has long been demonstrated by philosophers and theologians alike that we cannot prove the existence of God by rational or logical arguments. Nor can we disprove the same. We end up needing to make what the theologians call the "leap of faith." That means simply embracing a concept based on the best possible assumptions and then living one's life in the light of that concept. The original congregations of the Christian Church were communities of people who had heard a call to follow the first-century prophet named Jesus of Nazareth with lives based on *trust* in Jesus and the God he called us to follow. To believe in God is to bet on God's existence and live in the light of that conviction. This is a question of trust—putting our trust in God the Creator.

In Portuguese, two words can be translated as "believe." One is *acreditar*. This means to accept a particular idea or concept as fact. I can *acreditar* that the world is round, based on what I have learned in school and—if I have been inquisitive—observations I may have made about the earth's curvature. Believing in this idea is an academic matter—*acreditar*. The other word is *creer*. This is to believe by making a leap of faith—or getting into a ship and sailing out on the ocean toward the place where skeptics tell you the world ends, and you will fall off. If you *creer* that the world is round, you get in the boat. It is a matter of trust.

The original Christian communities were made up of *believers* who committed to following the life and teachings of Jesus, no matter what the cost. They got into the boat and sailed out into the unknown waters of the world. But today, even if we declare that we *trust* in a God, we are faced with how that God—maker of Heaven and Earth—can respond to individual humans. Can God really count the hairs on my head and see every sparrow that falls to the ground? Can God really be concerned with and involved in my life and my community?

I recently had an experience with our little GPS device (Matilda is her name) that gave me some insight into the possibility of God's ability to relate to each of us. Matilda responds directly and accurately to my requests for guidance, even as she simultaneously responds to millions of others. I understand about the satellites that the GPS is communicating with. Still, I do not know how that system can follow me with such detail and take me to the closest coffee shop, even correcting me when I miss a turn and telling me how to get back to where I was supposed to be. And if I change my mind along the way, Matilda will tell me of another place to get a cup of coffee, a taco, or pretty much anything else I might like. And while Matilda is providing me with all that personal service, she is *"personally"* providing the same service for anyone and everyone else who asks for assistance (and has a GPS device).

It seems clear to me that if a computer system designed by a bunch of very intelligent computer engineers can respond so effectively and in such detail to me in my car, even while responding in the same way to a few million others anywhere in the world at the same instant, it is not unreasonable to believe that the Creator of the 100+ billions of galaxies and the billions of stars in the observable universe could do the same—and even more. The real question is whether this God *cares* about us enough to bother, not whether it is reasonable to think God *could* respond to us. Certainly, the Creator God can/could respond to us. Does the Creator God who made this infinite universe want to relate and respond to the creatures?

My answer to that question is a solid *yes*. It is not based on a lot of philosophical mishmash or religious dogmas and claims but on my understanding of what we Christians call God's self-revelation and my own experience over the past nine decades.

I understand, probably as well as most Biblical scholars, that the Bible is not a transcript of God's words. The stories in the Christian Bible were not intended by their writers to be understood literally. They were and are stories—part of The Story of the Bible. They are like a mosaic, which takes on meaning only as one stands off a bit and gets the Big Picture. The Story of the Bible is not in the details. And it evolves as it moves on. But the message of that Story is quite simple: the Creator of all that is, which we cannot see or understand more than partially (through a glass darkly), is characterized by the word love. Love for the creation and the creatures.

It is filled with horror stories of a God telling the tribes of Israel to carry out war crimes against the peoples of Egypt, Palestine, and Syria. It has more than a good dose of stories of meanness and evil being ordered by God and carried out by his servants. In the telling of that Story, a lot of junk gets into the narrative precisely because the books of the Bible were written by fallible men and women like ourselves. The people God chose made a lot of mistakes and were pretty rebellious most of the time, even to the point of killing God's messengers. But when the Story gets to the life, ministry, and death of a strange man from Galilee, one Jesus of Nazareth, we catch a vision of the personality of this God that clearly indicates that God cares about us. More than that, this God has a purpose that we can participate in. Jesus called that the Reign of God, where God's intentional purpose of abundant life for all becomes a reality here on earth despite the evil and meanness of human beings. It is a Story of God caring about the poor and demanding justice and hospitality for all—especially the widow, the orphan, the wayfarer, and all in the world who are marginalized by society. Jesus of Nazareth came proclaiming God's love for all and showing that love by healing people who were excluded from society (lepers, tax collectors, prostitutes, etc.) and making them part of his family. The religious and political leaders of his time saw him as subversive and executed him.

Now, reading and understanding the overall intention of this Story as presented in the Bible is not necessarily convincing today. Many sensitive and caring people reject the whole idea because of the bloodiness of the actions in God's name in the early stories—and because of the history of abuses of people by the followers of the Story—the Christian Church. The Crusades, the Inquisition, anti-Semitism, later persecutions of women accused of being witches, and the institution of slavery—all in God's name—make it very hard for many people to accept the Story. Current scandals of pedophilia in the Catholic Church, covered up by dozens of Bishops and even the Pope himself, have turned many away from the Story.

However, I still embrace the Story of God's love for the creatures and the creation, despite all of the above, and more, for two primary reasons: One, the Story has been the inspiration for some of the highest and finest acts of service and self-giving in human history. It has resulted in people like St. Francis of Assisi, Martin Luther, John Wesley, Dom Hélder Câmara, Martin Luther King, Jr., Nelson Mandela, Dorothy Day, Agnes Sanford, and Oscar Romero in El Salvador, to mention just a few of the saints who have been formed by the Story and have followed the *Impossible Dream*. It has been an inspiration to me in my own pilgrimage over these many years.

Two, as I have followed this dream, I have experienced in my own life the reality that God *does* care and is involved in human history—and in my own life. I have seen in my pilgrimage that when I seek to put this Impossible Dream at the center of my life, events come together in a providential way that enables me to be of service and find fulfillment. In my own life, I have seen the power of God manifest itself in and through me in ways that are not rationally explicable. I have prayed for people dying of heart failure and seen them get up and go about their lives with full health; I have prayed for people with cancer and seen them get well; I have asked for God's guidance before making a life-shaping decision and seen events occur that could not have been anticipated making it clear which way I was to go. I have also made decisions that I was convinced were God's will, only to discover that I was wrong and had made a disastrous turn. But when I sought God's help and orientation, it came, and a way was opened for me to get back on track, very much as with Matilda, my GPS, only better.

The Wesleyan Quadrilateral

John Wesley used what later theologians have described as the "quadrilateral" as a methodology for doing theology. The four parts for Wesley were scripture, tradition, reason, and experience. Using the quadrilateral, I start, in my own life, with the Bible—not reading it as the "dictated" Word of God but as a record of how thousands of people have responded to the God-urge within them and how that affected their own history. Starting with the Bible and its Story, my experience in seeking to follow the Impossible Dream validates what the Bible teaches us, that is, if I don't get hung up on the contradictions I encounter in that book.

Similarly, in studying the tradition of the churches, I have been inspired by people who followed the dream—sometimes successfully, sometimes not, and often despite resistance and opposition by the so-called "leaders" of the churches. The traditions of the church(es) contain a lot of trash but also powerful testimonies of how the Word of God has shaped thousands of people's lives and history. It also shows in many ways how people can respond to the self-revelation of God and relate to each other. Further, using my own rational faculties, I have made sense of the Biblical message and its purpose for my life. Finally, my own experience has confirmed that God is the underlying reality of our world, the "ground of our being," as the 20th-century theologian Paul Tillich described it.

Through it all, I see the witness of people like myself and how God has chosen to make a self-revelation to us. I have spent my life studying many aspects of God's creation, including human history, philosophy, and literature. These studies provided me with many insights into the reality of our world and have shed much light on how humans can and should relate to that reality. In one of the best books I have read on prayer, John Magee, a professor at the College of Puget Sound, has a chapter on "Science, Law and Prayer."[13] He points out that much of our misunderstanding and subsequent rejection of prayer comes from our so-called scientific understanding of reality being a couple of hundred years behind the times. Most of us are locked up in a mechanistic view of the world in which rigid laws of cause and effect rule. So, asking God to violate or modify those laws to help us in times of stress or difficulty seems patently absurd. This approach to reality has shaped our modern thinking about economics, medicine, and even ideas about human freedom. Such deterministic views of history relieve us of any responsibility for changing or even shaping our reality.

For example, economics is less of a science and more often an ideological construct aimed at protecting a particular group's privileges. The Ayn Rand garbage that promotes the most extreme *laissez-faire* economics under the guise of "freedom" is really a means to justify plain old greed. Yet, it is embraced by millions who think they are on their way to becoming the next Bill Gates or Mark Zuckerberg.

Science has indeed freed us from centuries of mental and cultural garbage, and modern medicine has rid us of smallpox, polio, and a dozen other childhood diseases that have all too often crippled or killed children and adults. More dramatic conquests, like heart transplants, have given additional years of life to people who would have otherwise succumbed to early death. However, we aren't as enlightened as we like to think. Our current understanding of reality is a mixture of mechanistic science and primitive magic. And neither are accurate descriptions of reality.

Dr. Magee points out in his book that 20th-century science moved beyond a purely mechanistic understanding of reality to see a basically organismic world. This means that the universe is not a massive set of balls on a pool table, banging against each other and causing effects down the line, but that it is composed of "living substances organized within other living substances." The Heisenberg Principle of Uncertainty has shown that we cannot predict the behavior of atomic particles in any but a statistical fashion. Or, as Dr. Magee writes, " . . . every part of the atomic event is in organic connection with the rest. We are left with the strange, though experimentally established fact, that we cannot 'predict' exactly what will happen until the event is past."[14]

More than 200 years ago, astronomer Pierre Simon Laplace declared that if one could gather, for a single instant, all of the information about the forces in operation in the universe, one could predict the movements of the entire universe, from the stars and planets down to the atoms. This would include every person on earth. Current scientists know this is a false assumption because the relations between even the smallest particles known do not follow a strictly mechanistic pattern. Alfred North Whitehead, writing in 1925, stated: "The stable foundations of physics have broken up . . . . The old foundations of scientific thought are becoming unintelligible. Time, space, matter, material, ether, electricity, mechanism, organism, configuration, structure, pattern, and function all require reinterpretation . . . What is the sense of discussing a mechanical explanation when you do not know what you meant by mechanics?"[15]

Current science has shown that the borderline between animate and inanimate beings is undefined. For instance, the sub-microscopic crystals we call viruses show many characteristics of bacteria but clearly are not bacteria. However, they seem to obey "living" laws, not "mechanical" ones. That is one of the reasons why the HIV virus is so hard to nail down, thwarting efforts at developing a vaccine.

This leads one to postulate that the entire physical world is simply a collection of living entities, no matter how elemental the "life" within them may be. In other words, what we regard as mechanistic law is like the actuarial table the insurance company uses to calculate rates for life insurance policies. They can determine the life expectancy of a class of people by simply studying the actual death rates. They can say that the average man in the US will live to be 77 years old. But that is only a statistical average that cannot predict the date of death of any one person. Thus, the mechanical laws of physics, chemistry, and medicine are also statistical averages. But underlying them is a universe of non-predictable and thus variable activity. This means that the universe itself is to be seen not mechanistically but as an organism pulsating with life and governed, as our own bodies are, by a will.

If we can put our will in harmony with the underlying will of life in the universe, which is another way of describing God—what we call miracles can take place. Events can come about that do not fit within the mechanistic laws of cause and effect but result from bringing a higher law of life to bear within the context of the will of life, which is the fundamental nature of reality. This means that my life, efforts, and prayers can, as they are in harmony with that will of life, cause "miraculous" results.

Religion vs. Faith

I'm not inspired by religious institutions and what is commonly called "religion." But I am a great believer in faith—an attitude of confident trust in the Creator and a willingness to accept the unconditional love of Abba, our Heavenly Daddy. My life has been dedicated to inviting people to accept that love, and to live lives caring for the creation and all its creatures. The institution of the United Methodist Church provided me a platform for doing that, even though it has been less than supportive of me and my ministry at several crucial times. But following this path has been an adventure that I wouldn't give up for anything.

My father, a Methodist pastor for more than 50 years, required my attendance at his weekly services throughout my childhood. Through his preaching I heard that the Good News of Jesus was that God loves us. When I was at the University of Chicago from 1968–1970, the famous Swiss theologian Karl Barth came to Chicago on a speaking tour. One afternoon, he met with a group of pastors from every denomination imaginable, including Southern Baptists. After Dr. Barth's presentation, there was the usual question time, during which a Baptist preacher, clearly with an ax to grind, asked the theologian, who had recently published his 20-volume *Christian Dogmatics,* to sum up his theology in just a few words.

Barth didn't hesitate, saying, "Jesus loves me, this I know, for the Bible tells me so." End of questions. And that declaration really does sum it up. It doesn't require the acceptance of a bunch of doctrines and dogmas. It is a matter of trust, which is what I understand faith to be: *trusting* in this infinite and unconditional love of the creation and the creatures by being responsible for all existence and by participating in the "bending of the arc of history toward justice," or to use Jesus' words, the Reign of God.

As I conclude this memoir at the age of ninety, I am humbled by the realization that our humanity is marked by frailty and imperfection. Yet, the enduring message of hope lies in the Creator's boundless capacity to work through us, despite our limitations, fostering love and compassion. The details of any and all parts of this Story are not important. What is important is to understand that we live in a world in which love for creation and all its creatures is the underlying reality, and that we are all called to live in that love and to share it. And that is really Good News.

Epilogue

On the second Sunday of June 2021, I preached my last sermon at the North Hills United Methodist Mission. At 87, after 68 years as a Methodist preacher, I retired again, and we moved to Nicaragua. We are loving it here. In 1977, while I was a resident correspondent for *ABC News* in Costa Rica, the Sandinistas launched their insurrection against the Somoza regime with a bloody attack on the National Guard headquarters in San Carlos, Nicaragua. They wiped it out, but Somoza sent reinforcements, forcing them to flee the San Juan River to Costa Rica. I interviewed some of them in San José for *ABC* and met Padre Ernesto Cardinal and some Sandinista fighters. I had never heard of Sandino and knew nothing of Nicaraguan history, like most US citizens, even though I had been a history major in college. So, I began reading up on the country and its hero. And I was drawn into the Sandinista movement.

During the last two years of the insurrection and then the Sandinista victory on July 19, 1979, I worked more than half-time for *ABC*. They sent teams of reporters to Costa Rica, who then crossed the border into Nicaragua. I got to know many of the future leaders of the Nicaraguan government, like VP Sergio Ramirez, Violetta Chamorro, and Alfonso Robelo, as well as Padre Ernesto and Padre Miguel D'Escoto, future Foreign Minister of the Sandinista government.

Now, we are back in *Patria Libre,* Free Nicaragua.
Did you know that:

- Nicaragua has a higher percentage of women in posts of political power—ministers, members of the Assembly, mayors, police captains, etc.—than all but six other countries in the world?
- Nicaragua is number five on the list of nations with the best gender equality in the world, right after four Scandinavian countries?
- The US invaded Nicaragua in 1909 to collect a debt owed to the Boston Bank, and maintained an occupation army until 1933, when Augusto C. Sandino and his Band of Merry Men drove the US Marines out of the country?
- The US Ambassador collaborated with a plot to assassinate Sandino on February 21, 1934?
- Anastasio Somoza, a former used car salesman in New Jersey, was in charge of the newly cloned National Guard (1934) mainly because he spoke excellent English and could tell dirty jokes with the Marine commanders who never bothered to learn Spanish?
- A year later, he deposed the puppet president, took over the country, and ruled it ruthlessly with his two sons, who followed him until 1979, when the Sandinistas, following Augusto Sandino's example, led a revolution and threw Somoza out? And that 50,000 Nicaraguans, out of a population of a little more than three million, died in that insurrection, dying to get freedom for their country?
- Since 1979, the United States of America has tried constantly to eliminate the Sandinistas? First by the Contra war in the 1980s, which killed another 30,000 Nicaraguans, then by buying the election of Violeta Chamorro in 1990, with a mixture of direct threats by Bush I that he would destroy the country

if she lost, then spending several million dollars (illegally) to finance her campaign?

- The International Court in the Hague ruled that the United States owed Nicaragua $18 billion (in 1986) for war damages, which led to the US withdrawing from the Court?
- After Daniel Ortega was elected president in 2007, the US began a consistent campaign to undermine the Sandinista government? It spent over 100 million dollars in illegal funding of NGOs and insignificant political parties to defeat the Sandinistas.
- In 2018, the US Embassy in Managua led a failed attempt at regime change, financing insurgent groups with funds and weapons to seek to overthrow the government? That more than 200 persons were killed in those efforts, including 22 Nicaraguan police; that the Catholic hierarchy in Nicaragua openly supported the efforts, and at least one Bishop and several priests were videoed participating in the torture of Sandinistas who were captured by the insurgents? That the Bishop had to leave the country after more than 500,000 Nicaraguans signed a petition demanding his removal? That he is now living in Miami, supporting the anti-Sandinista Nicaraguans living there, with no visible means of support?
- On June 17, 2021, the Sandinista government arrested more than a dozen leaders of opposition movements on charges of money laundering and receiving funds from the US government illegally to seek to undermine the upcoming elections in November? The laws they violated are nearly copies of US laws regarding foreign agents, who must report any funds received from foreign sources. Now, the US is calling those traitors "political prisoners."
- A recent poll by opposition groups showed that Daniel Ortega will get more than 60% of the votes for president in November

and that no visible opposition candidate got double-digit numbers? (The Sandinistas got 76% of the votes in November 2021.)

- Nicaragua's economy is expected to grow by around 4% this year, more than any other Central American country?
- The Sandinista government has given up on trying to satisfy the demands of the US about its elections and anything else and is demanding the respect and sovereignty that every nation deserves—by arresting the US agents on its soil and charging them with crimes and not bowing to ridiculous demands by the OAS (Organization of American States, or, as Che called it, "Ministry of the Colonies"?

In March 2023, the US State Department asked the Nicaraguan government to release 222 people serving prison terms for crimes against the State and sent a chartered jet to take them to Washington. A Catholic Bishop under house arrest, refused to leave with the others and was sentenced to 26 years in prison for his persistent efforts over the past five years to get his congregants to take to the streets to overthrow the elected government by force.

The government of Nicaragua has terminated diplomatic relations with the Vatican, withdrawing its ambassador from Vatican City. It has also terminated its membership in the Organization of American States. And it has strengthened its ties with Russia and China, who have donated significantly to infrastructure projects in Nicaragua.

Since Daniel Ortega's election in 2007, the Sandinista government has built 25 new hospitals in the country, compared to zero in the 17 years of the neo-liberal governments of Violetta, Aleman, and Bolaños that preceded that election. They have built and maintained more than 100 "maternity hospices." Any woman in the country can go to one of these homes a month before her due date and stay up to two months after the birth of her child at no cost. They have also established a "Women's Department" in more than 100 police stations in the country where a female official will hear and respond to a complaint by a woman about any kind of abuse. (When I was a pastor in Los Angeles, victims of domestic violence could go to the police station, where they would generally be received by a huge male sergeant, which was so intimidating they would usually leave without filing a complaint.)

It gives me deep satisfaction to live in a country that defends its dignity and sovereignty against the most powerful country in the world, which has been trying to dominate or destroy it for more than 150 years.

Appendix

TORTURE, BRAZILIAN STYLE *Time* article from Nov. 18, 1974:

> *Torture is still widely used in Brazil, despite pledges made last spring by the country's new President, General Ernesto Geisel, to halt the barbaric practice. According to a report compiled by Brazilian Roman Catholics, former victims and attorneys, at least 79 persons have died under torture in the past nine years and thousands of others have been subjected to beatings, electric shocks and other torments. Torture, said the report, has become "institutionalized" in Brazil, conducted mainly by military security forces. A recent victim was former United Methodist Missionary and* Time *Stringer Fred B. Morris, 41, who was held without charges for 17 days by military officials in Recife. His report:*

After a chance meeting on the street, my Brazilian friend Luis Soares de Lima, 27, and I were getting into my car when about a dozen men in jeans and sports shirts, armed with machine guns and .45-cal. automatics, surrounded us, covered our heads with hoods, forced us to the floor of a station wagon and roared off. The man in the front was speaking into a walkie-talkie, using the code word hospital, saying that the "operation was a success," and that we would be arriving in a few minutes. We did—at the Fourth Army headquarters in downtown Recife.

Luis and I were immediately separated. I was forced to remove my clothing, except for shorts, and was dragged off to a small cell and left alone. Having lived in Brazil for most of the past ten years, I had heard all the horror stories about torture, and I wondered whether my fate would be the same as Paulo Wright's; the son of US missionaries, he was arrested more than a year ago, and has not been heard from since. To calm myself, I repeated, very deliberately, the 23rd Psalm:

The Lord is my shepherd; I shall not want.
Yea, though I walk through the valley of the shadow of death,
I will fear no evil; for thou art with me.

I felt a calm inner strength, which stayed with me. I needed it. After about 15 minutes, the cell door was flung open, my head again hooded, my hands manacled behind my back, and I was dragged off to a room that for me became a torture chamber. I again repeated the 23rd Psalm, as I was to do on every such trip for the next three days.

Still hooded, I was roughly pushed to the end of the room, and the questioning began. Several men were present. They wanted to know about Luis. They said he was a Communist, which I doubt. I said that we were friends, but that I knew nothing of his political activities. For my answer, I was kicked three times in the groin until I fell to the floor in pain. Questions continued: Where was Luis going? Why was he with me? My answers were met with fist blows to my chest, belly, kidneys and back.

More Shocks. The beatings went on for about half an hour. Then water was poured on the floor around me, a wire was fastened to the second toe of my right foot, and a spring-clip electrode to the nipple of my right breast, pinching so hard it cut the flesh. Trying to make me confess that I was a Communist, they resumed the questioning. Now my denials were met with shocks as well as fists. The voltage was successively increased, becoming so painful that I doubled over until I fell to the floor.

After about 20 minutes, the electrode was shifted from my breast to my right ear. These shocks seemed to be taking off the top of my skull. A blue-white lightning filled my head. Spasms forced open my mouth in screams, then slammed it shut on my tongue. My agony was highly entertaining to my inquisitors; there was much laughter in the room.

Next, the electrode was removed from my ear, and my shorts were pushed down. I remember saying "Oh, no!" I knew what was coming. The spring clip was placed at the base of my penis. Spasms threw my legs out from under me, causing me to fall with all my weight on my back. This ordeal continued for about an hour: questions, shocks, blows to head and body, falling to the floor, getting up to repeat the process.

Then I was dragged back to the cell. The handcuffs were taken off, passed around the outside of one of the bars of the door, at eye level, and refastened with my hands in front of my face. After about 15 minutes, back to the torture chamber for more questions, beatings and shocks. This continued for several hours. Then I was strapped to an armchair, wired with one electrode on my now bleeding right breast and the other on my right ear. The shocks were unbearably painful. At least twice I blacked out.

Finally, the real reason for their interest in me emerged: my inquisitors began asking endless questions about Roman Catholic Archbishop Hélder Camara, a vocal critic of the regime and a friend of mine. They were furious about stories that I had filed to *Time* and the *Associated Press* that they considered favorable to the Recife archbishop and unflattering to the dictatorship. They cursed Dom Hélder, claiming that he was a liar when he accused the government of condoning torture. Their tirade was accompanied by more shocks and my screams. Twice during the afternoon they tortured me in front of Luis in an effort to get information from him. He refused to give in, though I could tell he was distressed by my pain.

Fat Man. At one point, the most vicious of my tormentors got down on his knees in front of me, lifted up my hood so I could see his face and said that he would kill me if I did not cooperate. I believed him. Later, he told me his name: Luis Miranda Filho, a swarthy fat man with a huge black mustache. He is a notorious sadist, known in Recife to be responsible for countless tortures. He and a Colonel Meziat, identified as chief of intelligence of the Fourth Army and the man responsible for my imprisonment and torture, were the only ones I saw whose names I learned.

After more than eight hours of torture, I was allowed to use a bathroom for the first time, then taken back to my cell and hung by handcuffs on the door for the night. I was in a standing position, the handcuffs so tight on my wrists that circulation was nearly cut off; my left hand had been sprained and was painfully swollen. I passed the night standing and occasionally dozing, then being jerked awake as I sagged toward the floor and the cuffs pulled painfully on my wrists.

The next morning, exhausted from shocks, bruises and lack of sleep, I was hooded and hauled off again. Once more I recited the 23rd Psalm and again arrived before the interrogators inwardly at peace. I was made to stand, and electrodes were again placed on my breast and ear. Questions moved back to my arrival in Brazil in 1964 and all of my career as a missionary of the United Methodist Church, then focused mainly on my journalistic activities for *Time* and the *A.P.* Between sessions I was again hung on the cell door. Except for about an hour when I was strapped to the armchair, I was on my feet from Monday morning until sometime Tuesday evening.

That night the turnkey opened the peephole and offered me half a cup of water and a piece of bread—my first food or water since breakfast on Monday. Then back to more interrogation, which continued for a couple of hours. After that, I was dumped on the floor of my cell. I was still in my shorts, with no blanket, bed or pillows, just the bare concrete. I fell into an exhausted sleep, and was allowed to rest through the night.

Wednesday morning I was hung up on the wall of the torture room by handcuffs, with my arms high over my head. More questions about Archbishop Câmara, *Time* and Luis were accompanied by beatings on the back and kidneys. After about 15 minutes, I was taken down, turned around and hung up again, this time with my back to the wall, exposing my belly to their blows. Later, they turned me to the wall again, demanding to know the name of Luis' fiancee, so they could arrest her. I said I didn't know her, though I did. They used a new (to me) shock device. It was some kind of wheel with spikes on it, which they rolled across my back, scratching me. As they pushed down on it, it also gave me a severe electric shock.

At one point during this session, I was startled by a cold piece of metal being placed on my chest. I discovered that it was a stethoscope: the prison doctor was just checking my heart to see how I was bearing up.

To my surprise and despite my fears, I was bearing up rather well. I had not betrayed any confidences though I had none that could possibly have been of interest to the government, or made any false admissions.

I spent Wednesday night shackled to the door again, but on Thursday the questioning was accompanied by only a little torture. And then came help. US Consul Richard Brown in Recife was finally given permission to see me. My friends had alerted him to my disappearance. It took him three days to get Brazilian authorities to honor an international agreement granting foreigners the right to see diplomatic representatives of their country. On Friday Ambassador John H. Crimmins officially protested my treatment to the Brazilian Foreign Office in Brasilia. After five more days, Brown managed to get Colonel Meziat to provide a mattress for me; in seven days I was given decent food and a New Testament. After 17 days of confinement, during which I lost 15 pounds, President Geisel signed an expulsion order. Without being given a chance to get any money from my bank account or arrange my personal affairs, I was escorted by the federal police to Rio, told that I would go to prison for from one to four years if I ever returned to Brazil (though no official charges were ever made), and placed on board a flight to New York—and freedom.

Endnotes

1. Dr. Kee was the author of a book entitled *Understanding the New Testament*, Prentice Hall. 5th Edition, 1993.

2. A year later, Natanael drove Gessé out of the Methodist Church and he formed the "Wesleyan Methodist Church," which rapidly grew to be more than four times the size of the Brazilian Methodist Church.

3. That November, the Divinity School abolished these exams and they were no longer required for entering doctoral students.

4. Minerva graduated from SMU and went on to study at Perkins School of Theology in Dallas and was ordained a minister of the United Methodist Church. Later, after serving as pastor in churches in the Rio Grande Valley of Texas she became a District Superintendent, then, recognizing that the South Central Jurisdiction of the United Methodist Church would never elect a Mexican-American female pastor to be bishop, she transferred to the West Coast, serving as a district superintendent in the Oregon-Idaho Conference from which she would eventually be elected Bishop, and served in the Desert Southwest Conference and later in the California-Pacific Conference, where, in 2013, forty years after our contact in Nashville she asked me to come out of retirement in Nicaragua to serve a new Hispanic Mission in Los Angeles. Bishop Minerva Carcaño has become one of the most forceful

Bishops of the United Methodist Church, struggling for justice for immigrants and refugees.

5. Over the next 40 years, anytime I sent Noam an email I would get a response within 24 hours. In 2015 when we lived in Los Angeles and Noam had moved to Tucson, Argentina, I had lunch with him and his Brazilian wife, Valeria, a doctor of sociology. Noam's first wife died shortly after they celebrated their 50th anniversary. He married Valeria a few years later after having met her while speaking at a Brazilian university. Noam began our luncheon in Tucson by asking Valeria to speak with me in Portuguese. He wanted to be sure I hadn't been putting him on. She was duly impressed with my ability to speak her native language. In 2019 we were invited to go to Tucson again to join in the celebration of Noam's 90th birthday.

6. Wilson and I had had a great relationship during my years in the First Region. We were both pretty straight forward in our desire to be faithful to our calling to preach the Gospel of Jesus, but were both impatient with the arrogance and self-righteousness of the leaders of the Methodist Church. This came to a focus one day when we were sitting together at a command performance by Bishop Natanael. The Bishop commanded all of the pastors in Rio to gather for a day-long retreat in the Methodist Church of Cascadura, one of the suburban *bairros* of Rio. The Bishop then announced that we were to find a prayer partner and make a commitment to pray for and with him every day, forever. Wilson and I immediately agreed that we would make a solemn pact never to pray for each other. From that day on, from time to time we would reaffirm that pact. For instance, while Wilson was living in Switzerland, in exile for several years, and I was kidnapped and tortured by the Brazilian army, Wilson wrote me a letter to reassure me that he had remained faithful to our pact and had resisted the temptation to pray for me throughout my imprisonment. Loving him as I did, I deeply appreciated his devotion to our common pact.

7. This was a method I employed repeatedly during my tenure as Executive Director of the Florida Council of Churches. I knew the denominations in Florida were not about to risk their necks by picketing against a company like Coca-Cola. But, in fact, all of those denominations did have clear statements at the national level supporting the rights of workers to organize to defend their rights. Those denominations in Florida had something like 3.5 million members in their congregations. Though the Council was, in reality, a paper tiger, our letterhead was beautiful and on more than one occasion had an impact in the struggle for justice for workers.

8. Publix had/has a long history of anti-union policies. They automatically fire any employee that even looks at a union. And they are totally resistant to the efforts of any "outside" groups, like the Florida Council of Churches, to engage in dialogue on the issue.

9. Bishop Chuck Leigh was Bishop of the Apostolic Catholic Church. He approached the Council around 1999, asking for membership for his denomination, a kind of "Old Catholic" Church, which held to most of the doctrines and practices of the Roman Catholic Church except that it ordained women, allowed priests to marry, and supported LBGTQ persons without restrictions. I encouraged the Council to accept this new denomination as a member. Later on, I aided them in their successful attempt to become members of the National Council of Churches. Bishop Chuck told me that back in the Reagan years he had been a victim of Reagan's COINTELPRO, a fascist branch of the FBI that sought out persons against Reagan's wars in Central America. Bishop Chuck was a Vietnam vet, having been awarded the Silver Star for his actions there, but he opposed Reagan's wars. He was accused by COINTELPRO of having falsified baptismal documents for Salvadoran refugees from the war in order to aid them avoid deportation. He was convicted and sentenced to 15 years in prison. His ministry was in a very poor part of Tampa, where he

lived with and served the poor. I came to admire him deeply, as he is one of the very few clergy I have known of any denomination who actually lived the life of a follower of Jesus of Nazareth, suffering genuine persecution as a result.

10. All of this was complicated, in my view as well as that of most of the directors of state Councils, by the fact that Bob had demanded, and got, a salary of $250,000.00 per year when he was hired to be the General Secretary of the NCC.

11. In January of 2009, just before President Obama was to take office, *Tikkun* magazine, a Jewish publication, asked me to write a "Letter to the President," based on my experience, asking him to follow the Brazilian example of asking forgiveness of those who had been victims of human rights violations by the Bush administrations, and to offer them reparations, as the Brazilian government had done for me. I wrote the following letter to Barack Obama:

> *In 1974, I was the victim of human rights violations by the Brazilian army, being tortured in various manners for 17 days in their torture chambers in Recife, Brazil. But then, in September of 2008, while you were campaigning for the presidency, I was invited to Brasília, where the Vice Minister of Justice of the Government of Brazil stood before a group of more than 200 persons and asked for my forgiveness for what had been done to me by a prior government, 34 years before. They then gave me a cash gift as a symbol of their repentance as well as a lifetime pension. I have no doubt that actions such as these by your administration would go far toward restoring some dignity and honor to the United States, which today is held in contempt by the whole world for the actions of its government in its now-infamous "war on terror," and the use of torture and "rendering" against persons suspected of actions or attitudes against our country. Even persons who have actually been involved*

in actions against our country do not deserve to be tortured. A civilized society cannot use such a practice for any reason, not even the specious one of gathering information to avoid terrorist actions. Experts from the CIA and the FBI have testified to the fact that torture does not produce reliable information.

The efforts of the Amnesty Commission of the Brazilian government are not only healing the victims of the military regime's old wounds—they are also helping the entire nation of Brazil to regain its dignity after the horrors of the military regime. I beg you to do the same for our nation as you begin the process of change in and for the United States.

On December 11, 1974, I was invited to testify before a congressional committee (Congressman Don Fraser's Committee on International Organizations and Movements within the House Committee on Foreign Affairs) about my experiences in Brazil. In that testimony I said the following: "Torture brutalizes and dehumanizes not only those who are tortured but also those who torture, those who are intimidated by the torture of others, and those who try to ignore the fact that torture exists."

You have the chance to make a real change. Please establish a Truth and Reconciliation Commission and begin the process of asking for forgiveness from our victims.

Unfortunately, my advice to President Obama was ignored.

12. I contacted April Barnett while writing this and she said Izzie, now a teenager, never had another attack.

13. *Prayer and Reality,* John Magee, Harper and Brothers, New York, 1957.

14. Ibid, P. 13.

15. *Science and the Modern World,* Alfred North Whitehead. The New American Library, New York, 1925. P. 89

Acknowledgments

IN FIRST PLACE is my marvelous editor, Sara Volle, who has reshaped my original manuscript into a much more readable and dynamic story. Thank you.

I deeply appreciate the generous support from my publisher Susan Shankin at Precocity Press. She made this book happen. Her advice and creativity melded with Sara's editing to make my story what you are now able to read.

I also need to acknowledge the assistance I got from Elizabeth Roderick, who provided the first assistance in shaping my manuscript. And then, Tristine Rainer, whose book, *Your Life as Story*, gave me the original framework for this memoir.

About the Author

Rev. Fred Morris has lived an extraordinary life. The son and grandson of Methodist pastors, he studied at Cornell College, Drew University, and the University of Chicago. He served as a missionary in Brazil for 11 years, where his activism and friendship with Archbishop Dom Hélder Câmara led to his abduction and torture by the Brazilian military. Following his release and return to the US, Morris gained national attention through his testimony before Congress and an article in *Time* magazine, leading to appearances on the *Today* show and other programs.

In 1976, Morris moved to Costa Rica, where he launched a construction company, created the newsletter *Mesoamerica,* and served as *ABC News*' resident correspondent. Later, he led churches in Chicago, taught at the Methodist University in Rio de Janeiro, directed the Florida Council of Churches, served as Dean of the Orlando Campus of the South Florida Center for Theological Studies, and directed Latin American relations for the National Council of Churches.

"Retiring" in 2006, Morris moved to Panama, founding "The Church without Bullshit" for expatriates. In 2014, at Bishop Minerva Carcaño's request, he returned to pastoral service at North Hills UMC, revitalizing a previously closed church and establishing the San Fernando Valley Refugee Children Center to support Central American refugee children. Now officially retired, Morris lives in Nicaragua with his beloved wife, Argentina.

www.ingramcontent.com/pod-product-compliance
Lightning Source LLC
LaVergne TN
LVHW100514110826
845146LV00002B/629

* 9 7 9 8 9 8 9 8 3 0 4 8 0 *